Connection, Compromise, and Control
Canadian Women Discuss Midlife

Nancy Mandell

Susannah Wilson

Ann Duffy

OXFORD

UNIVERSITY PRESS

OXFORD

UNIVERSITY PRESS

8 Sampson Mews, Suite 204, Don Mills, Ontario M3C 0H5
www.oupcanada.com

Oxford University Press is a department of the University of Oxford.
It furthers the University's objective of excellence in research, scholarship,
and education by publishing worldwide in

Oxford New York
Auckland   Cape Town   Dar es Salaam   Hong Kong   Karachi
Kuala Lumpur   Madrid   Melbourne   Mexico City   Nairobi
New Delhi   Shanghai   Taipei   Toronto

With offices in
Argentina Austria Brazil   Chile Czech Republic France Greece
Guatemala Hungary Italy Japan Poland Portugal Singapore
South Korea Switzerland Thailand Turkey Ukraine Vietnam

Oxford is a trade mark of Oxford University Press
in the UK and in certain other countries

Published in Canada
by Oxford University Press

Library and Archives Canada Cataloguing in Publication

Mandell, Nancy
Connection, compromise, and control: Canadian women discuss
midlife / Nancy Mandell, Susannah Wilson, Ann Duffy.

Includes bibliographical references and index.

ISBN 978-0-19-541793-7

1. Middle-aged women—Ontario—Biography. 2. Middle-aged women—
Ontario—Psychology. 3. Middle-aged women—Ontario—Conduct of life.
I. Wilson, S.J. (Susannah Jane) II. Duffy, Ann III. Title.

HQ1459.O6M36 2008   305.244'20922713   C2007-907318-2

Cover Image: Bruce Gardner/Getty Images

2 3 4 – 16 15 14
This book is printed on permanent (acid-free) paper ∞.
Printed in Canada

Dedication

To our home and work 'families' with deep appreciation

Contents

Preface

This book tells the stories of 110 Ontario women in their fifties as they reflect on their successes and failures in the areas of home, work, and well-being. Midlife traditionally is a time of reflection when one takes note of goals achieved and not achieved. The contemporary cohort of midlife women has grown up in an era of tremendous social change: the movements for civil rights and women's liberation; the entry of married women into the labour force and massively into education and then into what previously were seen as 'male' careers. High divorce rates, low birth rates, and the public acknowledgement of same-sex partnerships have marked these women's lives as distinct from previous generations. The women of this generation who have forged new pathways in combining home and work lives are 'in transition'. How do they assess their lives? What have they learned? What do they regret? And what do they feel most proud of?

We spent hours listening to midlife women tell the stories of their lives. We recorded the many ways they fashion unique life scripts. We heard stories of resiliency and strength displayed in tremendously tough situations. We also noted their soaring achievements in the fields of education, business, and partnerships, accomplishments that have altered the playing field for younger women. We were humbled and awed by their willingness to share their lives with us and we developed a deep and abiding respect for their tenacity and courage. Their diversity, resiliency, and strength make this cohort of women fascinating. We invite you to join us as we unravel the complexities, the heartaches, and the achievements of midlife women.

Acknowledgements

We acknowledge and express our gratitude to our work 'families' who had to live with us during this project. During Nancy's time as departmental chair at York University, Dean Robert Drummond generously supported requests for research assistance and writing time. The research money for the focus groups came from York's Faculty of Graduate Studies, which was then headed by the admirable Dean and Professor John Lennox. As a colleague in Founders College, John has long been a wise and generous facilitator and Nancy thanks him for his constant support. Franca Cece at Founders College played an extraordinary role in helping to prepare this manuscript. She spent hours moving coded data into files, moving references into bibliographies, photocopying material, merging files, mailing drafts, arranging meetings, feeding us at meetings, and keeping the three of us on the same page. Rarely do we have an opportunity to work with someone as kind, generous, efficient, and gracious as Franca, who performed duties beyond the norm with love. Elise Armstrong picked up the slack when necessary with cheerful enthusiasm and calm efficiency. Jackie McConnell Siebert, patience and wisdom personified, along with Larry Lam, the guy who knows everything (hence his nickname, 'the ultimate power'), were an enormous help on the York front.

Ryerson University has supported the project through internal funding from a SSHRC Institutional Grant, and from the Faculty of Community Services research funding. The Faculty of Community Services Dean's office provided office space for the Ryerson research assistants. Most importantly, Deans Sue Williams and Usha George, Directors of the School of Nutrition Jennifer Welsh and Janet Chappell, and colleagues Rena Mendelson, Rheta Rosen, Susan Silver, and Rachel Berman have been interested, supportive, encouraging, and patient as this project has taken on a life of its own. Through the vigilance and grace of Wan Yee Tan, graduate students and research assistants were housed and paid—a challenging task involving many students and two universities.

Nancy, Ann, and Sue began meeting in 2001 to design this project. Together we developed the research design, sampling strategy, and interview guide and managed the data collection and analysis. A remarkable team of graduate student researchers worked alongside us and left their mark on our book: Marion Lynn, Beth Cutts, Brenda Blondeau, Shana Calixte, Jennie Addario, Alex Vamos, Lisa Rundle, Leslie Wilson, and Claire Carter participated at different stages. Using research money gathered by Mandell, Marion Lynn initiated the project by conducting six focus groups with over 80 women of diverse racial, ethnic, and class backgrounds in the Greater Metropolitan Toronto area. Judith Grant, in the midst of writing her own Ph.D. dissertation, held three focus groups in Ottawa and we thank her for making the time. Lisa Rundle acted as project manager in the early phases. Alex Vamos's graduate work on aging lesbians helped our initial literature review. Beth Cutts did most of the interviewing and wrote excellent summaries of the interviews. Beth's competence and efficiency saw us through this time-consuming stage and we appreciate her contributions. Ruby Newman allowed us to gather additional information on family and intimacy by designing a special interview assignment with her Atkinson class on aging. Jennie Addario, Leslie Wilson, and Brenda Blondeau helped us through the transcription and coding and analysis phases. Jennie and Leslie transcribed interviews with care and sensitivity. Leslie continued to support the analysis identifying codes, themes, and quotations. Her enthusiasm and positive energy have been a bonus to the project. Brenda prepared excellent condensed analytic summaries with patience and humour that has always made working with her a pleasure. Shana Calixte worked on the women's movement section and helped prepare a paper for a conference presentation. Leslie Wilson was the lead author of a paper on the women's movement, and contributed editorially throughout. We appreciate that she has been able to stay on to see the project through.

The project was initiated by a series of focus groups organized by nine different women's groups in Toronto and Ottawa: the Elspeth Heyworth Centre, the North York Women's Centre, Summerhill Co-op in Etobicoke, Immigrant Women's Health Centre, the Regional Women's Health Centre, Intercede, the Kanata Community Resource Centre, Rideauwood Addiction and Family Services Centre, and Amethyst Women's Addiction Centre. Without the active participation of these organizers and our energetic focus group participants, we could never have undertaken this larger project. Sharing their struggles and successes was an honour and privilege. We salute the women's centres that continue to make such a huge difference in the lives of women in Canada. We also sincerely thank all our interviewees, whose courage and generosity made this book possible. We hope we have accurately reflected your stories and, in some small way, helped advance the cause of aging women in Canada.

We found the patience and support of Oxford University Press exceptional. This project took long to complete but they never wavered in enthusiasm or conviction. Richard and Laurna Tallman were superb editors and the book is better for their care and prodding. We are grateful for the guidance and enthusiasm of Dina Theleritis and managing editor Phyllis Wilson, who have seen the manuscript through its final stages to publication.

Finally, we know we have forgotten people and ask their forgiveness.

From Nancy Mandell
We are fortunate that our 'home' families continue to be supportive. Lionel, Jeremy, Ben, and Adam Mandell have, once again, borne the brunt of their partner/mother's preoccupation. Lionel remains my nemesis and the love of my life with all the frustration and deep happiness such a twining entails. Balancing has proved challenging, but his constant and deep affection has been my rock. I hope that in some small measure I have been his touchstone as well. The boys I adored have now grown into men I admire. As I watch them embark on journeys with their own life partners, I wish them much peace and happiness while at the same time recommending liberal

doses of flexibility and tolerance. I have every confidence in their wisdom to make choices that will bring them and their partners joy and satisfaction. And I hope they will remember an adage my mother constantly repeated to her recalcitrant daughter: if one is patient and keeps one's mouth shut, most things work out over time.

From Ann Duffy

Many people at Brock University likewise have contributed, directly and indirectly, to the realization of this project. Many friends, colleagues, and students have been kind enough to listen to my thoughts and to share their opinions. I much appreciate both their patience and their insights. In particular, I want to thank Brigitte Cecckin, Melissa St Germaine-Small, Sandra Kovacs, Jaime Hunt, Kendra O'Brien, Norene Pupo, and Sarah Duhaime, each of whom contributed to the research that informs this discussion. I also want to thank my family—Dusky, Mayra, and Hermana—who have long provided my foundation and inspiration. In the course of writing the manuscript, my father Stan and my dear friend Wendy died, and their deaths brought home to me some of the sharpest edges of living through midlife. I hope the work here reflects some of the strength, wisdom, and compassion they kindly shared with me.

From Sue Wilson

This book has been part of the Wilson household for several years. All of us have lived with the preoccupation that writing about something this close to home—and heart—involves. While Leslie and Jay occasionally are called to action as research assistants, Leslie's role in this study has been significant, and this has been a wonderful bonus for me. Leslie has been involved in coding and analysis since 2003 and knew the transcripts as well as I did. She was the lead author on a paper focusing on feminist identity in midlife women, and contributed her skills as an editor during much of the writing. Paul, neither one of us knew when we met as undergraduates the winding road we signed on for. It has been an adventure, I know you would agree! I know, also, that you share my sense of wonder as we watch Leslie and Jay continue their journeys in partnerships.

When I joined the School of Nutrition at Ryerson in 1991, it felt like coming home. It still does. I brought my point of view as a sociologist and in return I learned about professional practice and community, and even more about friendship and possibility. These lessons of friendship and possibility were repeated in all of my research partnerships and in my experience as Associate Dean. I could not have imagined better colleagues, or a work situation to which I was better suited.

Chapter 1

Midlife Under Seige: Baby Boomers Redefine Aging

'I love growing older, love, love, love it!' (Susan, #16)

'Getting older sucks!' (Malina, #15)

Midlife is best characterized as that point in life when you fully realize that your life is more than half over. This humbling acknowledgement arrives in various, often convoluted, ways. For some women, it creeps up on them, lingering in their subconscious, awakening them in the middle of the night with a sense of panic or foreboding. For others, it appears suddenly and unexpectedly at the oddest times and places, perhaps flooding over them during a business meeting or crippling them as they chop the vegetables for dinner.

Whether quickly or slowly, whether all at once or episodically, all midlife women face the inevitability of life's winding down. This acknowledgement drives some women into a frenzy of activity as if they need to hurry up and do all the things they promised themselves they would once do but somehow never did. For others, the realization can be emotionally immobilizing as they struggle to fulfill daily responsibilities. And then there are women who experience feelings of acceptance, slowly eliminating onerous, mind-numbing tasks and connections and replacing them with people and activities from which they derive pleasure. Midlife often represents a period of tumult and transition, a time of physical, emotional, interpersonal, and career change.

Does midlife precipitate an identity crisis for women? Popular culture would have us believe so. But are the physical and social changes wrought by simply growing older 'crises' or new 'dilemmas'? Midlife is perhaps best understood as a crossroads or a time of reflection as adults evaluate how far they have come and where the next years of their lives will take them. Certainly, growing older brings with it changes in health status, the death of parents, widowhood, voluntary retirement, marriage of children, and the arrival of grandchildren. For women, midlife alters their health and well-being in predictable ways, such as the onset of menopause and associated changes, and such unpredictable ways as cancer or heart disease. Women confront physical shifts along with alterations in their families and work lives. But are any of these changes necessarily 'crises'?

The perception of midlife as crisis seems to originate with Elliot Jacques's study of men. In 1965 Jacques published a study of men in their late thirties arguing that these men responded to their own realization of mortality with what he called a midlife crisis. In 1978, Levinson used the central concept of crisis as a way to describe the *Seasons of a Man's Life*. This was followed two decades later with a parallel study of women (Levinson and Levinson, 1996). The notion of a midlife crisis as a shift in direction in personal or professional life came to dominate Western views of midlife. The discourse of crisis stems from concerns about loss. Men, it was thought, lose their careers, their physical attractiveness, and their sexual prowess, all of which plunge them at worst into depression and at best into a pressing need to re-examine their goals. Psychologists assume that women experience the same achievement crisis as men (Wethington, 2000). Women are just as likely, the thinking goes, to experience a sense that they have not contributed as much, done as much, or accomplished as much as they thought they would. As it does for men, the evaluation process precipitates a need to resolve previous expectations and perhaps shift priorities.[1] But despite a fairly long history of trying to document midlife as a time of crisis and heightened stress, there is little empirical support for this interpretation (Aldwin and Levenson, 2001: 199).

In this book, we replace the discourse of midlife as primarily crisis with the discourse of midlife as challenge and renewal. Guided by an early book by Lillian Rubin, *Women of a Certain Age: The Midlife Search for Self* (1981), we built our study on the central notion of midlife as change and growth. Using Jung's (1960) idea that the central task of midlife is integration, Rubin framed her understanding of women's growth in self-understanding with the ending of their primary roles as caretakers. An empty nest, she thought, would allow midlife women to engage in personal self-reflection, an exercise from which they might emerge with greater wisdom. Rubin's expectations about women's caregiving have turned out to be only partially correct. Contemporary midlife women engage in caretaking well beyond their middle years. With both aging parents and adult children needing support and intervention, midlife brings precious little leisure. However, our research suggests that the lessening of previous demands allows women to engage in more self-reflection. This possibility emerges from a distinct nexus of important social changes.

Why Study Midlife Women?

A quick glance at any library will reveal the intense interest in the study of midlife. For us as authors, this shift in public and academic interest has been timely. First, an examination of midlife offers us an opportunity to situate women in historical context, assessing the extent to which their lives are a result of demographic, political, and socio-economic forces and how much their life paths result from individual proclivities and circumstances. The post-World War II cohort constitutes a generation in transition. As baby boomers, women usually learned fairly traditional scripts for loving and working (Moen and Orange, 2002: 232). As they aged through the life course, their mothers' lessons provided remarkably little guidance for the challenges they encountered. As members of this cohort ourselves, we wanted to find out how other women have managed to fashion their lives. How do midlife women define success? What compromises do they make? What contradictions do they experience? How do they resolve dilemmas and what emotional and practical consequences ensue from these decisions? The chapters on work, caring, family, and health take up these challenges.

Second, midlife women have also grown up during an era of deep-seated **ageism**. When they are made visible, aging women often are portrayed as deficient, unattractive, worthless, and boring. Not infrequently, like other socially marginalized groups, they appear in the mass media as objects of humour or pity. Cultural representations of aging women also often position them negatively as bodies in need of curing. Just as individuals use gender as a guide for social interaction, bodies are used to signify age and thus to structure social relations. Midlife women grapple with negative images of aging that are pervasive in our media and pop culture. Any short jaunt into a 'woman's magazine' reveals the massive economic edifice built on our culturally inscribed fears of aging and its signifiers. Wrinkles, grey hair, and weight gain are to be mitigated with makeup, hair dye, anti-aging creams, weight loss products and programs, and so on. Blurring bodily signs of aging represents women's attempts to diminish signs of aging precisely because they know how important physical bodies are in shaping our social experiences. Given this marketing emphasis, one would expect women to obsess about their physical appearance and be horrified at aging; instead, by listening to the stories of midlife women, we understand that midlife is full of meaning and self-discovery, and much of it has nothing to do with wrinkle cream or 'magic' diet pills. We investigate this theme more fully in the next chapter.

Third, focusing on midlife women allows us to assess the impact of the women's movement in shaping women's opportunities for schooling, employment, and self-fulfillment. Women in our study were generally in their twenties in the 1960s in the midst of the women's movement and the sexual revolution. This generation's experience of change included unprecedented access to education and training, which in turn were reflected in new labour market possibilities that allowed women to define and experience themselves in new ways. We are curious to know how women understand the expansion of educational and employment options and if these opportunities changed their lives in positive or negative ways. Given the tremendous significance of the gender revolution, we devote an entire chapter to unravelling some of its specific consequences. The chapter on the women's movement explores these issues.

Fourth, midlife women's reflective assessment of what and how they have resolved the inevitable contradictions that make up a life seems to us to be especially useful for young women. Studies of college-aged females indicate that some see feminism as a much-needed historic equality movement. Presumed to have succeeded in achieving legal, social, and economic equality between men and women, the women's movement is now viewed by some younger women as largely irrelevant

(Arnold, 2000; Williams and Wittig, 1997; Buschman and Lenart, 1996). Young women involved in third-wave feminism see themselves as taking on issues unique to their generation at the same time as they indicate the importance of women's studies courses in helping put their struggles into socio-historical context. Midlife women were central to initiating and accomplishing the goals of the women's movement and we want to know how these struggles for equality play out in their personal lives. The struggles older women articulate provide a perspective from which younger women can understand their own entanglements, as mothers and as daughters (Wilson et al., 2006), and more broadly, from one generation to the next.

Fifth, scripts for the life course have altered considerably in the past 50 years. Born at mid-century and raised in the midst of traditional scripts of nurturer, caregiver, and homemaker, the blueprint for midlife woman became obsolete in the midst of a transformation in economic and family demands. Rather than relying on past socialization practices as forces for self-discovery, the new paths midlife women forged in work, family, and well-being became the means by which they explored new life scripts (Moen and Orrange, 2002). Opportunities in the service economy and in education, along with the erosion of familial and other constraints, opened up previously locked opportunities for women. As Judy reflects on her life: 'When I think of myself, I think that I am still becoming. When I look back at the different stages of my life, I realize that I am not the same person any more. I continue to grow and become' (Judy #50).

The experience of the life course as mostly linear, stable, and predictable is vanishing. In its place has emerged a more fluid and diverse life course, albeit one still influenced by past practices. Traditional beliefs and values about health, aging, work, family, and intimacy continue to tell people what to expect, how to prepare, and what to feel at particular moments in their lives. But individuals experience more and more often a set of largely unplanned events that force constant readjustment of their goals and expectations. In this half-changed world in which traditional prescriptions coexist uneasily with non-traditional circumstances, actual experiences (and not simply past socialization processes) have become forces for self-discovery and self-construction (ibid., 232). As we combine our understanding of the gendered life course with the postmodern, we come to see midlife women's identities, choices, constraints, and self-assessments are framed within a perspective of **structured ambivalence** (Connidis and McMullin, 2002a).

Current experiences of aging and midlife are distinctly modern realities. Until the middle of the twentieth century, few Canadians would survive into their sixties and seventies. In this context, the notion that women (think of Goldie Hawn and Raquel Welch) in their sixties could be ever considered sex symbols or models of female beauty would have been seen as laughable. Marilyn Monroe was represented as in decline when she died at 36. This experience and societal conception of aging was revolutionized by profound improvements in medicine, nutrition, hygiene, and public health. Together, these factors have reinvented the age profile of most developed countries, with dramatic increases in the numbers of seniors and aged seniors.

In this historical context, it is not surprising that beliefs and values attached to aging have been significantly altered. Indeed, popular conceptions of youth and middle age have transcended changes in biological realities. Despite improvements in longevity few 'middle-age 55-year-olds' today can reasonably expect to live to 110. However, in a culture in which 55-year-old men and women occupy positions of social, economic, and political power and in which old age continues to be stigmatized and youthfulness valued, it is to be expected that prevailing age categories will reflect more about societal clout and power relations than about actual life expectancy. Predictably, the marketplace has a vested interest in representing the young as youthful longer and middle age as a designation that encompasses more and more customers and clients.

Three Revolutions Shape Midlife Women's Experience: Longevity, Life Course, and Gender

That contemporary midlife does not necessarily constitute a major life turning point signals a fundamentally distinct understanding of this life stage, one which emerges from the very different challenges and opportunities facing contemporary midlife women. Three revolutions have shaped the lives of midlife women. The Skolnicks identify two of these social revolutions as the longevity revolution and the life course revolution (Skolnick and Skolnick, 2003). All Canadians tend to live longer, a demographic that is, in turn, altering life course expectations. Today, we routinely expect to live into our sixties and seventies and beyond; we expect to have post-paid employment and post-reproductive family lives. In addition to these two major changes, we also note the enormous significance of a third revolution, the gender revolution. Having lived through the women's movement, midlife women have heard and experienced fundamentally different life narratives than those available to most of their mothers and grandmothers. This has meant that their expectations, desires, ambitions, and achievements all have typically been affected by feminism. Combined with the fact that women now live longer and in less predictable ways, all three revolutions provide fertile background for framing our understanding of the social and material conditions shaping midlife women's life stories.

The Longevity Revolution

In 2004, 2.3 million women (about 15 per cent of all women) were 65 years or older. By 2041, 27 per cent of women will be over 65 (Statistics Canada, 2005: 20–1). The number of people over 65 is increasing dramatically compared to the numbers of people 18–64. This shift in the demographic profile of Canada and other 'developed' countries fuels social concerns that an aging society will create demands on social spending that are impossible to meet. The shadow of this huge cohort of aging 'boomers' is creating anxiety among social policy planners because older adults are presumed to use a disproportionate share of health-care dollars and multiply demands for institutional and family care. Since women live longer than men, this really amounts to a concern that in the long run some older women will be an insupportable financial burden on the state. Indeed, our interviewees express considerable concern about their financial futures; many are even reluctant to retire because of the financial uncertainty of old age. In a chapter on employment and retirement, we discuss this distressing trend.

Not surprisingly, interest in the study of age and aging has increased as the baby boomers move into their sixties. Assuming the experiences of loss and decline, there is an expectation that increased longevity will soon create a crisis in health care, seniors' housing, and related areas. At the base of this fear is the recognition that the number of people over 65 is increasing dramatically compared to the number of people aged 18 to 64, causing demographers to coin the term '**dependency ratio**'. This term, popularized in the media, refers to the numbers of seniors who 'depend' on younger, 'productive' members of the paid labour force to pay for services seniors require. This shift from older to younger members of Canadian society paying the bulk of taxes to support social services fuels social concerns that an aging society will create demands on national budgets that are impossible to meet. Gee and Gutman (2000: 12) resist this notion, calling it instead 'voodoo demography' because the assumptions that all people over 65 are dependent and all people 18–64 are productive are fallacious.

Nonetheless, this tsunami of seniors will have an impact on Canadian society. As a cohort, baby boomers have already altered our understandings of family, work, and well-being. This cohort will live longer than their mothers or their male partners and, compared to their mothers, will spend more of their lives living alone. They have more formal education than their mothers and are more likely to have participated in the labour force throughout their lives regardless of marital status or the age of their children. As a generation, baby boomers have had more choice in birth control, sexual expression, employment, and family life than any previous generation of women.

With expansion of choice has come a concomitant expansion of responsibilities. This generation of midlife women seems to have more debt, more commitments, more responsibilities, and more paid and unpaid work obligations than previous generations. Unique challenges for midlife women today include juggling the demands of employers and families, including support of adult children and managing care of aging relatives. Dreams of carefree retirement and 'Freedom 55' are proving illusory for most women.

The fact that the '50-somethings' are living longer has helped shift our ideas of what years constitute middle age. Generally, Canadians understand middle age to range from sometime in one's forties until sometime in the sixties. Some writers think of midlife as referring to individuals between the ages of 45 and 55 years, while others stretch the definition back to age 35 or forward to age 65. Over time, middle age has started later and lasted longer, thereby postponing the onset of old age (Arber and Ginn, 1991). As the chronological gap between youth and old age widens, it seems more people define themselves as midlife for longer periods of their lives. Midlife has become an ever-expanding life stage.

As attention has focused more recently on the many ways in which midlife is socially constructed, the category itself is being questioned. In particular, researchers are now beginning to draw attention to ethnic and cultural differences. Wray (2007) argues that since Pakistani and British Muslim women tend to marry and have their first child at an earlier age than other British women, midlife occurs earlier for them. Consequently, she defines midlife as occurring from ages 36 to 60 for her research population. As research develops this point further it is likely that midlife as an age category will be revealed to be much more contested and nuanced than previously.

The lengthening definition of midlife corresponds to the broadening definition of youth and old age. 'Early adulthood' can refer to people between 18 and 40, extending midlife from 40 to 60. Increasing longevity has prolonged the post-child-rearing stage of the life cycle, lengthened the retirement years, and made 'old age' a long and distinctive phase of life. The time between retirement and death can potentially last 20 or 30 years. Some analysts call those between 65 and 75 the 'young' old. A communications company in New York has coined the term 'tweeniors' to refer to people aged 55 to 70, who, as they describe, 'were too old to be considered middle-aged but too young to fit in with seniors' (Kesterton, 2006).

In any event, it is important to keep in mind that categories of age are fluid and socially constructed. In the past, we thought of growing older as meaning individuals inhabiting one predominant social role. Perhaps this was an essentialist and fictitious account because we know that older individuals, like their younger counterparts, inhabit multiple social roles. Women find themselves shifting in and out of social identities such as 'worker', 'child', 'parent', 'grandparent', and 'spouse' for more of their lives.

The Life Course Revolution

The longevity revolution has precipitated a life course revolution. People now find themselves in life stages for which cultural scripts have not yet been written (Moen and Orrange, 2002: 231). When cultural roles are undefined, social relationships are similarly unclear. Individuals interact as aging friends, lovers, great-grandparents, and caregivers with few traditions to guide their behaviour. Moreover, the stretching of life has added new roles unimagined within previous generations when adults often died shortly after retirement. Grandparents now look after their own aging parents, who in turn act as caregivers to their partners.

Knowing that the lengthening and disruption of traditional life courses has fundamentally altered social definitions, we decided early in our research to use a postmodern life course approach to frame our study. This approach encompasses both the individual and the social by recognizing the importance of social structures and historical context as they shape individual aspirations and achievements. To some extent, age cohorts have distinct experiences unique to their age category because they mature in particular socio-demographic and political contexts.

Contemporary Canadian midlife experiences are symptomatic of what academics refer to as a postmodern life course. Although not likely a term that our participants would use, postmodern life course refers to the diversification of women's experiences. All the little and large changes in social roles and cultural expectations as well as the trend towards normalizing diversity add up to a life course picture we call postmodern. Living in the midst of profound social change has forced midlife women to throw out old blueprints and write new, individual ones, leading to some unexpected turns, some disappointments, and some new issues to reflect on.

Abandoning the Modern Life Course Perspective

Much writing on aging uses a modernist framework for understanding people's lives. These writers assume lives take a predictable, linear, and stable progression from birth to death with characteristic life events—adolescence, marriage, work, grandparenthood, and retirement—marking significant transitions. Developmental psychology, for example, has tended to be predicated on such assumptions about human lives. In this view, men's life course differs from women's only in the type of work undertaken and in the significance accorded to it.

In modernist aging literature, life course, lifespan, and life cycle are often used interchangeably as organizing principles for understanding people's lives. In psychology, lifespan and life cycle are often used as stages associated with ideological expectations about how people ought to behave, ignoring the ways lives also are self-regulated and variable. In sociology, life cycle often represents a stage model of development that is applied roughly to chronological ages in an attempt to capture their distinctive characteristics (Settersten, 2003: 22). In this life cycle or lifespan model, youth is a time of immaturity and indiscretion; middle age is a time of acquiring experience; and old age represents a time of wisdom.

Viewed from a social historical perspective, age represents a social marker whose meaning continually shifts. In contemporary society, age is used as a way to distinguish different cohorts according to physiological processes, to confer social and economic responsibilities, and to define social membership (Arber et al., 2003). Moreover, as Featherstone, Hepworth, and Turner (1996) tell us in *The Mask of Aging and the Postmodern Life Course*, the idea of a middle stage of life is part of the broader process of the 'modernization of aging' whereby a social distance is created between youth and old age. Middle age represents a socially constructed boundary between adulthood and old age and increasingly has come to be seen as a life stage with more in common with youth than with old age.

According to Featherstone et al. (1996), two recent social changes precipitated the emergence of this new life stage boundary: the increased age-consciousness that emerged after World War II, which attempted to bring old people out of retirement and into employment; and the rise in consumer culture, which positioned middle age as an entirely new market. By defining middle age as a 'loosely arranged collection of ideals which intersect around youthfulness', the connection between old age and retirement was severed; midlife individuals were separated from the powerlessness associated with the elderly in modern economies; and the life course took on a more flexible, diversified, highly individualized, and biographical meaning. In postmodern sociological writing about aging, researchers have not discarded notions of distinct ages but rather lengthened the categories and blurred the distinctions among them. Broadening age categories robs them of their significance and allows a more multi-dimensional, fluid process to define life events. Some postmodernists have abandoned the age category altogether.

In this book, we distance ourselves from conventional gerontology, which has tended to psychologize the problem of old age, and from stage developmental and biomedical models, which focus on individual adjustment to 'natural' life change events like retirement, widowhood, or institutionalization. In a non-determinist perspective that focuses more on process than outcome, age represents a convenient indicator, not a necessary condition, for analyzing life course and its transitions (Settersten, 2003: 23). Postmodern writers use the concept of life course but differ from modernist thinkers in that they approach cohorts as socially and historically distinct. As life course pioneer Glen Elder (1985) points out, each cohort grows up in a unique socio-demographic and political context, which in turn affects psychological development. Moreover, no two cohorts are alike. In this view, each social cohort invents its own definitions of what age means by imbuing with social meaning certain roles, responsibilities, and cultural values. Adopting a **life course analysis** allows researchers to emphasize the intersection of social and historical forces with personal biography as key to shaping cohort experiences (Settersten, 2003).

Numerous elements influence cohort experiences, including size, composition, location, and cultural and political environment. For example, the size and composition of cohort affect opportunities and constraints facing new members and has implications for institutions that must take in and adjust to new members (ibid., 24). In this view, the institutions of family, work, schooling, and leisure are seen as interlocking collectivities that reflect the complex interaction of biology, psychology, economics, and culture in shaping lives.

A Postmodern Life Course

How does a postmodern framework shift our thinking about the life course? First, we move away from linear notions of life cycle to more chaotic notions of life course. A metaphor of a life as a series of ripples replaces the metaphor of life as peeling layers of an onion. Second, lives are not foretold and are therefore more difficult to anticipate except in the most general terms. Ripples spread in unexpected ways. Third, life events do not necessarily mark an identity movement from one stage to the next. There are few predictable stages but a vast array of significant moments heralding self-change. Fourth, there are no fixed meanings attached to particular life stages, rather each one is open to interpretation. Some we are socialized to see as life-altering in fact turn out to be mundane while others, perhaps unforeseen, have the power to shift world views. Finally, as a method of analysis, the process of deconstruction is to hear and rearticulate the voices of the suppressed, a process sensitive to contextual dimensions and marginalized voices, and a method that challenges traditional views of language and its relationship to thought and reality.

In this book, we use a **feminist postmodern life course analysis** to capture the complex interplay between structure, culture, and agency, which, taken together, help us understand women's lives. In trying to understand how gender and age get into women's lives and how, in turn, women interpret these intrusions, we envision the life course as an emergent project. Most midlife women grew up within a traditional or modernist framework and most of them find that it no longer suits their situations. They were typically taught to imagine and plan their lives around a series of predictable events and fixed stages that no longer match their experiences. In its place is slowly arising a more fluid and emergent process, albeit one infused with history, culture, politics, and economics.

The Gender Revolution

Women have both produced and been produced by the gender revolution. Relative to men, women are more affected by the twin trends of increased longevity and decreased fertility. Usually, women live longer and perform more care work than men throughout their lives. In addition, the lives of women have been significantly shaped by a third social trend, the gender revolution, which also has affected men but in different ways. Gender issues such as increased access to education, especially post-secondary schooling, longer periods of paid employment, sexual liberation, legal abortion, the ability to divorce, and formal equality are unprecedented factors affecting life narratives.

Some of the most common features and consequences of the gender revolution sparked by the women's movement are well-documented (Luxton, 1980; Mandell, 1995; Wilson, 1996). The movement of married women into the labour force represents the single most significant change to affect midlife women. Today, 65 per cent of women with children under the age of three are employed, compared to 28 per cent in 1976. Most of these women work full-time (Statistics Canada, 2005: 105). In one generation, the norm concerning women and employment shifted completely. It is now unusual for mothers not to engage in paid employment; to be unemployed is considered a luxury, a sign of financial prosperity or unusual circumstances. Married women must now contribute financially to their households or risk plunging their families into poverty. And they must continue to shoulder the majority of the domestic labour without significant support of the workplace, which has not evolved to fit the needs of Canadian women or families.

For their mothers, who were midlife in the 1960s, stress often was associated with being at home and not having been engaged in meaningful work in the form of paid labour (Friedan, 1985). A lifetime of domestic labour meant that midlife reassessments centred mostly on career regrets, mainly not having as many options for work and family as their male partners did. In contrast, the amount of time spent today in paid jobs has reduced midlife women's free time, making the reduction in leisure time a significant source of stress. After a lifetime of juggling multiple demands, midlife women wonder if they are really better off than their mother's generation. Contemporary regrets for midlife women are just as likely to centre on their failure to achieve work–family balance as are regrets for midlife men.

By midlife, women have learned that being female can mean a lifelong commitment to caring for others. Unlike their mothers, who were likely to be empty nesters and grandparents by age 50, contemporary 50-year-old women are likely to have dependent children at home and to embrace an array of work/not work combinations. Some already may have retired, others are just gathering steam on new careers, while still others remain completely or partially trapped in the paid workforce by financial necessity.

Ageism in Studies of Midlife Women

Until we began our literature review for this book, we simply did not know that much contemporary work on midlife and old-age women had escaped feminist and postmodern deconstruction. As women age, they become less visible to the larger social order. They tend to be ignored as research subjects and under-represented in the research literature. This invisibility applies most to older women but begins in middle age. It has been dismaying and discouraging to confront the uncontested pathologization of aging women as abnormal, psychologically unfit, socially useless, and economically burdensome.

Almost without exception, magazines, television programs, and movies that target the female audience convey the meaning that aging is an undesirable process to be fought 'tooth and nail' every step of the way. Can you imagine anyone on the television program *Friends* as midlife actors? Of course, omnipresent advertisements from the massive, billion-dollar cosmetics industry make the same point: those who are not young are undesirable and tainted. Any hint of aging, from wrinkles to age spots, is stigmatizing. The marketplace encourages midlife women's active self-loathing. The popularization of cosmetic surgery and the marketing of anti-aging products that promise to lift or fill in wrinkles, to 'refresh' the face and eliminate sagging eyelids, condemn the naturally aging face and body. Aging female celebrities, who ironically are touted as evidence that we accept aging actors, are in fact severely mocked when they themselves show evidence of aging. Where adultery, alcoholism, and DUI convictions are fodder for gossip, the truly unforgivable moral offence in popular culture is revealed to be aging.

Studies on midlife women must, therefore, be approached with caution. Many studies we read were uncritically and normatively based on deeply sexist notions of aging, women, and the life course. What little feminist writing exists (see Chapter 3 for more on this topic) does not tackle the inherent sexist dualism that underlies a lot of empirical research.

What are some of the dualisms we have tried to avoid? First, and most obvious, is the biological metaphor, the contrast between *growth and decline* that permeates aging literature. Biology is thought to incite the social. According to Arber and Ginn (1991), a pathology model predominates in which elderly people are seen in terms of disease, disability, poverty, bereavement, isolation, and role loss. Studies dwell on older people's decline of mental faculties, loss of physical capabilities, and slide into financial dependency (Twigg, 2004).

Chronological age has proven to be a poor predictor of a person's intellectual capacities, social behaviour, attitudes, lifestyle, physical condition, or ability to work (Arber and Ginn, 1991). Why, then, does the decline metaphor predominate? According to Featherstone and Hepworth (2000) the association of later life with dependence and decrepitude is part of the process of stereotyping through which hostility towards the elderly is expressed. Stereotypes affect the way the stigmatized are perceived and treated, which in the case of aging women tends to be largely patronizing. Stereotypes also perform a prescriptive function, warning us who age against socially unacceptable behaviour at the same time as they serve to legitimate economic and cultural disadvantage.

Second, emotional dualisms of *immaturity versus wisdom* are layered onto the social to complete an ageist conception of the life course. The young are physically immature. Hence, it is assumed they are socially and emotionally immature as well. A significant component of socialization through the life cycle entails learning which emotions signify which stages of life. Popular culture suggests that one grows into wisdom because while bodies decline, minds and souls expand. The association of wisdom with age is simply a stereotype that allows the juxtaposition of 'old' and 'young' to persist. There is no need to invoke wisdom as a rationalization for aging. In our interviews, we discover a range of a sense of wisdom: some midlife women feel they had grown wiser while others feel they express no more common sense, insight, or diplomacy than younger women.

Third, underlying most writing on aging women lies what Gannon (1999) calls the ultimate dualism between *normality and abnormality*. Young women are normal; aging women are abnormal. Aging women are not normal simply and precisely because they are not young. Youth constitutes normalcy. This logic mirrors that which is critiqued in early feminist writing on sexist dualisms. As Simone de Beauvoir points out in *The Second Sex* (1989 [1949]), women are 'not normal' precisely because they are 'not men'. Normality is invoked as an ideological turn of phrase, a trick to reinforce the status quo. So-called empirical 'facts' are interpreted through a conceptual lens that frames the gathering and analysis of empirical research. As Gannon (1999) reminds us, if one did not conceive of aging women as abnormal, one would not conceive of menopause as an illness and therefore one would not do research on ways to treat it.

Finding Our Participants

While the study of midlife women has received increased attention of late, there has not been a major study focusing on Canadian women. We researchers all are midlife women. All of us have had career-long interests in women's work and family responsibilities and were drawn to the topic of midlife women, especially to the ways in which our gender, feminism, and the women's movement have shaped our institutional and personal connections. Throughout the process of designing the study, conducting and analyzing the interviews, and framing the analysis of this book we have grappled with the concept of ageism and asked ourselves repeatedly to what extent we have internalized the ageism of our culture.

There are two parts to this study: a pilot study conducted in 2000 and in-depth interviews completed in 2002. Sixty-four women of diverse racial, ethnic, and class backgrounds participated in nine focus groups held between December 2000 and

February 2001 in Toronto and in Ottawa. All participants were brought together for the focus groups through an agency or organization dedicated to serving the needs of women. In Toronto, focus groups were held at the Elspeth Heyworth Centre, the North York Women's Centre, Summerhill Co-op in Etobicoke, Immigrant Women's Health Centre, the Regional Women's Health Centre, and Intercede. In Ottawa, focus groups were held at the Kanata Community Resource Centre, Rideauwood Addiction and Family Services Centre, and Amethyst Women's Addiction Centre. These groups attracted anywhere from three to 11 women between the ages of 45 and 64 for a total of 64 women. The goal of the focus groups was to gather information about the quality of life and the social and economic well-being of midlife women. It was our intention to use the findings to ground a subsequent, in-depth interview project as well as to allow participating community agencies to initiate projects servicing women's needs and advocating on their behalf.

The findings from this study (Lynn, 2001) suggest that family, career, and health transitions were the key themes in the narratives of midlife women, and these themes became the basis of the in-depth interviews. We designed the interview portion of the study to ask women about their families, work, and health; the meaning and timing of significant life events; regrets, hopes, and so on. The interviews probed about intimacy, love, and friendships; paid, unpaid, and volunteer work; and feelings about health. We also asked about the impact of the women's movement on their lives. We wanted to explore similarities and differences in how women of differing class, ethnicity, race, ability, and sexual orientation experience these dimensions and how this experience has changed over the course of their lives. The interviews were open-ended and encouraged women to describe their experiences in as much detail as they wished.

Over 100 women living and working in southern Ontario were interviewed, and their stories inform this book. As we note in the Appendix, pseudonyms have been given to the interviewees and they are also identified by number. Our goal in the study is to derive a sample that is inclusive, diverse, and grounded in the materiality of women's lives. While it is not our intention to have a statistically representative sample, every effort was made to invite participation across racial and ethnic groups and to solicit views from women in a wide range of income groups. To recruit women who represented the ethnic, racial, and class diversity of Canadian society, we used a two-stage sampling strategy. Community organizations across the Greater Toronto Area and in Niagara participated in the recruitment by agreeing to advertise the study to women who worked, volunteered, or were otherwise involved in the centre. A midlife graduate student conducted the majority of the interviews. The participants were very open, and said they appreciated the opportunity to talk about their own midlife experiences—a subject they agreed did not otherwise receive much attention. The transcribed interviews, interviewer field notes, summaries, and codes provide the basis of the analysis for the book. This original research material, with ample excerpts from the women themselves, serves as the foundation for the core chapters of the book.

Because we contacted the women we interviewed through women's organizations, it was not surprising that many identified with feminism. While none of the organizations was explicitly feminist, they included a range of community service groups, from organizations serving immigrant or poor women to religious organizations. Some of the religion-based groups could be seen to be anti-feminist in orientation. None of the admittedly small number of women from semi-rural areas identified as feminist.

A postmodern framework for understanding their lives implores us: to press for the diversity, fluidity, and the process of midlife women's experiences; to concentrate on turning points as self-defined moments of significance; to allow women to express hidden thoughts on ageism and sexism; to listen carefully to self-narratives to uncover self-awareness and self-critique; to view subjectivity as a multi-faceted, situated process; and to understand that there are no fixed meanings attached to midlife. Postmodern midlives encompass these elements.

As midlife women who have struggled with the challenges of regret and renewal, we wanted to interview other midlife women to hear how they, at this halfway point in their lives, reflect upon their fears, their dreams, their losses, and their accomplishments. In this book, we look in-depth at the lives of these Ontario women, most in their fifties at the time of the interviews. These women were born at mid-century, which means they came of age with the women's movement of the 1960s. Having lived through this significant cultural shift—whether or not they were actively engaged—we expected their life experiences to be very different from the generations that preceded or followed them. This assumption turned out to be largely correct. Contemporary midlife women have been profoundly affected by the women's movement in sometimes surprising and unexpected ways, including their career choices, life partner decisions, and the ways they raise their own children.

In interviews lasting from one to three hours, our participants talked about the meaning and timing of significant life events, what they see as obstacles to achieving goals, and what individuals or social situations propel them. We ask women what they see as notable shifts in personal relationships, how they measure their accomplishments, and what factors contribute to feelings of failure or satisfaction. We ask women how they view their aging bodies and accommodate to the physical signs of aging. We find that by having sampled across a wide range of different groups of women, we are able to make initial assessments of the impact of health, ethnicity, sexuality, and economics on women's experiences.

The research population is described in detail in the Appendix. We note that half of those sampled were married or cohabiting at the time of the interviews. Over 80 per cent were mothers and less than 20 per cent were grandmothers. Many were engaged in extensive caregiving and at the same time were gainfully employed. This was a well-educated group of women, half of whom had post-secondary education, including 12 with master's degrees and three with Ph.D. degrees. However, there were also 10 socially and educationally marginal women in the research group, along with a large number of women in the middle.

Not surprisingly, we discover a range of life narratives. There is not one path through midlife but rather a complex variety of passages. There is not one adjective that characterizes contemporary assessments of midlife but rather a host of descriptors. There is not one 'best' or 'worst' choice that stands out above others but rather a series of small, seemingly insignificant events that, taken together, characterize a life approach. Women make the best possible choices they can under difficult circumstances; these so-called 'choices' often do not appear immediately significant but in fact set in place a series of other consequences that resonate throughout their lives in often unexpected and sometimes uncontrollable ways. Midlife is all about reflecting on this chain of events, of trying to make sense of how the pieces fit together, and then coming to a place of acceptance. Our hope is that readers will gain insight from these life stories and revel in the enormous courage and grace so many midlife women display.

Thematic Overview: Gendered Ambivalence as Connection, Compromise, and Control

Discussion of the gendered ways in which women construct their lives leads directly to the concept of structured ambivalence (Connidis and McMullin, 2002b). An individual or group's location within the social structure places her or them in ambivalent or contradictory positions throughout their lives. Ambivalence is, thus, a social condition that inspires contradictory feelings, beliefs, and actions towards self, others, and situations. By ambivalent we mean 'of two minds': hesitant and decisive; unsettled and focused; doubtful yet confident; traditional and postmodern. The list goes on but the point remains that midlife women experience structured sets of social relations that pose opposite or contradictory courses of action for them in the intersecting institutions of work, family, and well-being.

Women experience greater ambivalence because the interaction of gender (as a category deployed to structure resource allocation) with work and family sets up more contradictory courses of action for women than for men (ibid.). This **gendered ambivalence** allows women to like and dislike midlife at the same time. The two quotations at the beginning of this chapter—'I love growing older . . . ' and 'Growing older sucks!'—capture the ambivalent nature of women's experience of midlife. It is our intention in this book to explore the institutional, cultural, and emotional experiences and expressions of structured ambivalence by focusing specifically on the realms of work, family, health, and care work.

Ambivalence is experienced institutionally, culturally, and within everyday behaviour. Institutionally, women often experience structural struggles in the demands of work and family. As an indication of the rewritten life course, the social standard of retirement has been reconstructed to reflect the many baby boomers who, instead of leaving the workforce in their sixties, embark on new career paths. As reported in the *Globe and Mail*, a Merrill Lynch study of midlife adults in 2005 found that 76 per cent of respondents 'expected to retire from their current jobs around age 64 and then start an entirely new job or career'—and, interestingly, midlifers are motivated to continue working 'more out of desire than of necessity' (Wright, 2006). Of course, this finding does not apply to any one person but rather indicates an entirely different possibility for living the last decades of life.

Because their lives did not unfold in the predictable, linear fashion they were raised to anticipate they would, midlife women find themselves with many opportunities for creative reconstruction. Instead of retirement, for example, midlife women talk about remaining in the workforce, switching careers, or going back to school. Having assembled a variety of technical and social skills, they find, as Linda (#42) tells us:

> Midlife is grand, actually. I don't see life as black and white, I'm much more conscious of the ambiguities in life, of my limitations, and I am glad that at this point in life that helps me be more tolerant. [Walking down the street I see my reflection] in the windows and I see this middle-aged woman, and it makes me glad. I think in the year 2002 that it's very much different than my mother's generation. We're allowed to enjoy it; we're allowed to revel in it because it's very much midlife. It isn't the end of life, the end of our reproductive life . . . . It isn't the end, but very much in the middle. I just feel like I've learned so much.

Culturally, midlife women both embrace and eschew aging. In day-to-day behaviour, whether caregiving or care-receiving, women experience both caring and uncaring feelings and behaviours (Curran, 2002). When we ask women about their close friendships, their relationships with paid and unpaid work including caring and volunteering; when we ask about their health and well-being, we hear stories of ambivalence and contradiction. Narratives of women feeling and experiencing both pleasure and pain—whether negotiating intimate attachments, gaining economic security, or maintaining their health and well-being—led us to concentrate on three central themes: *connection, compromise,* and *control.* Key to women's assessment of their life experiences, these central themes of connection, compromise, and control weave across differences of economics, ethnicity, and sexuality, thus allowing us to craft patterns of life narratives from seemingly diverse backgrounds.

As we ask women about their work and family lives, their relationships and their communities, we ask them to talk about areas of their lives where they feel they have control and how they feel about the compromises they have made along the way. For example, one woman tells us about how she wanted very much to go to university after high school, but her parents would not allow it, so she did not go. Another woman talks about falling in love with another woman at a time when homosexuality was rarely public and how this experience left her feeling out of control. Many women talk about the control/loss of control dilemma they feel in relation to physical changes that they feel less able to control than they imagined. Joint pain, arthritis, and deteriorating bodies seem to derail some women while others are more stalwart, declaring they will adjust to whatever changes come along.

As we expected, everyone in the study has countless examples of compromises made. The majority of these revolve around the structural impossibility of being able to balance the demands of paid work and family life. One woman, who had divorced in her late thirties after 18 years of marriage, talks about how she was expected to compromise in every respect in her first marriage. Ruth (#6) explains that:

> . . . the desires and the goals of my husband superseded my own. My understanding during our marriage was that eventually he will compromise for me, as far as my goals both professionally and just values in life, when indeed that is not what took place.

Margaret (#4), now in her late forties, talks about how the business of managing her life, between family and work obligations, took up much of her time, compromising her ability to pursue deep friendships, or more creative pursuits, or sports. While no one anticipates a life without compromise, it is the compromises weighed down by regret that the midlife women in our study talk most passionately about.

Another thread running through our interviews is the notion of connection. In *Time Bind*, Arlie Hochschild (1997) refers to ways workplaces have replaced families as sources of community. Many women in this study work in 'the helping professions' and they talk about the important connections experienced with their colleagues and clients at work. Others discuss the importance of spiritual or religious communities in maintaining connection; one respondent mentions the importance of her Native community to her sense of spiritual wholeness. Others find networks of like-minded people when they return to college or university. Several women who identified as lesbians discuss the significance of the community provided by their wide circle of similarly identified friends and acquaintances.

The preoccupation with self-improvement, the rise of experts, and the pervasive narcissism of the culture cannot, of course, be fully understood outside of the profound socio-economic changes that both sustain and encourage these developments. The post-industrial economy, the mushrooming of the service (especially the personal service) economy, the expansion in the numbers of low-wage workers, especially immigrants, available for personal service work (as might be confirmed by a visit to almost any manicure/pedicure salon), along with a variety of other economic and social factors, have contributed to the burgeoning of a new economic order. While fortunes are still made in oil, they are also made in Oil of Olay; while corporate chieftains such as Bill Gates still stride the economic world, self-improvement mavens such as Martha Stewart and Oprah Winfrey accompany them. A significant portion of the economic order is dedicated solely to the very activities that help to construct the parameters of midlife women's lives: controlling the aging body, creating and maintaining familial and other connections, negotiating compromises in every area of personal life. The emergent economic order not only promotes and popularizes these diverse services; it actively expands the market for them. It is, therefore, important to keep in mind that the personal lives of midlife women—their search for connection, their struggles with compromise, and their efforts to achieve control—are sculpted by market forces dedicated to the primary directive of making a profit.

How Does the Experience of Ambivalence Make Women Feel?

While structured ambivalence asks us to concentrate on constraints midlife women face, the concepts of agency and empowerment focus on the ways women struggle to control their lives. When they speak of control and agency, midlife women do so within the context of relationships. Agency, as Wray (2004) notes, is an interdependent, relational concept. Women are not moving away from relationships and achieving autonomy by distinguishing themselves from others but rather feel powerful, of worth, and more in control in relationships where they exercise autonomy. In other words, women achieve independence in and through relationships with others, not by distancing themselves from others. Helene (#36) reflects on her experiences leading up to midlife, and had this to say about life lessons learned and the importance of connections:

> A community involvement, connecting with people. That what it's all about. Because that's where you find out, you talk to somebody about what you're going through, what you're feeling and you learn so much, by connecting with people. Be exposed . . . Feel all your emotions, don't close them. When you're feeling sad, feel sad. When you're feeling happy, feel happy. Feel what's going on inside you. And when you're feeling something, go with it, whether it's tears or happiness or joy or whatever, stop and listen to it. For me that's it.

Ambivalence creates tension around taken-for-granted understandings of how to define oneself. Individuals work out family and job roles in the form of an ongoing dialogue between the institutional and the reflexive components of self (Beck-Gernsheim, 1999).

As postmodern writers tell us (ibid.; Fairclough, 1989; Featherstone et al., 1996; Gergen, 1996), ambivalence and contradiction lead to constant dialogue within oneself and with others about coming to terms with workable alternatives: what one might have to sacrifice in the future as one confronts uneven transformations in gender, work, family, and life course. Janet (#72) expresses the mixture of bitterness and resignation characteristic of ambivalence:

> Sometimes I'm very bitter and then I think back, 'Why am I being selfish?' and I let it go. I regret many of the compromises that I've made, because maybe today I wouldn't be where I am right now. Maybe today I would be better off financially, mentally, emotionally, career-wise, life-wise . . . .

This ongoing, often internal, conversation opens up space for agency and self-creation but at the same time increases one's potential to experience stress and anxiety. We reject calling these moments 'identity crises', but midlife women do seem to live in fairly constant states of self-reflection that come from the push to always be working on one's self. What does it mean to be old? How should I age? What jobs might I take up in the future? The paths are not clearly articulated; women must find their own ways.

As Gilleard and Higgs (2000: 18) note, midlifers face the historically novel task of creating new identities in middle and old age. The stress associated with lifestyle alterations precipitated by divorce, job loss, moving, death, and illness create their own pressures to reinvent oneself and to feel satisfied with the result (Ferudi, 2003). The momentum here is the prevailing cultural assumption that happiness—a better self, a better relationship, a better work life—can be achieved if one just 'works' hard enough.

This emphasis on self-definition and self-improvement reflects a shift in the moral economy from traditional to non-traditional roles and life paths. Working on the self is valued in society as a good exercise in moral well-being. Not working on the self is regarded as moral failure. The media and popular culture have taught us to judge individuals as being more scrupulous, ethical, conscientious, and upright if they devote large amounts of time to massaging and managing themselves. Any time spent on the self through exercises in well-being and intimacy garners respect from others. In the past, time spent on self might have been read as a sign of narcissism or moral decay. Today, developing one's self is defined as the primary project of one's life, so we respect and revere those who do so. One of the reasons the body has assumed such prominence is because it is read as a sign of moral development. Healthy bodies, worked-on bodies, perfect bodies presumably tell us something about an individual's moral character. Imperfect bodies signal moral imperfection. Yet, individual makeup (genetic propensity) and structural factors (economics, care for others) make it impossible for many midlife women to pursue or fulfill the ideal. Indeed, many eschew the norm altogether.

If the 'rational man' was the exemplar of modernity, the 'moral individual' represents the pillar of postmodernity. The shift from materialist values to postmodern, post-materialist values is associated with a search for personal meaning and morality, for spiritual development, for close affectionate ties with family members and friends, and for existential significance in work (Polivka and Longino, 2004: 8). But the creation of self-identity is not done alone. In the modern world, tradition dictated and legitimated belief and behaviour. In a postmodern world, the expert provides guidance and validation. Individuals are responsible for constructing their own identities but are enjoined to rely on experts for direction and social support as we travel on this search for significance.

As Polivka and Longino (ibid., 6) state, since lots of different types of expert knowledge exist, one of the central postmodern tasks for individuals is choosing wisely the particular expert to follow whose advice will be integrated into one's sense of self. The rise in consumerism reflects the emphasis on shopping for expert knowledge. Consumer culture and commodificaton are elements of postmodern culture. If there are multiple ways to achieve self-perfection, there are multiple ways to insert oneself into and construct one's culture. As Gilleard and Higgs (2000: 12) tell us, aging is a cultural process, less something that is 'done' to individuals and more something with which people engage.

The rise of postmodern experts and the centrality of moral self-development along with the demise of tradition as a guide mean that ambiguity coexists with ambivalence as a central feature of postmodern existence. There are no 'right' answers in terms of fashioning a life. As Elizabeth (#81) explains,

> I take people one on one. I don't care if you're yellow with green polka dots, as long as it's not contagious. [Laughs] If you're a good person, you're a good person. If you're not, I want to have nothing to do with you. And I hope that's how my kids live their life. But they're individuals, and they'll have their own prejudice and you know . . . likes and dislikes. But I hope that when dealing with the world in general that they would take people one on one.

There are no 'correct' ways to achieve intimacy, work satisfaction, perfect health, and well-being, but only regular opportunities to negotiate structural contradictions that characterize postmodern life. It is no surprise that youth have captured this ambivalence completely with the word 'whatever'—whatever works in making one's life is socially acceptable as long as one gets on with the project. Finishing her thoughts on her experiences of bitterness and resignation, Janet (#72) concludes that ambivalence leads one to issues of control:

> The only thing I can control is myself. I have no control over anybody else. I don't want to control anybody; the only person I'm responsible for is me and the choices I make. What I do and what I don't do. If I try and fail, then okay, if I don't try and I still fail then that's my own responsibility. There you are.

'To each her own' seems to sum up prevailing social attitudes towards personal development; a respect for individualism, and the sense that individual rights trump desires for collective focus or conformity to any particular group.

At the same time as expert knowledge has been raised to a normative level, so also has the contradictory trend of contesting this knowledge. Expert knowledge is transitory and threatened in the search for personal aggrandizement. At the same time, the rise of postmodern self-reflexivity has democratized personal relationships. When we look more carefully at intimacy for midlife women, we shall see the ways in which the spread of democracy has shifted personal relationships in fundamental ways.

Conclusion

In the rest of this book we investigate the social, cultural, and economic landscape on which midlife women have emerged. Shifting demographics and changing attitudes combine to produce historically unique life-course experiences for contemporary midlife women. In order to understand midlife women, we need to interrogate the sources that have contributed to the emergence of midlife as a diverse and pluralistic experience. How have changes in the workplace, in communities, in education, and in family altered what midlife women see as possible and desirable? Midlife women entered adulthood at a time when particular institutional constraints framed their choices and decisions. Shifting ideas of intimate partnerships have fundamentally shaped midlife women's ideas of love, commitment, and caring just as clearly as changing educational and workplace opportunities have opened some doors and closed others. By examining midlife women's lives, we begin the task of unravelling the complex interconnections that both distinguish and tie together various facets of their lives. In the next chapter, we focus on the theoretical underpinnings of our analysis by interrogating the interconnections between institutional forces, cultural manifestations, and individual actions as articulated in midlife women's narratives about aging.

Key Concepts

Ageism Stereotyping and prejudice against individuals or groups because of their age. The term was first coined by US gerontologist Robert N. Butler in 1969.

Dependency ratio A term popularized in the media that refers to the numbers of seniors who 'depend' on younger, 'productive' members of the paid labour force to pay for services seniors require.

Feminist postmodern life course analysis Life course analysis grounded in postmodern and feminist principles. Feminism involves an ideology and practice aimed to achieve equality between the sexes, which means that social analysis begins from the standpoint of women; postmodernism espouses an intellectual, cultural, and artistic state lacking a clear central organizing principle or hierarchy and embodying extreme complexity, contradiction, ambiguity, diversity, and interconnectedness.

Gendered ambivalence The social condition in which women and men experience structured sets of social relations that pose opposite or contradictory courses of action for them in the intersecting institutions of work, family, and well-being. Women experience greater ambivalence because the interaction of gender (as a category deployed to structure resource allocation) with work and family sets up more contradictory courses of action for women than for men (Connidis and McMullin, 2002b).

Life course analysis Research that aims to understand the causes, processes, and consequences of change over the course of life. Human development and aging are seen to involve the interaction of social, biological, psychological processes from birth to death.

Midlife Roughly, the period of life from some time in the forties to some time in the sixties. Some writers think of midlife as referring to individuals between the ages of 45 and 55 years of age while others stretch the definition back to age 35 or forward to age 65.

Structured ambivalence An individual's or group's location within the social structure that places them in ambivalent positions throughout their lives. Ambivalence is a social condition that inspires contradictory feelings, beliefs, and actions towards self, others, and situations. Ambivalence means 'of two minds': hesitant and decisive; unsettled and focused; doubtful yet confident; traditional and postmodern.

Questions for Critical Discussion

1. What is midlife? Provide a specific example of how it is a useful category in analyzing themes in your life.
2. Sociologists see contemporary life as riddled with ambivalence. Define structured ambivalence and provide an example of how this applies to you.
3. In addition to being structured, ambivalence is also gendered. Define this term and describe how it applies to you. Refer to specific examples in the areas of schooling, intimacy, and friendship.
4. Outline four characteristics of a postmodern life course. Provide specific examples.
5. Television shows and advertising are constructed on ageist images of men and women. Choose an example from both types of popular culture to illustrate this assertion.

Chapter 2

Structure, Culture, and Agency in the Study of Midlife Women

Structure, Culture, and Agency

Midlife provides a broad canvas on which to study issues of aging, gender, and the life course. In this book, we employ two theoretical perspectives in our analysis of the lives of midlife women: a **materialist (political economy) approach** and a post-modern, feminist interpretive position. Taken together, these perspectives provide a framework within which we are able to analyze midlife women's understandings of themselves as the combined result of structure, culture, and agency. Women act within the social structures of education, work, and family. They use the cultural environment, or age symbolism to interpret ideological messages about how to live their lives. And, women's individual agency, as they move within different cultural environments and social structures, allows them to interpret, accommodate, resist, and revise their options.

The Material Structuring of Age

A materialist or political economy perspective sees Canadian society as character-ized by major inequalities in the distribution of power, income, property, and pres-tige. This theoretical framework gives primacy to economic forces as conditioning the status, resources, and even the thoughts of individuals and groups. One's posi-tion within the social structure, it is argued, conditions one's aspirations, and the likelihood of achieving one's goals and life choices in work, intimacy, and well-being. Historical changes, social conditions, and economic fluctuations influence what opportunities become available for individuals. But, within a range of struc-tural and cultural possibilities, individuals make choices and carve out their lives.

Age, like gender, race, and class, represents a major stratification dimension that affects access to scarce resources. In 1975, a geriatric psychiatrist Robert Butler coined the term 'ageism' to capture our negative attitudes towards the aged and the aging process. According to Butler (1975: 12), ageism:

> . . . can be seen as a process of systematic stereotyping of and discrimination against older people because they are old, just as racism and sexism accomplish this with skin colour and gender. Old people are categorized as senile, rigid in thought and manner, old fashioned in morality and skills . . . . Ageism allows the younger generation to see old people as different from themselves, thus they subtly cease to identify with their elders as human beings.

Ageism refers to the interplay of practice and attitudes, material reality and ideology that reinforce and perpetuate discriminatory practices and beliefs. Ageism is an outcome of social practice. Ageism also creates social practices and thus acts in combination with other dimensions of social reality such as gender, ethnicity, sexuality, class, and dis/ability to produce social inequality and to maintain its current systems. Ageism, for example, is institutionalized in the labour market when older people face employment barriers and mandatory retirement. Often these beliefs are taken so for granted that they take on the force of normal practice. Age-segregated policies contribute to a view of the elderly as socially redundant, incapable, and dependent (Arber and Ginn, 1991). The end of compulsory retirement in Canada has led to some interesting discussions and in these public debates about the roles and responsibilities of over-65-year-olds, often one finds explicitly ageist beliefs and values. Taken together, institutional and state policies, cultural images, and day-to-day treatment of the elderly add up to a profoundly negative environment for many older Canadians.

The Racialization of Aging

The materialist or political economy approach to aging states that those with the greatest power and resources in society have disproportionate influence on cultural beliefs and institutional practices. Inequalities follow women throughout their lives and are both intersected with and shaped by race, class, sexual orientation, dis/ability, and other social variables. In particular, the material disadvantages of ageism and racism are substantial and as women age, the inequality they faced in earlier life stages typically becomes sharper and more visible (McDaniel, 1988).

Racialization refers to the process by which we differentiate or categorize based on race. The process of racialization involves the construction of specific images based on a set of assumptions or stereotypes according to certain races. It not only refers to a process of differentiation based on race but to an imposition of a racial character on a person or action. We impose a racial character or context on a situation by interpreting, perceiving, and experiencing events within a racial context.

Racialization takes place on local, national, and international levels. In each case, the construction of racially unequal stratification hierarchies is accomplished by imposing clear boundaries between dominant and subordinate groups based on race. As Marable (2004) observes:

> The problem of the twenty-first century is the problem of global apartheid, the racialized division and stratification of resources, wealth and power that divides Europe, North America and Japan from the billions of black, brown, indigenous, undocumented, immigrant, and poor people across the planet.

Racialized groups have, throughout their lives, more limited access to economic resources than Western groups. Racialized older women experience even greater material constraints (Browne, 1998: xx). Economically, this means they are more likely to have faced joblessness and underemployment. Global capitalism continues to erode income security and has effectively erased most hopes for pensions, full-time employment, or health benefits, key elements that cushion retirement.

Many of the women in the focus groups emigrated from other countries and had a clearly visible membership in ethno-cultural groups. They spoke of the intense marginalization they encounter because of ethno-cultural and religious affiliation and basic material inequities they confront on a daily basis. Poverty, fear of unemployment, physically demanding jobs, social isolation, and linguistic barriers contribute to their lack of power and control over their daily lives. While they are proud of their considerable achievements, they articulated the intense loneliness and pain they have encountered trying to build families in a new country, an effort that has been exacerbated by racialized discourses and state practices. Many have been unable to secure full-time jobs, have amassed little property of their own, and fear aging in a future of financial insecurity and deprivation. One South Asian woman described her circumstances as 'living on a treadmill in order to survive'; such women are unsure that they will have partners or family as economic supports in the future (Lynn, 2001: 8). For many, having struggled to keep minimum-wage jobs entailing skill demands far lower than that of which they are capable, they have little faith in state income security programs. A Filipino woman envisions a tough future: 'I have to work and will have great difficulty in ever having enough money for my older years' (Lynn, 2001: 12).

For midlife women, managing on very little income means having to choose between getting a haircut and having dinner that day, having to strategize to buy birthday gifts for their grandchildren, and having to cut back on necessary prescription drugs. The embarrassment of being dependent on adult children, the pain of feeling abandoned by their families, and the fear of the possibility of living on the streets lead them to dread old age. This is hardly the rosy picture of competent aging women striding through their old age.

The Gendering of Aging

Both men and women suffer from ageism. But older women also suffer from institutionalized and cultural sexism. Older women are judged less attractive than older men, a cultural phenomenon that American feminist Susan Sontag (1972) labelled the '**double standard of aging**'. Aging is more a social judgement than a biological eventuality. According to Sontag, there are two standards of male beauty: the boy and the man, but only one standard of female beauty: the girl (Teuscher and Teuscher, 2006). But not only is the double standard of aging a matter of aesthetics, it represents a shorthand to describe an entire set of oppressive structures that keep women in their place (Sontag, 1972: 38). When you add racialization and disablement to the mix, older women seem triply disadvantaged.

Throughout our interviews, women talk a lot about the ways in which their life course was shaped by economic decisions they made in their twenties. Janet (#72), a woman in her fifties, makes the point that the consequences of lost economic and employment opportunities can feel overwhelming and far-reaching:

> I knew, back then, that I wanted to be an archaeologist. I knew. Unfortunately, I was talked out of it. Two reasons were given to me, the main reason was there are so few women in the field of archaeology, you'll never get a job. At that point, it was the time of Jane Goodall. So I would have been one of the pioneer women if I had been allowed to pursue the university education, and become an archaeologist, I would have been one of the new women, or first women in that profession. I knew I wanted it, but I was not allowed to pursue it. My parents gave the reason, 'You'll never get a job, you need a career, a trade.' My mother and father didn't want me to go to university anyway, they didn't want to pay for it. So I graduated at the end of grade 12 with a degree as a secretary, which I didn't really want, but did well at.

Women's economic inequality typically increases with age. A lifetime of occupational segregation restricts women to traditional female job ghettos; as waitresses, sales assistants, nurses, teachers, domestic labourers. Typically they earn lower salaries than men and have variable access to pensions. More than two-thirds of employed women work in teaching, nursing and related health occupations, clerical or other administrative positions, and sales and service occupations. In contrast, only 30 per cent of employed men work in these positions. Significantly, this occupational distribution has not improved for women since 1996.

Working-class jobs involve hard physical labour often in poor conditions that lead to increased physical disability in old age (Calasanti and Slevin, 2001: 23). The racial segregation of occupations means that certain ethnic groups, and certainly the disabled, experience the onset of old age earlier through their stressed bodies and in more demanding circumstances than their more affluent counterparts (ibid.). Lower-income women in the focus groups that informed this study frequently talk about the stress created by their chronic health problems. Their ill health created a Catch-22. Because they couldn't work, they did not have health benefits. Consequently, they could not afford the drugs that would keep their chronic conditions under control (Lynn, 2001: 6).

In contrast to men, most women, regardless of social class, have less capital—financial, personal, and social—to negotiate changes in their lives, which in turn puts them at greater risk of poverty in old age. Despite dramatic improvements in the poverty rates among older women, it remains the case that senior women (age 65 and older) have low-income rates twice that of senior men. Nine per cent of women aged 65 and older lived in an after-tax low-income situation in 2003 as compared to only 4 per cent of comparable men (Statistics Canada, 2006).

If they are dis/abled, members of ethnic minorities, or unattached, older women can call on even fewer resources to manage the vicissitudes of life. From the moment women first take employment, their incomes will be lower than those of men, and until they reach retirement (age 65) this pattern will only worsen. Midlife women (aged 55–64) earn little more than half the incomes of their male counterparts (Statistics Canada, 2006: 134). Becky (#54), like many midlife women, paid a heavy price for employment and economic decisions made early in life:

> My first employment was with [a large transportation company]. I did reservations. If I stayed there, I would have had a huge pension right now, so it was stupid for me to leave. I left because they were bringing in the computers and I thought I was going to be replaced by them. I think my life would have been totally different had I stayed on there. I do regret that decision.

Reflecting on their current financial situations, a number of women talk about regretting not securing their futures by gaining a solid education. Joanne (#53) was particularly articulate:

> A major turning point was the realization as a young woman that without education, and even with a certain amount of education, life would be difficult. And it was after I left home and was working as a housekeeper that I ended up taking a nursing course. And even with that, it was not sufficient because of lack of education . . . the pay wasn't any better, the hours weren't any better and there was no guarantee of full-time work.

Analysts have long made the point that women with access to male wages, typically through marriage, are less likely to sink into poverty, less likely to be economically insecure, and less likely to be poor in old age. But, for some women, continued access to male wages entails sacrifice: remaining in partnerships with abusive men; sticking with unfulfilling marriages in order to secure the financial well-being of their children; and forgoing career advancement to care for home and children. Lorna (#13) typifies female decision-making wrapped around perceived male needs: 'Looking back I should never have left my teaching job . . . because then I would have had a full-time teaching pension. I left that to help my husband in this business, and I should never have done that.'

Women who are on their own due to divorce or single-parenting find their incomes substantially reduced. Low-income, mother-headed families have the lowest incomes of any family type. By 2003, they were earning only 38 per cent of the income of the average two-spouse family with children. Poverty analysts have for decades made the point that to be a single mother is a virtual guarantee of poverty (Statistics Canada, 2006: 134).

The financial figures associated with divorce are now familiar to us, namely that women's incomes drop 40 per cent on divorce while men's increase by 70 per cent (Ambert, 2002). Joanne (#53) talks about the challenges she faces in being able to support herself after the dissolution of her marriage:

> . . . especially when the divorce came through, it was 'Fine. I'm going back to school.' Well, we subsisted on welfare for which I was very, very fortunate. We made ends meet and we did not incur debts and we subsisted on it until I finished community college. Two full years to get my diploma. And there again I found out to my dismay, unless you're [certified] and if you don't have your four years of university, again there are many places you cannot work. Again, the education was not sufficient to get the money.

Traditional notions of femininity and masculinity embedded in the nuclear family conspire to reduce women's material security. Focus group participants spoke of the power and control men in their cultures have over their lives and of marriage as being male-dominated and not to the advantage of women. They describe situations where women are captives in their own homes, not allowed to leave because they might speak to other people about family problems, of being deprived of learning English and having to use symbols on streets and subways in order to get to factory and restaurant jobs only to return home with unopened pay in envelopes they turn over to their husbands. Such entrapment leaves them feeling vulnerable, powerless, and isolated. (Lynn, 2001: 15).

The devaluation of older women is evident in remarriage patterns following divorce or widowhood. Many more women than men past the age of 45 are likely to get divorced and stay unmarried. Remarriage is more likely to take place for men than for women. For men and women divorcing between 25 and 34 years of age, the probability of remarriage is 80 per cent for men and 66 per cent for women. But, when the divorced couples are between age 35 and 50 years of age, 61 per cent of men but only 48 per cent of women will remarry. Older men, especially those who are economically secure, are seen as powerful, sexy, and desirable while older women are seen merely as old (Twigg, 2004).

Widowhood does not offer better prospects. A recent study by Statistics Canada reveals that women whose partners die find their incomes considerably reduced. The incomes of older widows decrease in the first year following the death of their spouses and are lower than the incomes of married seniors. Five years later, the difference between widowed and married senior women is even larger. Median family income for widows declined 9.8 per cent (leaving them officially below the low-income threshold in most cases) whereas it decreased only 1.5 per cent for their married counterparts (Li, 2004).

Why is it that older women are more likely to have fewer economic resources than older men? Simply put, caring for children reduces women's opportunities to remain uninterrupted in the labour force. Single women without children have profiles similar to single men without children, given similar education levels. Women with children have less opportunity to focus on work or career. Some women have little or no choice in this regard, given their responsibilities for financially supporting children at home. The impacts of divorce, going back to school, and long hours working and commuting not only make women's lives more stressful, but also extend to relationships between mother and child. As Joanne (#53) continues to tell her story, she details difficulties in balancing competing demands:

> . . . spending three hours a day on the transit to go to work, [just] to be able to pay the rent. I did that for five years. However, my son just saw it as 'No mother any more'. From the time he was 12, he didn't have a mother, due to the time of me going back to school, etc, which he has stated in no uncertain terms, and which is very difficult at times. At this point in time he was going to school; I don't see how I could have done things differently. He simply didn't have things done for him that had been done for him up until this time. We had moved from the matrimonial home and we were very fortunate to find a two-bedroom apartment, but he didn't have the circle of friends coming that he had had in his own home.

In the 1970s when the women in our study were entering adulthood, the structural barriers that had kept their mothers and grandmothers out of the labour force were beginning to crack. It would be several decades before we could describe the barriers as showing signs of crumbling. Middle-class white women went to universities—but they did not go with career plans. They expected to marry—and most did so in their early twenties. Mia (#10) talks about how she would have made quite different choices regarding education, marriage, and children had she had an opportunity to relive her twenties:

> I only got the grade 11, and that wasn't the way I wanted it. I wanted further education, but having my son and being an unwed mother—those days, unwed mothers didn't go to school; I couldn't go to school. And so I decided my whole life was over, I'd never get a future education, I'd always be stuck in this rut where I'd be totally dependent on somebody else for everything.

Low-income women, racialized women, disabled women, and single mothers did not have the luxury of university education and its corresponding entrée to full-time, secure jobs. Most of the focus group participants speak of the difficulty of getting any work in Canada and of the barriers preventing them from having their previous education, training, and skills accepted and rewarded. When they do manage to take on post-secondary certification, they worry that their delayed entrance to better-paying jobs will be too late to materialize in the form of pension benefits to cushion their retirement.

Ageism as Cultural Reproduction

Born today, a woman might envision a 40-year connection to the labour force, cohabit rather than marry, be open about her sexuality, and time the birth of any children she might choose to have. But it wasn't—indeed isn't—only structural barriers that create the context for life choices. Social attitudes, what we are calling the cultural context, have as much or more impact on life chances.

Material conditions influence women's economic opportunities, but so does the cultural environment within which midlife women live. Relationships of age are constituted through material conditions but also through culture and social interaction. In these ways, age structures interactions and is structured through interactions. Age is formed and takes shape under certain material conditions but the material is, in this Bourdieuian sense, more than simply the result of the economic system or of the effect of the economic system on behaviour.

Ageism reflects deep-seated cultural values, including all our beliefs, values, images, and myths of aging. Understanding the social and cultural reproduction of ageism involves an analysis of culture, including the arts, media, ideas, and ideology. Ageist beliefs and practices are embedded in our culture; both maintained and reproduced through cultural absorption. Books, magazines, television shows, commercials, radio programs, and newspapers are consistently ageist. In one study, Vasil and Wass (1993) examine media representations of older people and find that older adults generally are under-represented. When they are present, they are negatively portrayed either as the 'super' old defying biological norms or as the 'regular' old, decrepit and decaying. Just as we cannot imagine a popular television series based on an elderly superhero, we rarely see television commercials of older women modeling lingerie. Indeed, both men and women who are older are likely to be presented as sexless and/or unattractive in the popular media (Walz, 2002). Sexism then operates in this general, anti-aging context.

In general, media portray mature men more often than they portray mature women, seeing the former as sturdy, distinguished, and wise and the latter as insignificant, ordinary, and ineffectual (Vasil and Wass, 1993). Media invisibility reflects the cultural erasure older women face in society. Martha (#49), who describes herself as being shorter than average, explains how she feels rendered invisible in terms of both her age and her size:

> As you become an older woman, you become invisible, and if you start off small, you can become more transparent much more quickly, and I think there is something that resonates with me, that I can become less prominent not only because of aging, but because I'm very small, and the two together are probably a double whammy.

Disabled women resent being left out of mainstream cultural norms that are centred on attractive able-bodied women. But does this mean they want to be subjected to able-bodied norms of attractiveness in order even to be seen? The recent success of the Dutch television program *Miss Ability* has angered disabled women. Is a live beauty contest where disabled women compete in bathing suits and nightgowns and present short videos on how they have overcome their disabilities progressive? Advertising for the show goes like this: 'Ever whistled at a babe in a wheelchair? Checked out the boobs of a blind babe? If the answer's "no", this barrier-breaking show will put an end to that. . . . Is this long overdue recognition for disabled women, even if it is based on appearance, or is it more like "Wow, now disabled people can be treated like meat too!"' (*Washington Post*, 2007).

Media have not only largely ignored disabled women, much less aging disabled women, but they also have not generally presented any aging gay images. In the summer of 2007, the American interest group GLAAD (Gay and Lesbian Alliance Against Defamation) compiled what they call a Network Responsibility Index measuring the quality, quantity, and diversity of images of lesbians, gay, bisexual, and transgender people on network television. By examining all prime-time programming—4,693 hours on the five major networks from 1 June 2006 to 31 May 2007—they assigned grades to each network of excellent, good, fair, or failing. *Brothers & Sisters*, a new hit show, led the way as the gay brother Kevin Walker (Matthew Rhys) is given as much screen time as his four siblings and is often seen kissing his boyfriends. Notably, the 2007 season ended with the revelation that the uncle, Saul (Ron Rifkin), is also gay, bringing an aging gay presence for perhaps the first time in a major television series (Hernandez, 2007).

Subjectivity, Agency, and Resistance

A focus on structure and culture reveals the historic, symbolic, and material conditions that frame women's lives. But where do social practices fit? How do midlife women, in their day-to-day behaviour both reproduce ageist beliefs and practices and challenge oppressive social relations? Individual agency refers to the capacity of an agent or individual to act in the world. Human agency is the capacity for human beings to make choices and to impose those choices on the world. How humans come to make choices, by free choice or other processes, is another matter. **Resistance** represents the act of defending one's position in response to confrontation. Through their own acts, midlife women reproduce social relations of inequality that contour their experience while simultaneously acknowledging their complicity.

Midlife women both embrace and resist oppressive structures and social relations. Is it any wonder that they feel ambivalent? Structured ambivalence is a social condition acknowledged and articulated through midlife women's exercise of control, compromise, and connection. Midlife women attempt to control the degradation of ageism through individual acts of resistance while simultaneously compromising and giving in to structural demands and cultural expectations. By creating communities, midlife women build buffers against racism, sexism, and ageism, which provide them with safe spaces in which to 'let down their guard'. Focus group women talk of their gratitude in having community organizations where they can find other women with whom to share their struggles. Lesbian women speak of the broader gay community as offering a safe and supportive environment in which to raise their children. As we discuss in subsequent chapters, communities—women's organizations, ethno-cultural and religious assemblies, neighbourhoods, and interest groups—offer midlife women much-needed shelter and protection.

Submitting to and Resisting Ageism

For midlife women, resistance often is articulated around age avoidance and body issues probably because these practices offer the most immediate and vulnerable sites and also because they offer women the greatest likelihood of successfully resisting ageism. It is impossible for women to exercise absolute control over their economic, cultural, and personal environments but they can achieve some measure of success when controlling their own appearance. By both adhering to and challenging ageism, midlife women's **subjectivity**, or how they feel about themselves, is constituted.

As Canadian feminist Leah Cohen (1984: 242) suggests, society's betrayal of older women affects their self-esteem:

> All women, regardless of their income level or educational attainment, experience aging as a social judgement. Older women lack the freedom to exercise control over their own lives. As we age, we are progressively infantilized by doctors, gerontologists, drug companies, the media, and volunteers. The power of each of these groups is reinforced by older women's traditional socialized passivity. Often older women find that they have little or no power to define their own goals in life. This realization has a profoundly negative effect on their self-esteem and leads irrevocably to a diminished sense of dignity.

Ageism and sexism are deeply enshrined in discourse and language. One of the first lessons young women learn is the ideology of middle age as decline. Negative words are applied to older women: 'spinster', 'crone', and 'old maid' (Covey, 1988). Culturally there are far more ageist jokes about older women than about older men—although 'grumpy old men' are not excluded entirely. And jokes about middle- or older-aged women focus on their futile attempts to conceal their age when everyone knows they are simply old, 'If Goldie Hawn had any more plastic surgery her lips would be up to her eyeballs.' Such jokes on late-night television shows reinforce the stereotype that all older women need and want to hide their age. Is it any wonder that age anxiety is evident among 20-year-olds? They know, correctly, that their power lies in their youth and beauty and that when both, inevitably, disappear they will be discursively disparaged.

Ageism thus constructs, and is constructed, through the emergence of an aged social identity and subjectivity. The cumulative effect of constantly telling aging women that they are impotent and not socially valued is lowered self-respect. The cumulative effect of constantly telling midlife and older women to avoid aging is experienced as attacks on the self. The aging self inhabits a discursively discrepant space. Our need to pass as young or as middle-aged reflects our ageism turned inward even though we decry ageist stereotypes. Catherine (#61) expresses our culture's ambivalence about aging:

> I just get pissed off because people expect me to act like an old lady. I'm going to be turning 60 next year and I don't want to focus on being old, I want to focus on what's possible with life, not what I'm restricted with. I don't want to say, 'Oh, I can't do this because I'm 59.'

Instead of aging as something to look forward to (the growth, maturity, wisdom, and insight associated with 'growing up'), it is something to avoid or deny. By saying things like 'You sure don't *look* 50!', we support age denial. No wonder some of the women in our study refuse to accept aging. As Donna (#76), someone who has clearly internalized the ageism of our culture, explains: 'I don't think I would go back to work right now, no. I'm too old for that. Nobody would hire me [laughs].'

While institutional experiences, cultural practices, and day-to-day behaviour teach women how to age, one of the most crucial ways in which midlife women take up the social position of old is through emotional subjectivity, that is, learning which emotions are socially sanctioned as appropriate for growing older. As Kathleen Woodward (1998) points out, we learn to associate certain emotions with certain ages and life stages. If cultural images see the young as vital and the old as in decline, what are the appropriate social roles and affiliated emotions associated with each life stage? And what happens if one refuses to emote in culturally sanctioned ways? Ageism thus involves an interpretive understanding and display of specific gendered, raced, and classed emotions.

> I've heard people say 'I'm too old for that'. It's like they've put the older hat on themselves. There have been places that they've tried to set up for women who aren't 20 or 30, but nobody goes. I just find it really interesting for me to figure out. Also, I like to dance. Where am I going to go dance? I'm probably going to go where everyone is younger. So it took a whole mind shift for me to be the oldest one in the room. (Catherine, #61)

Cultural constructions in the life cycle foster the emotion of nostalgia associated with the elderly and feelings of shame both by and for the old. We simultaneously pine for the good old days while disavowing the aged. Barbara Macdonald, a radical feminist writing in the 1970s, says that shame around aging represents a political emotion, an internalization of the culture's message that ' old is ugly, old is powerless, old is the end and therefore old is what no one could possibly want to be' (Macdonald with Rich, 1983).

> I've accepted my lot in life, and I'll probably end up being a miserable old lady. Alone. And it's probably better because I'm probably too difficult to live with anybody. . . . Now I'm starting to say, 'No I don't want to do that'. Or

starting to realize that it's okay to say, 'No, and to hell with what people think.' It's taken 53 years to figure this out. That it's okay to do for myself . . . (Phyllis #3).

Emotional subjectivity, how one feels about oneself, is learned through language and discourse. One of the central aging emotions is learning that society does not 'see' older women. Older women are rendered socially invisible. As Catherine (#61), a woman in her late fifties, comments:

I walk down the street and because I dress often younger, you can see people kind of look at me until they get closer and then they once they see that I'm older, the interest fades. It's a part of life, but it's really interesting to observe, and I can see that in bars or out at an event.

Aging subjectivity also involves age-appropriate presentations of self. Tamika (#58), a Caribbean woman, learns what constitutes an aged identity by comparing herself with others in her age cohort. In this way, she adjusts her ideas of what being older means according to her feelings about these people and decides how, publicly, the middle-aged should appear:

On that Queen streetcar you see some ladies come on, my age, I'm sure. You know they're my age, but they look older, but they're wearing tight jeans and tee-shirts with the bars, and cut-offs. Right now I dress reasonably conservatively. I cover myself. I try to be conservative for my age. I like to think so. But I see these ladies in these tight jeans wear the clothes that a 19-year-old girl would wear, and that bothers me sometimes. And I think to myself, 'Look at this old lady!' And I think to myself, 'I'm old, too'. I forget that—sometimes I don't see myself as being old. I still think I'm in my thirties.

Today's baby-boomer demographic provides us with a critical mass of women who at every life stage have tended to challenge stereotypes associated with femaleness. These women are in the process of developing a new understanding of aging. As a result, there is more cultural space for women to feel more positive about their midlife, as a time of renewal. Some women find power in the role. They are confident in a way they weren't when younger. This is reflected by Anita (#12) in an anecdote about her recent birthday celebration:

When I turned 40, my mother gave me a *Reader's Digest* [article]. This is an article that's very old. It says when you turn 40 you become well-grounded and you become more comfortable with yourself and your surroundings. But my forties were total turmoil about my image, my being, my life, my family, my everything. When I turned 50, I just went 'Fuck it', you know? It's like a bolt of lightning hit me. 'I am perfect the way I am, so just get over it', you know? (Laughs) It was when I turned 50. And you know, people came to see me, my aunt, and they're all so incredible, and they gave me 50 roses for my birthday. And they said, 'You don't look 50.' And I said, 'What does 50 look like? Don't say that to me. 50 is 50.' It's just a date, but for me it's so liberating. I'm okay with what I am.

Aging thus brings both cultural pressure to remain youthful while simultaneously acknowledging the power and wisdom that accrues with age. Midlife women often build communities in which the positive effects of aging are accentuated. Creating positive social spaces represents ways to counter negative cultural stereotypes. Joyce (#59), a lesbian who works in feminist communities, finds personal and social strength in asserting her age:

As I'm getting visibly older—so I have the white hair—but I'm still the mouthy dyke I always was. I actually get away with more now than I ever did before. Twenty-five years ago they would have said 'idealistic young fool!' Now, because I'm going to be 50, I get to mouth off. I plan this stuff carefully, so I'll walk in, in this black dress and the long grey hair, the long white hair, then I'll say, 'Oh, that is such fucking shit!', right? And I get away with it, because I bring who I am and my reputation into this committee work. They listen more because I'm older, and I get to be absolutely outrageous. Even more so than when I was younger, so I'm quite enjoying it actually. Now I'm like the crazy old lady. And then I get my menopause fan out, because I start having these flashes during the meetings, and I say, 'Excuse me, menopause.' So if they didn't realize how old I was before, they then go, 'Oh. What? Oh, that hair is white, it's not blonde.'

It is easy to emphasize the weight of negative cultural norms and discriminatory institutional practices. But, countering these forces lays the generational strength of baby-boom women who are characterized by their non-traditional behaviour. In the midst of forces pushing stereotypical norms, midlife women have forged divergent life paths from previous generations and in their choices, normalized diversity. Taken as a group, midlife women appear thoroughly postmodern. And in their strivings for economic and personal independence, they have acquired self-efficacy, confidence, autonomy, and pride. To be sure, they recognize and adhere (variably) to cultural norms of femininity; but in acknowledging the structural we should not obscure midlife women's buoyancy and self-sufficiency. As Dorothy (#22) points out, aging brings increased agency and autonomy: 'The less young one becomes, the more one can be oneself. In other words, I could flirt outrageously with a 25-year-old and everybody would be cool with it.'

Age Avoidance through Body Concealment Practices

Given the cultural derision of older women, is it any wonder that many aging women engage in age avoidance and **body concealment practices** in order to hide signs of aging? Ageism and aging sneak up on midlife women but even as young adults most have been well-schooled in tying to 'pass' as younger. By middle age, most women describe the numerous tactics in which they engage in order to avoid the inevitable cultural and institutional experience of being devalued for being unable to 'beat' aging.

Some psychologists explain age avoidance as reflecting a deep-seated fear of aging and death. Martens et al. (2005: 224) insist on seeing fear of aging as rooted in biology, stating that 'ageism exists precisely because elderly people represent our future in which death is certain, physical deterioration probable, and the loss of current self-worth-enhancing characteristics a distinct possibility.' In contrast, we prefer to see 'age passing' (pretending to be younger that you are) as a form of internalized ageism thoroughly rooted in the social (Cruikshank, 2003: 153). As youth culture pervades our society, more and more men are feeling the effects of the powerful connection between youth and robustness. North American plastic surgeons report that men are increasingly seeking cosmetic surgery to provide them with a competitive advantage in the workplace (Holstein and Gubrium, 2003).

Although we have no way of knowing how many people lie about their age, some assume that most people do (Palmore et al., 2005: 9). People who try to pass as younger may indeed be trying to affirm that they feel good—perhaps as good as they felt when younger. (Passing as older, we find, is strictly the domain of the young.) As Butler (1975: 14) pointed out over 30 years ago, 'The problem comes when this good feeling is called "youth" rather than "health", thus tying it to chronological age instead of physical and mental well-being.' We don't want to be associated with older people because they have such low social status. Age denial, like racial 'passing', is a reaction to ageism. 'Social customs encourage this; it is considered impolite to ask a person's age, and a standard reaction to finding out age is to say, "You don't look that old", which is, of course, a dubious compliment because it implies, "You don't look as feeble and decrepit as most people your age"' (Palmore et al., 2005: 10).

Embodying Age

Just as individuals use gender as a guide for social interaction, bodies signify age and, thus, structure social relations. So strong is the link between youth and power that individuals use every available technology to mask the aging of their bodies (Featherstone and Hepworth, 1991). When bodies finally do reveal signs of aging, individuals experience ageist attitudes that threaten their personal and social identities (Biggs, 1997; Calasanti and Slevin, 2001).

The blurring of bodily signs of aging attempts to mute signs of aging, an indication of how important physical bodies are in shaping social experiences. Concealment practices are designed to make women look young, fit, and unwrinkled. Dress, makeup, hair dyes, cosmetic surgery, and drugs are consumed in an effort to present a socially youthful image. Anti-aging products, which constitute a multi-billion dollar industry throughout the developed world, are relentlessly promoted as strategies women can employ to defeat age and, thus, stave off discriminatory practices.

Advertising feeds on women's fear of aging and legitimates their engagement in complicated and sometimes dangerous procedures that allow them to pass as youthful (Calasanti and Slevin, 2001: 23).

Our interviews provide a wide range of responses to the hesitant and diffident ways midlife women confront their aging bodies through techniques of control, compromise, and connection. A number of midlife women acknowledge the inevitability of physical decline without feeling regretful. Bodily changes mean women cannot perform physically as well as they had in the past; midlife women must face up to differences between what they want to be able to do and what they are able to do. As Vera (#8) notes phlegmatically: 'I mean, there's only so much you can do with an aging body.'

These women accept their growing physical limitations without apology, tending to describe their aging in relative terms. As Joyce (#59) succinctly puts it: 'I'm getting older. My body's not what it was when it was 25, but it's not bad for a 50-year-old.

Others feel resistant and dislike the way they look. These women complain of numerous body issues. Aging is synonymous with disappointment over body issues, particularly weight gain. Joan (#48) laments:

> At 35 years of age, I started gaining weight, probably not doing as much exercise. I gained a lot of weight, which was difficult. And then, perhaps I wasn't ashamed of my body, but I felt like I couldn't do things that I used to do, like I started yoga again and I can't do a shoulder stand, I used to be able to do a head stand, shoulder stand. So just realizing that my body isn't the same as it was 10 years ago . . .

Although these feelings are found in women of all ages, we feel it is important that for some midlife women negative feelings about body image can compound over time and adversely affect their quality of life. A minority of midlife women recount painful struggles with body image issues. Jennifer (#60) recalls her difficulties:

> I feel totally self conscious about my body image and my weight, particularly my weight. It's constant, but I work out faithfully. But it's still a constant thing about my life. From a health perspective I don't feel as horribly overweight as I did before, but I still feel self-conscious about it. It is about the relationship I have to my body—that's a whole other interview right there. From a health perspective it's never been a problem. It's never impeded my ability to do anything. But from a mental health perspective, it's been critical.

While the hard realities of aging often are confronted on the physical level, a woman may not 'feel' older. Anita (#12), a 'young midlifer' in our study, describes how she feels about the disconnection between 'mind and body'. While she feels young, her body issues harsh reminders:

I think that all of us—when we don't look in the mirror—still see ourselves as being sixteen. I dance in my head. And I think that the biggest compromise is going to be learning to live with an aging body. Even if I say to myself that I'm fortunate that I'm in a good body, it's just like a car! I can't do things the same way any more.

Western norms of feminine beauty idealize white, middle-class, young, thin, and toned women (Clarke, 2002a: 429). Cultural messages implore women to adhere closely to this hegemonic ideal. As women age, the gap between the ideal and the reality widens, making it more and more impossible for women to meet cultural norms. Anita (#12) understands that cultural pressure for women to maintain a 'youthful' or 'sexy' appearance in order to be happy and successful contrasts with the physical experiences of the aging body:

My body's falling apart, it's really doing me in. I read an article in *Chatelaine*, which gave me a laugh because it was about [how] high heels make you feel sexy and, [I'm] like, 'Not even, I can't even go there!' I have a choice: I can walk or I can wear high heels.

The messages, both blatant and subtle, are clear: stay slim; use makeup and dress to hide flaws in your appearance; look young at whatever cost. Women who ignore these messages are seen as failures who are 'falling apart' or 'letting themselves go'.

Are non-white women vulnerable to hegemonic standards of beauty? Absolutely; but they can also subvert cultural norms. In her detailed ethnography of the history of black beauty in America, Maxine Leeds Craig (2004) documents how black women have negotiated race, politics, gender, and beauty. Using interviews and archival material, Craig documents changing meanings of black female beauty and shows how beauty contests, afros, and conks represent African-American forms of cultural resistance to social ideas of black inferiority.

Because the social standard of female beauty has only one norm—the girl—while male beauty has two norms—the boy and the man—women age faster and earlier than men, who are allowed to age naturally without social penalties (Sontag, 1972). Because men are defined as 'old' later in life than are women, older men remain on the social radar far longer than older women, while women of all ages are judged more harshly in terms of their appearance and are more likely to be considered sexually eligible only if they are young.

Midlife women are caught in a double bind: neither compliance nor avoidance necessarily guarantees social success. This is what Nora Ephron calls 'the hilarious tragedy of the aging process, how women get to a certain point where you know gravity's going to win, but you end up kicking, fighting, and struggling—and you know you're being a complete idiot by doing it' (Ephron, 2006). Ephron describes reading an article about a face cream that people actually think lessens wrinkles. 'I clipped it out of the newspaper! But then, in the tradition of a person in my age bracket, I forgot where I put the scrap of paper' (MacDonald, 2006).

Age Avoidance Shaped by Class, Ethnicity, Sexuality, and Disability

The experience of ageism and age avoidance practices is shaped by class, ethnicity, sexuality, and dis/ability. Shifting identities lead some individuals into convoluted avoidance practices that appear to be related to the degree to which they equate ageism with loss of power. Historically, definitions of aging have been strongly related to social class as well as to gender. Wealthy men, across all ethnic groups, have been able to use their considerable resources as well as their social standing to avoid being treated as 'old'. Similarly, upper-class women may actually gain power as they age (Calasanti and Slevin, 2001: 23). Since wealthy men are seen as growing older later than economically insecure men, they are able to embrace aging in different ways and with less animosity than working-class men of all ethnic groups.

Consider, for example, the developed world's political and economic leaders who are almost without exception older men whose grey or thinning hair, grizzled visage, and, in some cases, hefty girth are seen as consistent with their personal attractiveness and public power. For some (for example, Donald Trump), a much younger wife or much younger sexual liaisons simply are taken for granted as an aspect of their social position. Their power and masculinity negate most of the common requirements for youthfulness and physical attractiveness. In contrast, when older women (for example, Hillary Clinton, Martha Stewart, or Oprah Winfrey) achieve political and/or economic power, they are routinely held to higher standards of personal youthfulness. Even powerful older women try to minimize the appearance of aging by dyeing their hair, staying slim, and dressing fashionably. Such efforts to adhere to standards of youthful feminine attractiveness soften, but do not eliminate, the frequent criticisms these women suffer that they are too 'mannish' and 'hard'.

Racial norms shape age and beauty standards. When media tend to see Western white women as standards for attractiveness, they marginalize non-white women by adding beauty to the long list of ways that racialization occurs. Feeling culturally alien, as deviant from prevailing norms, hair has become a symbol of ethnic discrimination among black women. As Shelton says, 'few things generate more anger and passion among Black women than their hair. Some Black critics say that women are in a frenzied search to shed the ancient racist shame and stigma of nappy hair—bad hair—by aping White beauty standards. Others say that, like most non-Black women, Black women are helpless captives of America's beauty industry, which is geared to make them more attractive and pleasing to men. Many Black women counter this by saying they are merely seeking their own identity or trying to look better' (Shelton, n.d.). Regardless of how one analyzes black conformity, race contours norms and practices of beauty.

Neglect of Ageism by Feminists

Given the structural, cultural, and individual ambivalence women feel towards aging, it should not be surprising to discover that feminists have been reluctant to embrace ageism. After all, feminists face the problem of ageism turned inward just as non-feminists do.

All midlife women, as Calasanti and Slevin (2006: 8) point out, have grown up in an ageist culture. It is no wonder that we find ourselves at times reflecting unconscious ageism:

> Because our culture is ageist we learn this form of bigotry from the time we are born. As a result we ultimately oppress ourselves: Either we try to avoid the aging process or we lose self-esteem because of the selves we feel we are becoming.

A number of feminists—including Browne (1998), Calasanti and Slevin (2001), Hooyman (1999), Pearsall (1997), and Reinharz (1997)—have criticized contemporary feminism for its neglect of aging as well as gerontology for its neglect of women. In other words, gerontology is seen as sexist and feminism is seen as ageist. In gerontology the focus has been largely on white men, leaving out women, women of colour, lesbians, and never-married women (Browne, 1998: xxii). Yet ageism hits women, who are already at a social disadvantage, harder than men, 'leaving them with their financial, health, caregiving, and social status seriously impacted' (ibid., xxvi). Calasanti and Slevin (2001: 27) observe:

> Most research on aging has paid little attention either to gender or to other hierarchies of privilege and oppression such as race, class and sexual orientation. . . . On the other hand, most feminists, while sensitive to gender and intersecting power relations, have virtually ignored old age in their theories and research.

The usual explanation for the seeming neglect of ageism by the second wave of the women's movement focuses on the age of its participants. Many of the core activists of the second wave were young women who, quite naturally, addressed issues they were experiencing. They rejected issues of age along with their rejection of commitments to domesticity such as those undertaken by their mother's generation (Reinharz, 1997). For young women of the second wave of the women's movement, sexism posed a more fundamental issue than ageism.

There were, of course, some older feminists in the 1970s and 1980s. In 1983, Barbara Macdonald and Cynthia Rich published *Look Me in the Eye*, which identified ageism as a central feminist issue. They pointed out that young women's alienation from old women, their dread at becoming them, and their revulsion towards old women's bodies are the direct result of a sexist consumer society that falsely empowers youth and disempowers the old. 'Your power as a younger woman', they wrote, 'is measured by the distance you can keep between you and older women.' Macdonald and Rich understood the source of ageism to be the patriarchal family, wherein mothers serve all members including youth and self-sacrifice is a valued commodity.

Macdonald tells the story of how she first confronted ageism in the women's movement. At the age of 65 she went on a 'Take Back the Night' march. She hadn't particularly wanted to go, but agreed to show her support. As they were lined up, six abreast, waiting to start, she overheard a young march monitor suggest that if she could not keep up with the others that she reposition herself in the crowd. Both the comment and the fact that the younger woman could not address her directly with her concern offended Barbara. Her response was one of seething rage: 'All my life in a man's world, I was a problem because I was a woman; now I'm a problem in a woman's world because I'm a sixty-five-year-old woman' (Macdonald and Rich, 1983: 30). The attitudes of young women 'have been shaped since childhood by patriarchy to view the older woman as powerless, less important than the fathers and the children, and there to serve them both; and like all who serve, the older woman soon becomes invisible' (ibid., 40).

In the quarter-century since these remarks, the cultural context of aging has changed little. While the women's movement helped women unlearn the lessons of sexism, it did little to help them learn how to confront ageism. Only in 2005 did the pioneer journal *Off Our Backs* devote an entire issue to ageism. At first glance the lack of academic curiosity about age and aging might appear to reflect negative stereotypes of older women who are—in the minds of some—simply not that interesting to study. As May Sarton pointed out in *As We Are Now*: 'The trouble is that old age is not interesting until one gets there' (Sarton, 1982 [1973]: 23). Indeed, middle age and aging certainly became more central to today's authors once we began to see ourselves as middle-aged.

Garner (1999) expects that as feminists age, their awareness of their own aging will focus academic attention on the aging process. To some extent we have seen this happen. Feminists like Beauvoir (1986 [1977]), Friedan (1993), and Greer (1991) have published books analyzing the aging process. On the other hand, such books are few in number and they apparently have not had a significant impact on the study of aging. Cruikshank (2003) takes Gardner's point one step further in suggesting that it may take a large number of feminists confronting issues like caring to ignite a passion parallel to that brought to issues of reproductive choice. We agree with Copper (1997: 121), who said that 'there are endless unexamined contradictions in the prejudice which women feel toward the old women they themselves are becoming.'

Key Concepts

Body concealment practices Attempts made by older women to hide the physical signs of aging. Dress, makeup, hair dyes, cosmetic surgery, and drugs are consumed in an effort to present a socially youthful image.

Double standard of aging A term coined by Susan Sontag in 1972 to recognize that older women are judged less attractive than older men.

Materialist (political economy) perspective A theoretical perspective that sees economic conditions as shaping social and individual actions and attitudes.

Racialization The process of constructing specific images based on a set of assumptions or stereotypes according to certain races. It refers to a process of differentiation based on race and an imposition of a racial character on a person or action.

Resistance The act of defending one's position in response to confrontation.

Subjectivity How one feels about oneself is constructed through experience with ageism.

Questions for Critical Discussion

1. One way in which young women take up their female subjectivity is through their adherence to body practices. Make a list of all the daily body practices in which you engage, from when you wake up in the morning until you go to bed at night.
2. Define 'racialization'. Provide examples of racialization processes in popular culture.
3. What is the double standard of aging? Has it affected you yet or is it a phenomenon that only affects the old?
4. How would a materialist perspective analyze social class patterns in body concealment practices?
5. Women both accept and resist aging. Why and how?

Chapter 3

Midlife Women and the Women's Movement

Perhaps it is impossible for young women to comprehend a time when living with one's boyfriend was called 'living in sin', when children born to unmarried parents were illegitimate, when husbands could legally rape their wives, when lesbian relationships were kept secret, or when employment for women was limited to household service, nursing, secretarial work, clerking, waitressing, hairdressing, sewing, or teaching. Occasionally, women became doctors, lawyers, chiropractors, school principals, university professors, church leaders, independent researchers, musicians, artists, or businesswomen, but such professionalism was not the norm. Yet, this is the world midlife women were born into.

Feminism, the ideological arm of the women's movement, represents a powerful critique of the legal, economic, political, cultural, and personal barriers to inequality women face. There have been as many different approaches to feminism as there are ways to combat inequity. The midlife women in our study experienced either first-hand or from a distance the wave of social change that swept through Canada in the middle of the twentieth century. This wave framed their lives, altered their choices, and, in many instances, shifted their priorities. For some, feminism meant freedom to enjoy a career and reconsider the necessity of marriage and/or marriage to men. For others, the expansion of economic and cultural opportunities precipitated individual confusion and unhappiness. The impact of feminism and the women's movement was by no means the same for all of the women in our study.

In this chapter, we trace the legacy of the women's movement for midlife women. We begin by sketching different forms of feminism and the diverse types of women's movements that emerged in Canada. Midlife women had access to different routes to feminism through their connections to the social structure. We look at if and how midlife women took up feminist identities and which parts, if any, they passed on to their children. We conclude with a personal portrait of what we call the 'new' mother–daughter relationship, which seems to have been literally unimaginable for most Canadian women in previous eras.

Routes to Feminism

While the women's movement defined the 1970s and 1980s in Canada, midlife women connected to it in fundamentally different ways. At the broadest level of society, **liberal feminism** along with **socialist feminism** altered the social institutions and social groups to which women belonged. Laws changed, which meant that behavioural norms common in previous generations suddenly shifted. It was impossible to be a Canadian and not be affected by these powerful institutional shifts even if one did not subscribe politically or morally to the changes. Birth control and, later, abortion were legalized. Divorce laws were revolutionized. Wages rose. Education expanded. Even when laws already existed, the women's movement made it clear that they were paying closer attention to if and how laws were enforced. Personal violence against women had long been illegal but marches by women campaigning against wife assault and campus rape helped spread social understandings that women did not 'belong' to men and that women could not be mistreated with impunity. Cultural institutions began featuring the voices of women in ways not previously experienced. Magazine articles, feature films, bookstores, art displays, and advertisements began to publicize the goals of the women's movement and the views of its various advocates.

Coming of age in the 1970s exposed many women and men to liberal feminist views. You read about it. You lived it. You knew someone whose life had been affected by the insertion of gender into public consideration. But exposure was not synonymous with acceptance. Many midlife women, while readily acknowledging that they benefited from the goals of feminism, whatever its stripe, did not see themselves as actively participating in the women's movement nor did they identify themselves then, or now, as adherents. Are they understating their roles in history or simply not making connections between individual, small acts and larger social changes? We think both.

Institutional Changes Brought about by the Women's Movement

If you grew up after the 1950s and 1960s, it is worth watching one of the popular films from that period, for here are the models of womanhood that pervaded the culture. Doris Day was tightly coiffed, perpetually virginal, and always 'falling in love' or Elizabeth Taylor—more dynamic and overtly sexual—was always to be tamed by the male hero and romance. Without exception, leading 'ladies' in that period were young, primped and permed, and framed completely by their relationships to the leading 'men'. Older women—Bette Davis or Joan Crawford—maintained their roles in film only by becoming objects of humour, pity, or the macabre. This stifling social construction of women's lives was shredded by modern feminism. Long, wind-swept hair, the 'natural' (no cosmetics) look, the rejection of torpedo bras, girdles, and pantyhose all speak to a powerful, sometimes angry rejection of the constraints on women's being and a demand for an opportunity to be freer, more human, wilder, and more independent.

These seemingly surface changes were, of course, embedded in profound institutional shifts. Beginning in the mid-1960s jobs began to open up for young and educated women and post-secondary institutions were increasingly accessible. Yet, the expectation that women's ultimate calling was marriage and children did not change. The sexual revolution of the 1960s encouraged sexual freedom—as long as it was heterosexual sex.

Increased access to education, the popularization of early feminist writings such as *The Second Sex* (Beauvoir, 1989 [1949]) and *The Feminine Mystique* (Friedan, 1963), and the youth revolution of the 1960s provided the opportunities, the vocabulary, and the strategies for challenging the dominant culture. Increasingly, young women found the sexism they encountered in their relationships with men, whether in groups or one to one, intolerable. As students they objected to sexist social expectations of their future economic roles as well as to the content of the material they were expected to learn. Women students wanted to read about women's experiences and to hear what women writers, critics, and academics had to say. Although more women went to university, women were vastly under-represented on university campuses (as faculty and as students) and course content was, by today's standards, sexist and heterosexist.

Women were ignored or stereotyped in the content of many disciplines. In sociology, as in all social sciences, men were social actors and what they did was the norm. Research on men was generalized to women. Childhood, motherhood, and housework were not separate subjects of study within sociology. The lens for studying women's paid work was its impact on the family. That women worked in a narrow range of jobs for low pay was not problematized. Motherhood was women's destiny. Whatever else women did, they were expected to mother. With the emergence of feminism and the availability of birth control pills in the sixties, more and more young women protested compulsory motherhood, and a number of the women in our study were among those who postponed childbirth or decided not to become mothers.

When the authors of this book were undergraduates in the late 1960s the social climate was beginning to change, yet we were taught that the sexual division of labour was both natural and desirable. As graduate students we were involved in consciousness-raising sessions and campus women's caucuses that helped frame our experiences. By listening to other women's stories and struggling to make sense of them, we came to understand in a visceral way the truth in the slogans of the women's movement: 'Sisterhood is powerful' and 'The personal is political'. Nevertheless, we are three white middle-class women, privileged in our access to education and in the support we received to attend university. We knew sexism. We did not—and could never know—the layered oppressions of immigrant, non-white, lesbian, or disabled women.

Before women could change oppressive structures or depart confining relationships they had to begin to change themselves. In the 1960s young women were drawn to consciousness-raising groups as a way of talking about and trying to understand explicit and implicit sexism. 'The groups created an environment that reinforced the relevance of personal experience and underscored the inconsistency between that experience and the theoretical models used by social scientists to characterize it' (Wilson, 1996: 7). In consciousness-raising groups across North America, which principally were campus-based and did not involve women of colour and working-class women (Agnew, 1993: 221), white middle-class women began to see their personal experiences were shared, and they began to push for change.

In those early days of second-wave feminism, many married women with young children struggled to find meaning in the roles of wife and mother in the face of a universally held expectation of a sexual division of labour. When Betty Friedan's *The Feminine Mystique* was published in 1963, it struck a chord with housewives across North America. Women resonated with her description of 'the problem that has no name': the problem of housewife's malaise; the problem of how to engage meaningfully in life when your BA was being used to run the local PTA or killing time in pediatricians' waiting rooms. Friedan solved this problem for herself by later becoming the first president of the National Organization of Women (NOW) in the US.

Career women had different concerns. They were tired of having to prove themselves capable over and over again, only to be paid less and overlooked as managers or leaders. The focus of employed women was economic equality, which meant changing discriminatory and sexist practices in education, work, politics, and law. The newly established women's organizations took up these economic and employment inequalities. Canadian activists including Laura Sabia, who was president of the Canadian Federation of University Women (CFUW) and of the Committee for the Equality of Women in Canada, joined with other women to initiate a Royal Commission on the Status of Women. Doris Anderson lobbied for change as editor of *Chatelaine* magazine. In a recent interview (Rundle, 2006) Anderson described how the mainstream press at the time thought the idea of a Royal Commission was 'hilarious'. 'And then the stories started coming out about battered women, women in poverty, Native women, and it became more serious.' The Royal Commission (RCSW) was struck in 1967 with the goal of ensuring for women 'equal opportunity with men in all aspects of Canadian society' (Royal Commission on the Status of Women, 1970: vii). The 167 recommendations of the Commission set the agenda for lobbying efforts for the next two decades. The National Action Committee on the Status of Women (NAC), a national coalition of women's organizations, was organized to ensure the implementation of the recommendations.

Not surprisingly, economic inequalities were a focus in programs for change. Of course, the majority of working women at the time were not career women. Rather, they were poorly paid, working-class, 'pink-collar' women working in clerical, service, or light manufacturing jobs. One way to understand the differences between the women who demanded a Royal Commission and the women who protested on campuses or in workplaces is to refer to the former as **institutional feminism** and the latter as **grassroots feminism**. 'Institutionalized feminism operates within traditional institutions—inside political parties and government ministries, for example—while grass-roots feminism is more community-based, emphasizing collective organizing, consciousness-raising, and reaching out to women "on the street"' (Adamson et al., 1988: 12). Institutional feminism developed along with an increased awareness of sexual discrimination in employment, of segregation, and of low pay. Women wanted legally enshrined freedoms to enter the labour force on an equal footing with men. These liberal feminists sought legislative protection to ensure equality of opportunity. They demanded daycare and other supports for employed mothers.

In contrast, grassroots feminism emerged in a climate of radicalism created by the rise of the peace movement, the civil rights movement in the US, and the New Left. Women's groups began to organize around issues such as reproductive choice, sexual freedom, rape, violence, and pornography, and these organizations became focal points of change. In the midst of the sexual revolution it became evident that sexual freedom was not possible without safe, effective, affordable birth control. Abortion was necessary, too, if women were to be assured an end to unwanted pregnancies, so access to abortion became a key demand.

The Women's Health Movement

The **women's health movement** grew out of the women's movement in the 1960s and 1970s. Because most women activists then were in their twenties and thirties it was logical to focus on reproductive issues. The right to safe and effective birth control, access to abortion, greater sexual autonomy, birthing centres, and so on became the key issues. At the time, abortion was illegal in Canada and the United States except where the life of the mother was in jeopardy. Childbirth in the 1970s was highly medicalized. Partners were not usually allowed to be present during the birth, and women often didn't see their babies for hours after the birth. Feminist health advocates questioned the number of Caesareans and, later, the medicalization of menopause in terms of the number of hysterectomies performed and the use of hormone replacement therapy. Since women in the 1970s were presumed to want to leave the labour force to care for their young children, they were expected also to want to do this caregiving in the privacy of their homes. Breast-feeding in public was frowned upon. Public child care was woefully inadequate.

The women's health movement provides a powerful example of the impact of second-wave feminism on Canadian women's lives. From the beginning, the movement consisted of a myriad of grassroots groups, so it was never a single movement. Some groups were institutionally supported; others remained active at the grassroots level without such support. Initially, the goal was to provide information and women-centred care. Feminists worked to create clinics and services for women that challenged sexist, paternalistic practices in the care of women and infant children. Information was assumed to be the key to enable women to make informed decisions about their care. Newsletters proliferated and included a wide range of information for and by women concerning their health. Now, this information comes by way of the Internet. The Boston Women's Health Collective, perhaps the best-known women's health initiative in North America, was started in 1969. Two years later they published the best-selling *Our Bodies, Our Selves*. This was followed in 1994 by *Our Selves Growing Older* and a revised version of *Our Bodies, Our Selves* in 2005. In

Canada, *Healthsharing* started in 1979 as a newsletter and evolved into an alternative feminist health magazine read by women across the country. In its 15 years of publication, *Healthsharing* tried to broaden the concept of women's health to look not only at reproductive issues or diseases, but also at women's physical, mental, and spiritual well-being (Gotleib, 1994).

A major contribution of the women's health movement was to create an alternative health-care model that moved away from the existing biomedical focus long before official action was taken on these issues. Women brought to light unhealthy practices, such as early versions of the contraceptive pill, the negative impacts of an exclusively medical management of birthing, and health concerns associated with hormone therapy. Women insisted that their experience and their concerns regarding their health and the kinds of treatment and support they valued be a major component of their care. An important issue was the identification of gender bias in medical practice and research. For decades, most studies were conducted on male subjects and the results generalized to women. For example, research on cardiovascular disease did not address differences in the disease in men and women. Today, women's health has become an area of medical specialization, and women's health centres have become institutionalized. Perhaps the greatest challenge for the women's health movement lies ahead. Ruzek argues that the aging of the population is a critical women's health issue for the future. 'The next wave of women's health activism surely must address the pressing challenges of women's health and health caring in a rapidly aging society' (Ruzek, 2004: 113).

The women's health movement is rooted in the women's movement, the civil rights movement, and the peace movement. The breast cancer movement drew on all of these, plus gay activism and the AIDS movement (Kaufert, 1997: 294). Indeed, Kaufert (ibid., 302) argues that the breast cancer movement would not have evolved in the way that it did without the example of AIDS. The breast cancer movement started with acts of resistance as a few individuals began to speak out about breast cancer. At the time even talking about breast cancer was radical. Until prominent women like Betty Ford spoke to the media about her diagnosis, breast cancer was simply not discussed publicly. Public figures spoke out on the subject, and feminist poet Audrey Lourde, who later died of breast cancer in 1993, wrote about her experiences and her fears in *The Cancer Journals* (1980). As some women spoke publicly, others who felt isolated in the experience of breast cancer began to join together in support groups that eventually became the backbone of a movement.

Pioneers in the breast cancer movement asserted the right to information in the face of often paternalistic attitudes of oncologists. Without access to information, how could women make informed choices regarding their treatment? Until 25 years ago, mastectomy was the typical surgical treatment. Women argued for less radical surgeries, and now lumpectomy has become standard practice. Breast cancer activists demonstrated, marched, held candlelight vigils, and published letters and columns in newspapers to draw attention to an 'epidemic' they argued was ignored because it was a woman's disease. Later the breast cancer movement became increasingly engaged in political action, arguing for a broader research mandate to include research into environmental causes of cancer.

The breast cancer movement lifted the silence surrounding diagnosis, questioned surgical procedures, raised funds for and influenced the research agenda, drew attention to the psychosocial aspects of living with cancer, and effectively raised awareness regarding breast cancer risk. This campaign was so successful that women now have a fear of breast cancer that is out of proportion to the risk (Robertson, 2000: 219). Indeed, Canadian women believe it is the 'number-one killer' of women, when in fact more women die of heart and cardiovascular disease than breast cancer.

The women's movement and the women's health movement have tended to focus on the issues and concerns of the young women who made up the majority of activists. The concerns of older or aging women were secondary concerns, although the medicalization of menopause was an exception. Indeed, menopause has received disproportionate attention, and is essentially the only health issue connected to middle-aged women. Interestingly, most women in our study had little to say about menopause. Their biggest health concern is stress and the elusive search for balance at this stage of their lives.

Diversity within the Women's Movement

Feminists represent a myriad of concerns and issues and a wide range of organizations. Despite their differences, organized feminists for the past 150 years have shared a passion for asserting gender equality. We typically refer to the suffragist movement as **first-wave feminists** and the women's movement of the 1960s and 1970s as the **second wave**. The **third wave**, influenced by postmodernism, developed out of the second wave's inability to resolve issues of racial difference and sexuality. The goals of first- and second-wave feminism were similar. Nineteenth-century feminists were concerned about unhealthy working conditions, low wages, restricted access to education, unfair marriage laws, and women's exclusion from politics. However, it soon became apparent that without the right to vote, women would not succeed in making changes, so obtaining the vote became their focus (see Wilson, 1996).

According to bell hooks, feminism is 'a movement to end sexism, sexist exploitation, and oppression' (2000: viii). This definition makes it clear that feminism is not anti-male. And as she points out, women can be as sexist as men. Indeed, we all are engaged in perpetuating sexism, although men benefit more than women. Institutional and grassroots feminists followed different paths in their struggles to end 'sexism, sexist exploitation, and oppression'. Radical feminists focused on the right to reproductive choice, free from the cultural scripts of motherhood and the patriarchal family, and free from male violence (see ibid.). Socialist feminism was concerned with women's place in the class system. The centre of socialist feminist activism was the workplace, particularly the union movement. Although the women's movement represented a wide range of women's organizations, large and small, the majority of activists were young. Their concerns about aging women were limited to an analysis of the feminization of poverty and the economic concerns of older or divorced women. They did not pay particular attention to the meaning of age, aging, or ageism.

Women's Studies courses responded to demands of women students for course content by and for women. The first such courses in Canada were offered in the early 1970s. The movement gained momentum because of these courses as they became incubators for women's scholarship and the development of feminist theory. Yet, in the long run the development of Women's Studies courses may have negatively affected the movement because universities' access was limited to middle-class women. 'Once the women's studies classroom replaced the consciousness-raising groups as the primary site for the transmission of feminist thinking and strategies for social change the movement lost its mass-based potential' (hooks, 2000: 10).

Agnew's (1993: 224) writing about Canada makes a related point about the academy: 'Publications on women of colour remain scarce since these women are only marginally present at Canadian universities from which such writings usually emerge.' One of the criticisms of second-wave feminism that came from inside the movement was its inability to respond to issues of difference in a way that did not marginalize women of colour along with lesbians and bisexual women.

The women's movement of the 1970s transformed our thinking and our behaviour. It opened doors for women in education that were relevant and critical, and jobs that were meaningful and respected. Women's Studies began in Canadian universities with a limited analysis of women and developed into what now is a rich body of work. It increased the number of women professors in higher education and the number of men working in child care and teaching primary school. It encouraged sharing of housework and child care so that both men and women cook and parent. It changed rape laws and brought interpersonal violence and sexual abuse into the open. Women's organizations relentlessly lobbied for affordable and accessible child care. Women can now take responsibility for birth control and have access to means that are safe and effective. Bisexuality and homosexuality have come out of the closet. Indeed, because of these successes of the women's movement, in terms of career advancement, educational opportunities, and increased control of reproduction and sexuality, many feel that the second wave essentially completed the task it set for itself.

However, others argue that the job is far from complete. Violence against women and girls is pervasive, as is women's fear of interpersonal violence. Women and children still are economically vulnerable and full-time women workers still earn less than men in comparable jobs. Indeed, claims of the closing gap between male and female wages have more to do with declining male wages than gains for women. Opportunities to engage in paid work did not deliver greater equality for families. Today men and women work longer hours and are more stressed. Fewer couples choose to have children because the stress and time pressures involved in raising a family these days simply are too daunting. In North America the conservative and religious right has supported an anti-feminist backlash that has resulted in lost ground in regard to reproductive freedoms and a return to 'family values' and entrenched gender roles.

'The two slogans at the ideological core of the women's movement, "Sisterhood" and "The Personal is Political" failed to address the barriers of social stratification based on class and race' (Agnew, 1993: 217). Visible minority women insisted on an analysis that looked at the intersection of race, class, gender, and sexuality. They argued that just as it was not useful to generalize from men to women, it was not useful to consider the experiences of white women as the norm. This issue was not simply about diversity of experience. Women as well as men exploit women. The failure of second-wave feminists to adequately confront issues of race and ethnic difference or the multiple oppressions of race, class, sexuality, or ability became the seedbed of the third wave. Indeed, women of colour were the first to use the term 'third wave' (Springer, 2002).

Identifying with the Women's Movement

Culturally, the legacy of feminism is full of contradictions. Feminists often are portrayed in the media in derogatory ways—as angry lesbians, man-haters, and as women who reject any accommodations to femininity. Bad press is hardly a new tactic. American feminists involved in the abolitionist movement attending the Seneca Falls Convention in 1848 were described as 'spinsters, crossed in love, wishing to ape man' (quoted in Rupp, 2001: 170). The media seem to have been a catalyst for the current anti-feminist backlash. While stronger and more vocal in the United States, Canadian anti-feminist groups like Realistic, Equal, Active, for Life (REAL) women have been relatively popular. Their motto is: 'Women's rights, but not at the expense of human rights'. When we visited their website in September 2006, the first item under 'Alerts' describes a 'counter-attack by feminists' to thwart the attempts of REAL women to 'disband the Status of Women [a federal government bureau that has been savaged by the Harper government] and its outrageous policies and funding' because it is based 'on the false premise that women in Canada are victims of a patriarchal society' (REAL Women of Canada, 2006).

In Canada the backlash of the 1990s created a sense of one step forward and at least one step back. While there were political gains, including greater participation of women of colour in national organizations, there were also severe funding cutbacks that affected the national organizations and local initiatives. The Montreal massacre came to symbolize the backlash. On 6 December 1989, a severely disturbed young man shot and killed 14 women engineering students, ostensibly because he was angry about feminism. Kam Reo, one of the women interviewed for Judy Rebick's book *Ten Thousand Roses* (2005), which chronicles the recent history of feminism in Canada, talked about the connection between the massacre and the reaction to the broad misogyny across many Canadian university campuses. For example, the 'No Means No' anti-date rape campaign at one Canadian university was mocked by male students, who posted aggressive slogans such as 'No Means More Beer' around campus.

That young women today take the gains of the women's movement for granted is, in part, a sign of the successes that have changed social rules in the space of one generation. Unlike midlife women, young white women have not had to struggle for a voice in education or for access to employment. They do not yet experience ageism. By virtue of their age, younger women are knee-deep in the issues related to their demographic: the identity struggles likely surrounding the importance of look-ing young and thin. As they age, these young women will live the experiences of what it is to be in midlife while facing the same cultural imperative of youth and beauty for women. Where getting married, finding a job, and having a baby at one time were the catalytic events for feminist consciousness, today, perhaps, it is growing old.

Young women have grown up in an economic, political, and social context that reflects the gains of the women's movement. In this context, feminism as a move-ment may seem outdated, and the term 'feminism' may simply seem old-fashioned. Young men and women support the idea of gender equality, yet typically they do not think of feminism as relevant to their lives. Young women 'deny being feminist while maintaining views that are fundamentally compatible with feminism' (Arnold, 2000: 8). It may be, as Arnold claims, that the feminist label young women reject is the anti-feminist stereotype. More positive attitudes are found when researchers asked about the 'women's movement' instead of 'feminism' (Buschman and Lenart, 1996).

Another explanation for the resistance to feminist labelling is that young people are encouraged to see the world in individualistic terms and to reject the notion of labels entirely. 'Perhaps it is not the goals of the movement but the collective nature of a "movement" that some supporters of feminism resist' (Williams and Wittig, 1997: 892). In this context, it is not surprising to find researchers referring to many young women as 'precarious feminists', that is, women who are caught between 'moderately strong group identification as well as strong beliefs in individualism' (Buschman and Lenart, 1996: 72). In a cultural context where reliance on assistance from others—whether governmental affirmative action or social welfare programs, unions or social movements—has been represented in increasingly negative terms, it is not surprising that female university students understand their lives in terms of personal ambitions and individual struggles rather than 'collective action toward obtaining equality for women' (Williams and Wittig, 1997: 894). These are women whose socialization has made them self-reliant.

Of course, some middle-aged women have internalized this same construction of achievement, as it pertains to visions of individual freedom, hard work, and perse-verance. In this sense, feminism as a collective movement becomes irrelevant or dis-respected because it cannot champion individualism in the same way. As Gail (#14) describes:

> I, maybe because of the person that I am, I had always felt that I could do any-thing that I always wanted to do. I have never felt that as a woman I wasn't equal to a man and couldn't be totally honest and be whatever I wanted to be. So I have never felt as a woman that I had to be a feminist. . . . My environ-ment, my parents just expected me to be whatever I wanted to be.

Third-wave feminism, as noted above, developed in response to the inability of second-wave feminism to account for differences in terms of race, sexual identity, or ability. Third-wave feminism is multicultural, angry, sad, joyful, celebratory—in brief, 'out there'. Influenced by postmodern thinking, it defies or rejects labels and categories, organizational structures, and leader–follower roles. 'Viewing identities as multiple, fluid and unstable was seen as presenting more possibilities for the surfacing of differences' (Mann and Hoffman, 2005: 63). As a result, even active feminists may not identify with feminism—since they don't identify with any groups.

In this study, a number of midlife women respondents resist labelling themselves as feminist because they, too, resist labels of any kind:

> I don't call myself a feminist, but I live a life that would be familiar to any feminist. I don't like categorizing myself at all. Do I consider myself a Catholic? Do I consider myself an American? No, I don't consider myself an American. No, I don't consider myself a Catholic. I don't see myself as defining, or considering myself a feminist. I consider myself supportive of a feminist movement. (Rita, #1)

> I think that my life and feminism have been in parallel universes, parallel streams, that the movement and I have walked down the path together and matured together. If asked if I was a feminist 30 years ago, I would have said, 'so what?' I believed in freedom and equality of sexes, I had always been outspoken whether I was going to be coined a feminist or not. I knew that I was going to make decisions and not be subjugated; I didn't need feminism to tell me that I could rally behind that. (Martha, #49)

Our interviews support the idea that when midlife women reject a feminist label, it is sometimes because they are reluctant to assume any 'one' identity in general. Midlife women in this survey grappled with these concepts, as one artist and mother of two asked: 'as women we have so many different pieces, so many different parts, so many different roles, how do we become whole?' (Anna, #73). Postmodern identities are characterized by precisely this fragmented, splintered, and decentred sense of self, where an understanding of our 'selves' is based on categories of identity that are more fluid and context-dependent.

The desire for a more inclusive 'poly-feminism' was evident in the discussions as well. Nancy (#2) clarified that, for her, 'there is no one feminist movement.' Later in the interview she said: 'I feel like I belong to a woman's community on my terms.' Women in this study were sympathetic to the women's movement, without necessarily feeling comfortable with the 'feminist' label. The respondents at times were hesitant when asked if they would call themselves feminists. For example, Gail (#14) said that it 'depends on how it is defined':

> If it's defined as having the freedom to be all that I want to be and to relate to others in every way I wanted and to help others have the freedom they need to live a whole, balanced, wonderful life whether it is male or female, then I am. That would be my definition.

Anna talked about her desire for a non-gender-specific type of equality:

Well I guess the label 'feminist' is denying part of who I am. I like being a woman, I don't feel that I need to apologize for who I am, or try to be whatever it is. If we were to treat each other as people, rather than as male or female, to get rid of the labels—forget the labels—I talk to you as a person. Not as a male or a female, or as this or that or anything else. . . . If I'm going to be valued for who I am, not because I'm a woman, or a male, but because I'm me. I don't have to be a feminist; I don't have to be anything to prove who I am. It's not about proving anything. It's just about being. (Anna, #73)

One participant shared an anecdote that offers a stark reminder of the power of labelling, and illustrates the tension underlying identity politics for many women. During a seminar presentation she had attended:

I heard her [feminist presenter] speak and she said, she is in her seventies . . . . She would put these big white pieces of paper on the wall and each one had one word on it. So she would run to the one that said 'Woman' and then run to the one that said 'Jew'. That has really stayed with me because it has to be all integrated, and then move forward, because it is not separate. If you have to choose between black and Jew . . . what do you do? And who decides? Who puts them into that box, like that is like the Jewish box, the Gypsy box, the homosexual box? (Nancy, #2)

Given the backlash, the media stigmatization of feminists and feminism, and given the predominant belief in individualism, it is small wonder that women today are reluctant to call themselves feminists. The disclaimer—'I'm not a feminist, but . . .' appears to characterize the feelings of many women we talked with. Indeed, the phrase appears in the title of many published studies exploring this phenomenon (see Schnittker et al., 2003; Buschman and Lenart, 1996; Williams and Wittig, 1997; Zucker, 2004). Most of this research focused on the attitudes of younger women, primarily American college and university students. Interestingly, research that has looked at women of colour or 'othered' women has found that these women are more likely to self-label as feminist and support feminism (see Chow, 1993; Dufour, 2000). Zucker (2004) expected to find that women who grew up with the second wave of the women's movement would have a stronger identification with feminism than women who were one generation older or younger. However, her results did not support this difference. Feminist identity—for all ages—is a complex, evolving, and many-layered phenomenon.

Midlife Women and Feminism

We asked the women we interviewed if they thought of themselves as feminists, before we asked them to talk about their connection to the women's movement and to describe its impact on their lives. We wanted to know if these women, who lived through the political awakening of the 1960s, who experienced first-hand the social inequalities of negotiating domestic labour and careers with glass ceilings, who faced the economic insecurities of lone parenthood, or who felt the shame and stigma of women's sexual choices and identity, thought of themselves as feminist as they reflected on their lives at midlife. As discussed in Chapter 1, because our informants were located through women's organizations, it is understandable that many of them self-identified as feminists. This was by no means universally true, however.

'I'm not a feminist, but . . .'

One-third of the women in the study did not think of themselves as feminist. For some, feminism carries negative connotations. They seem to have internalized homophobic or heterophobic media images of feminists as outspoken, man-hating lesbians, and certainly resisted the idea of being associated with these stereotypes. As Lenora (#41), a married mother of two, explained:

> Whenever you tell someone, you sound like you have an opinion, they laugh, 'Oh, she's a feminist', or they think you're going to get involved with women that are lesbians, or . . . you know, many people associate feminist with lesbians.

Some women rejected the identity and echoed what sounded like the tone of feminist backlash, responding to the construction of feminists as 'controlling' or 'anti-male'. This negative labelling is an effective social control mechanism. Maya (#43) said that her husband called her a feminist when complaining that she is opinionated:

> I would say I have been painted with a broad brush—it's the feminism brush—in my relationship with my ex, because I was more than willing to compromise and give whatever it took to make my marriage work. But because I was standing up for myself, not because I was a feminist but because I feel that I'm a human being and I wanted to be listened to. I wanted my opinion to count. I wasn't trying to rule him, as he would say, or to control him.

Ironically, some who did not think of themselves as feminists expressed ideas that were decidedly feminist. As Maria (#80) said: 'I don't think I'd describe myself as a feminist, but certainly I am glad for the moves that women have made.' Malina, Brenda, and Amy also seemingly feel very strongly about gender equality, but did not feel comfortable calling themselves feminists.

> No, I wouldn't call myself that [feminist]. I have always maintained that women should have equal rights. I was brought up in a culture where women were subservient to men. . . . When I married my husband we argued; my husband said, 'I'm earning now. I hope that you will stay home.' I said, 'No. My career is important to me. I will stop when the first child comes.' I didn't stop

because at that time we needed the money. Today, there are times when he [my husband] almost resents the importance that I give to my career. But he understands it. But there has never been the feminist side in me. . . . [But] I really do feel angry when I see a woman that has not been given her rights. (Malina, #15)

I think feminism, as I understand it, has shaken the world up, but I wouldn't call myself a feminist. The women's movement has allowed me to become more open. It has supported me to be who I wanted to be without hiding behind a man. (Brenda, #51)

Well, I believe in equality absolutely, but I like having the door opened for me and I like somebody to sit my chair under me and pour me a glass of wine and . . . [laughs]. So if you look at that, no, then I'm not a feminist. (Amy, #20)

While not defining herself as a feminist, Amy added that she thought 'women have generally on the whole suffered much more than any man I know.' The attitude of Vera (#8) on the subject of feminism is perhaps more ambivalent and is qualified by the remark that she is 'partially' a feminist:

I believe in equal rights . . . equal wages . . . I believe [in] equal opportunities in education. I like getting the door opened for me. I like having men around.

Shantell (#46), who emigrated from the Caribbean as a young adult, like some other women, rejects the gains of the women's movement because she is concerned about its impact on gender roles and family life. Her comments also reflect the media stigmatizing of feminism.

I don't think it [feminism] has done too much. . . . I grew up with it. I grew up with a mother that I saw struggle and be very independent. I've seen women get a lot of dirt. I see it here in this company. I think that we lost something, what the women did. They are so confused and so afraid, and they don't know if they're coming or going. We have gone out and helped men bring home the bacon; then we still prep it and cook it, too. We now have two jobs instead one. That's really lost. Before, the [men] that were decent took pride in taking care of their families. They are so emasculated these days. They are not allowed to stand up to a strong woman. So they are lost. Right now, the men in our generation are a mess.

Issues of ethnicity, race, country of origin, and class complicated the ability to identify with the women's movement. As Reid (1984: 252) has noted, there are often many reasons why black women do not identify with the women's movement, including a very real problem of racism in the women's movement and mistrust between black and white women. As one black woman, who had immigrated to Canada in the 1980s, stated:

Mistakes a lot of women or females have made in the past is that they have to label themselves, and then they have to act out according to that label, and then they have to publicize it. See, I read all the literature on the feminist movement. They have some good points, but as a black woman, I couldn't go there. I didn't want to go there. I made a decision not to go there, because white women, they did have a problem. Now, from a cultural standpoint, as a black woman, we know the power we've always had. Blacks have always been matriarchal, and so we know we have that power. We didn't have to go fight for it or anything. We didn't have to—if you look at the movers and shakers in the black world, they're mostly women. (Tamika, #58)

Similarly, a Muslim woman, who moved to Canada as an adult, felt disconnected from what she called 'Western' feminism:

You know it's a little bit difficult to be an Iranian feminist, or to be a Western feminist, or to be a black feminist. I think all of these feminists have [a] different definition for themselves. I consider myself as a feminist regarding to the Iranian culture. Regarding Western culture, I think I need to work still. Because I don't get the Western culture yet. (Amina, #9)

Class, too, was a barrier. Catherine (#61), a 59-year-old mother of two, described the women's movement as a middle-class movement. She said she didn't have the opportunity to become involved until she herself became middle-class.

It was extraordinarily hard for me to be involved in feminism until probably my forties, which is the same time I did the class shift. Feminism is really a middle-class construct. I still believe that it is. There's been some attempts to link feminism to more working-class [women], but it's pretty hard and part of that is because when you look at the hierarchy it means if you're too busy scrambling trying to figure out how to feed yourself, how to keep a roof over your head, then feminism becomes more of a luxury.

Nancy (#2), too, grew up poor and found this to be a major barrier to involvement. For her the issue was how to communicate. 'I couldn't be a part of the movement because I didn't feel I fit in, I couldn't talk the language.' In a movement that was seen as largely white and upper-middle class, women from 'othered' or lower-income backgrounds felt excluded, and couldn't participate in the sometimes philosophical debates when their immediate practical needs (of food, shelter, child care, etc.) were not being met, and they were, like Nancy, largely focusing on survival.

While some felt excluded because of their working-class origins, others, like Pamela (#11), from privileged backgrounds, were not initially drawn to feminism. 'I probably came kicking and screaming into feminism until I finally made the connection. And I think a lot of that had to with my past, my privilege, I didn't connect it.'

'Yes, I am a feminist!'

Two-thirds of the women who responded to the question about feminism said they would call themselves feminist. There was a higher representation of self-identified feminists among lesbians and among women with higher education and higher income. Non-white or immigrant women, as well as working-class, separated, divorced, or widowed women and women active in organized religious groups, were less likely to call themselves feminists.

When describing the impact of feminism on their lives, Margaret (#4) said the women's movement was 'the biggest influence in my life, bar none'. Judy (#50), a single mother of two, said she could write a book about how the women's movement impacted her. The movement had given her strength and understanding 'about myself and the things I was going through. It made me realize possibilities for my life.' Now she draws hope about a different future where the lives of women and children benefit from the movement. 'There is hope that we can find a different way to deal with conflict, [of] finding a feminist approach to dealing with conflict.'

Most of the women who identified as lesbian also identified as feminist. Here is how Sharon (#5) responded to the question:

Yes, Yes, Yes, Yes, Yes, Yes, Yes! Yeah, absolutely. I came out as a feminist, not because all of a sudden I had this undying attraction to women but the more you talked about feminism, particularly in the seventies, the more you went: 'Who would want to be with a man?' And all of a sudden it happened that you didn't have to be. So I think that I have been a feminist since I was about three. Actually, my paternal grandmother was a feminist so it is very much part of who I am. There is no question. When women say to me, 'Oh, I am not a feminist', I look at them and think, 'What is the matter with you?'

Sharon talked about the support she found as a university student in the women's caucus. She says she often thinks of Charlotte Whitton's famous quote: 'A woman has to do whatever she does twice as well as a man to be recognized. Fortunately, that is not difficult.'

Of course, some women found their enthusiasm for the women's movement waning over time. Phyllis (#3), who was quite active as a feminist in the past, described the change as part of a mellowing political viewpoint: 'after years of hearing the same kind of rhetoric, in my twenties and thirties it fuelled me and now it just kind of feels like, "Not again".' Others became more involved as they aged. Ruth (#6), a mother of four in her early fifties, said the women's movement has become 'extremely important' in recent years: 'I presumed I should get rights, and felt during my life that being a woman was a detriment. The women's movement has enabled me, in every aspect, to pursue the various avenues I have pursued', including divorce, gaining custody of her children, getting a mortgage, going back to school, and making sense of the inequalities she faced throughout her life.

Women in this study spoke about their precarious, hesitant, complex relationship to feminist identity. As we have pointed out, race, ethnicity, and class influence the likelihood that women will identify with feminism and the timing of their involvement (whether active or not) in the movement. Some, like Pamela (#11), were drawn to feminism because of their experiences at work: 'Really, my work on women in trades is where I hit it. I hit sexism. I hit sexual harassment. I hit all the "-isms" that you would going in there, which I never had experienced.'

Others identified as 'lesbian feminists' or sought to understand their sexuality through a feminist lens. Susan (#16) talked about how feminism helped her resolve the conflict between her conservative religious upbringing and her feelings about wanting greater equality in her marriage: 'feminism was salvation for me . . . . Gloria Steinem is my god!'

Routes to Feminism: Learning from Their Mothers

Some analysts assume that feminist identity is 'passed on' from one generation to the next—older feminists teaching younger women about the politics and narrative of the feminist movement (Adkins, 2004). However, our research does not support the idea that feminist identity is 'inherited' in this way.

Some women recognized in their mothers' lives and in their own lives the constraints imposed by a patriarchal social order. Indeed, they seem to have a strong historical sense of their own lives, although this did not necessarily result in a feminist position. As the first generation of second-wave feminists become mothers and grandmothers it is intriguing to explore the intergenerational impact of feminist identity. One can readily detect the ambivalence in Tara's (#75) reflections. 'No, I don't think I'm a feminist, because I was raised in a family setting where the man was the breadwinner, and the mother was the homemaker. But I certainly applaud the feminists to a certain degree.'

Vera (#8) talked about the historical contrast between her life and the life available to her daughter versus the life her own mother had. It is meaningful to be able to put into context the political gains made in the status of women over three generations. Vera refers explicitly to her experiences as being 'in the middle', thus acknowledging the evolution of gender equality as an ongoing, not fully realized project:

> There's definitely been an impact. The opportunities are out there. You think at one time women were basically relegated to the house. They didn't work in the outside world, they didn't go to school. Maybe I'm looking at it more— it's great for my daughters coming along. I was sort of in the middle part of it.

She explicitly contrasts her daughter's opportunities to her mother's restrictions:

> My mother is very much a feminist. She had a short stint of not working when she was first married, then when she divorced she was back to work. She always complained about not getting equal job opportunities, equal pay, everything. She would say she had got as far as a woman could, in her job.

Mothers and Daughters

One of the surprising recurring themes of the interviews was the connection between mothers and daughters. We found that the complexity of the feminist identity for many midlife women was discussed in relation to their daughters. Having a daughter, for these women, provided a window onto women's lives as a collective experience, bringing into focus a 'common fate with women' (Reid and Purcell, 2004: 766). Having a daughter allowed an opportunity to (re)connect the personal to the political, to be more emotionally attached to the gains (and unfulfilled promises) of the women's movement, and to believe in differences for their daughters in the future.

We found a strong connection to positive feminist identification among mothers of daughters. As these mothers elaborated on the meaning of feminism in their lives, they also referred to the impact of the movement on the lives of their daughters. They described feelings of pride in their daughters' accomplishments, respect and admiration for their daughters' feminist politics, appreciation for the increased opportunities available to their daughters as a result of the women's movement, and their hope for their daughters' futures.

These midlife mothers consistently framed their comments about feminism around the notion of increased educational and career opportunities for their daughters, particularly in contrast to their own experiences growing up:

. . . to think my daughters were able to go to university and to graduate school and this wasn't allowed 50, 60 years ago. (Lenora, #41)

When I was going to college, you know like you were a teacher, nurse, or secretary; it didn't seem like there was a whole world out there for us . . . There is a whole world out there, I think, for our daughters. (Lesley, #19)

. . . it's great for my daughters coming along. I've got a daughter who wants to be a teacher—I mean she could be a doctor, she could be anything she wants to be, and in the past that wasn't quite as open for her to do; and I think that's terrific. . . . There are more opportunities. (Vera, #8)

I see my nieces playing hockey—their choice . . . I played hockey in a more casual thing, but they're on a team. I see my other niece; she works in the forestry and fisheries. She's capturing bears and doing this and doing that, and has this whole outdoor sort of thing happening. And I'm thinking, 'who would have thought?' She's 25 years younger . . . It's wonderful to see what she's doing . . . this is good, it's just more doors. But whether it's engineering, it's just things women never ventured into before. There's choices now. Not that it's easy, but there's choices. (Cindy, #47)

Many women specifically referred to their daughters as feminists. Nancy (#2) proudly referred to her daughter as 'a fierce feminist'. A 58-year-old Jamaican immigrant talks about her daughter as 'a strong feminist—a very strong woman, who has really inculcated the importance of being who you are' (Shana, #63). A South Asian immigrant talked about body image and politics surrounding her daughter's 'liberated' generation in Canada, and added: 'I'm very proud of my daughter' (Malina, #15).

Women also referred to the impact of feminism on their ability to raise their daughters with an awareness and consciousness of women's issues and the women's movement. Susan (#16) said proudly: 'I have raised three wonderful feminist daughters.' Judy (#50) echoed this sentiment in saying: 'The movement and feminism have allowed me to have a more satisfying life. It helped me raise daughters to have a feminist consciousness.' Raising a daughter seems to have been pivotally important in influencing midlife women's reflections on feminism and the women's movement. Their daughters provided points of contrast regarding 'how far we've come' and 'how far we still need to go':

> I think that the issues for women are still the same; I think that we haven't made enough changes. I really don't know sometimes if it's because I'm an old fart or not. You know, because I have teenage daughters. They still [think], 'God I should be beautiful'. . . . Yes, you should be beautiful, don't get me wrong, of course you should be beautiful; but you shouldn't centre your life around people with penises. It just doesn't work. And yet, it's shocking for me for them to live in a house with an outspoken mother who's the economic provider, the social convener, the wonder woman, and they're still believing in this, 'One day the prince will come.' I mean their favourite woman is 'Pretty Woman'. So I ask: have we made a substantial change? I think the answer is 'yes'. But is there still a long way to go? Absolutely. That's how I see it. (Anita, #12)

Sometimes the gratification they felt regarding the freedoms their daughters enjoy is spiced by resentment at the taken-for-granted attitude of the daughters' generation. 'There was a women's movement . . . but the next generation will have it as second nature to them' (Tracy, #35). (Note the use of the past tense in this comment.) Sacrifices and struggles may simply be obliterated by time. 'Well, I expected to be an equal and it was a surprise to me when I wasn't an equal. But you fought for equality and it does disappoint me when I see it taken for granted by my children' (Lesley, #19). Some women expressed a feeling of frustration for their lost history:

> I think the one thing that's important to me is not to lose the sense of our history, the history of the feminist movement. There are young people who didn't understand that it used to be against the law to be queer, who don't know anybody who died of AIDS, who didn't live through the gross inequities between women and men in the work environment. They know nothing about any of that stuff. . . . They're not taught the history; they don't understand the struggle [and the] place that we came from. (Joyce, #59)

Finally, granddaughters, too, bring home the insidious persistence of gendered realities.

> I'm very aware of that when I speak to my grandchildren. I was noticing that, if it was 'the' robin, I noticed it in myself: 'He's on the birdbath.' Well, it's not 'he', right? It's 'the' robin, but I saw that masculinization of all those sorts of things. So, I would point that out to them: 'Well, it might be a male; well, it might be a female—it's not always a male.' (Lorna, #13)

Women's Studies and Feminist Theory in Education

One of the substantive changes as a result of the popularization of feminism—through feminist novels, films, television, *Chatelaine*, the National Action Committee, the Status of Women Bureau, and so on and on—was the creation of Women's Studies courses—first, programs, and then departments on campuses across Canada. Certainly, those of our respondents who as young women or as returning students participated in such courses were likely to develop a clear political consciousness and a strong feminist commitment. As Amina (#9) said: 'I am a feminist because of Women's Studies.' These academic programs also encouraged the publication of women's work and the proliferation of women's bookstores and women's publishing houses, which in turn helped women embrace a new social reality. Judy (#50), a 62-year-old divorced mother, sums up the general significance of these new cultural artifacts:

> When I was growing up, I don't remember taking books in school written by women. Then, to hear women speak, of course women have thoughts, ideas, and leadership qualities that we need in our community and work life. So, I think it was very important to me. I didn't take formal courses, but I read a lot, and I did audit some courses, but I really felt that to hear women speak and formulate their ideas, I felt I was becoming more of an individual, of a person. I didn't have to be in a relationship. My experience was other people's experience. Even to help me identify that I could feel angry about being cheated, to identify that the things that helped form and develop me were from a masculine point of view. Things were imposed, even how I thought of women and women's lives. The possibility of leading a different kind of life was satisfying.

Shana (#63) talked about the ongoing influence of the movement in both 'public' and 'private' aspects of her life:

> It had a strong impact on my life—feminism. It's influenced me to go to school to begin with. And it influenced me also—well, it influenced me to stay with my obligations with the family, but now it's influencing me in

another direction, and that's to become a person on my own, to become an individual, to self-actualize.

The Personal Is Political?

The connection of the personal to the political in second-wave feminism has been misconstrued as *equating* the personal with the political. Midlife women in this study reflected on their desire to be in control of how they are seen by others and of how they understand and construct their own identities. In the postmodern condition, we tend to occupy many roles at once, and move in and out of social roles depending on age and life stage. Asking someone to choose a *single* identity forces a denial of some other equally important aspect of the person's life and personality. Am I a woman first? Or a lesbian? A Muslim? A mother? Or a wife? Or, simply a person, not circumscribed by the boundaries of gender, race, class, sexuality, religion, and so on?

There is an important difference between personal and political opinions, as reflected in the responses to the questions posed to the women in this study. For example, a woman may want to marry at some point in her life, yet support the right for all women not to have to get married in order to live fulfilling and happy lives. The same goes for more hotly contested issues, such as abortion: while a woman may not believe in abortion on a personal level, she might respect the right of all women to have access to safe and effective birth control, including, as a last resort, the right to an abortion. The politicization of opinion stems from an exposure to the policy implications of women's rights, resulting (in the examples here) from: women's studies literature and classes; participation in women's groups; and close friends or family members who can provide a context for understanding the issues in a collective sense. In order to understand the implications and possible effects that an issue will have on people other than oneself, the ability to engage in a dialogue with others offers a perspective and context that 'puts a human face' on such issues.

This generation has witnessed major victories in women's rights. In a relatively short period of time women have enjoyed legally protected access to education, pay equity, and career opportunities; birth control; divorce; maternity leave; and so on. Not surprisingly, many people have grown to understand the movement in historical terms, as something that achieved what it set out to do and that is no longer as relevant or necessary given the accomplishment of its goals. Thus, it is not as imperative to align politically with the women's movement, when the issues may seem less tangible or less easy to relate to.

However, as supported by the literature and the qualitative interviews in this study, it is apparent that feminist identity is an evolution as opposed to an 'awakening'. For many women, it is important to be able to interpret their world through a feminist lens: by watching the experiences of their female children as they grow up, by being able to engage with feminist voices in literature or Women's Studies classes, or by embracing one's sexual identity. Cultivating female relationships—as mentors, teachers, role models, colleagues, relatives, or lovers—gives midlife women an opportunity to embrace identity politics from a different and more collectivist perspective.

As feminism matures within the society and becomes a recognized part of the social and economic landscape, and as the generation of women who grew up with the second wave age, it is evident that there are many different ways of understanding what makes a feminist. Indeed, the activist aspect of social movements (attending a rally or participating in a demonstration) may no longer hold appeal. Being a feminist is not about a media-constructed identity: it does not involve burning bras or hating men or rejecting society through a radical or extremist stance, or even being 'publicly political' at all. The meaning of feminism has taken on more mainstream, notions of equality for both genders. The movement is no longer solely focused on 'women's issues'. It has become more appropriately focused on achieving social justice with regard to race, sexuality, and access to health care, daycare, and a living wage for all.

Women in midlife express political beliefs that reflect the goals of the women's movement, without expressing their desire to adopt the label 'feminist'. This is not a rejection of feminism, but of the labelling process itself. The postmodern woman expresses her desire to be free, independent, and able to take responsibility (and credit) for her own life. 'To each her own' can certainly characterize this shift in thinking.

In sum, there is a fundamental struggle with feminist identification, but it pertains to the problematic construction of the term, not to the ideology or goals of feminism. Unfortunately, this has been incorrectly attributed to mean an associated lack of support for the women's movement and its contributions to women's lives, leading to calls of the death of feminism, or the beginning of a post-feminist age. However, more accurately this should signal a problem with the way that feminism has been constructed in and by the media, and in how it is taught (or not taught) in high schools and universities, with the rejection of negative stereotypes associated with the movement, and with the avoidance of labels entirely.

Key Concepts

Feminism The ideological arm of the women's movement, representing a powerful critique of the legal, economic, political, cultural, and personal barriers women face. bell hooks (2000: viii) defined feminism as 'a movement to end sexism, sexist exploitation, and oppression'.

First-, second-, and third-wave feminism We typically refer to the suffragette movement as having been the focus of first-wave feminists and the women's movement of the 1960s and 1970s as the second wave. The third wave, influenced by postmodernism, developed out of the inability of the second wave to resolve issues of racial difference and sexuality, and characterizes contemporary young women's attachment to feminism.

Institutional and grassroots feminisms   Institutional feminism operates within traditional institutions—inside political parties and government ministries, for example—while grassroots feminism is more community-based, emphasizing collective organizing, consciousness-raising, and reaching out to women 'on the street'. (Adamson et al., 1988: 12).

Liberal feminism   Feminism that emphasizes equality of opportunity and legislative reform.

Socialist feminism   Feminism with a focus on women's place in the class system. The centre of socialist feminist activism was the workplace, particularly the union movement.

Women's health movement   The women's health movement grew out of the women's movement in the 1960s and 1970s. The right to safe and effective birth control, access to abortion, greater sexual autonomy, birthing centres, and so on became the key issues.

Questions for Critical Discussion

1. The second wave of the women's movement set out to achieve gender equity in law, education, and the workplace. Explain the extent to which these goals were or were not achieved.
2. What does feminism mean to you? How is your practice of feminism the same or different from that set forth by the second wave of the women's movement?
3. How does popular culture portray feminism? In what ways has this portrayal helped advance or obstruct the path of feminism?
4. A new slogan suggests that 'men are the new women'. What does this mean and how does it relate to gendered differences in educational achievement?
5. Was your mother a feminist? Did she pass along any feminist messages to you, and if so, how have you responded? Provide concrete examples.
6. Culture transmits complex and contradictory messages about masculinity and femininity for young adults. Explain and discuss.
7. What do traditional messages of femininity and masculinity have in common?

Chapter 4

Families and Intimate Connections

Intimacy Ambivalence

For most midlife women, intimacy—with partners, children, siblings, and friends— is experienced as a 'double-edged sword'. Intimate commitments often are contentious and constrictive but they also offer women opportunities for achieving deep contentment and happiness. In short, intimate attachments provide midlife women with their most enduring sources of love and affection, but they also constitute connections that offer them the most pain and suffering. And sometimes the same relationship offers both.

Our purpose in this chapter is to focus on what family means for midlife women and how they construct and manage intimate attachments. Specifically, we focus on women's embedded relations, defined as the web of interrelationships, weak or strong ties binding individuals within a social institution, as well as the history of interactions characterizing the relationships within a social institution (Curran, 2002).

As sociologists, it is our job to link women's feelings and interpretations of family to larger social processes (Lüscher and Pillemer, 1998). When we analyzed particular intimate incidents, one overarching theme through the narratives was found to be ambivalence. In analyzing families as sites of co-operation and conflict, family sociologists Ingrid Connidis and Julie McMullin (2000a, 2000b) coined the term 'structured ambivalence' to describe the conflicted feelings and behaviours experienced by family members who are intimately involved in intergenerational relationships trying to resolve dilemmas of conflict and co-operation (Lüscher and Pillemer, 1998). Meaning 'of two minds', ambivalence refers to the deep connection, contradiction, and sometimes confusion midlife women express about their most cherished attachments with partners, children, friends, parents, and siblings.

Ambivalence is structured in that it permeates the social structures within which women experience intimacy. Competing notions of families, marital scripts, and intimacy discourses place women in ongoing dilemmas. Structures of inequality, especially race, gender, and economics, both configure and are constituted by social interaction. In this way, inequalities get inside women in such a way that their conforming behaviour appears 'natural' and 'normal'. Ambivalence is gendered in that accountability is invoked differently and anticipated through close, personal relations differently for women and for racialized women than it is for men. Midlife women have grown up expecting that they will be held responsible morally for taking care of others within the family. Finally, ambivalence is interpersonal in that it exists at the level of emotions and is expressed through intimate attachments. Emotions of frustration, anger, and sadness indicate the existence of ambivalence and of resignation, its resolution.

Picking up themes outlined in Chapter 1, where we contextualized the social and historical context within which midlife women have constructed families, we find that economics and ethnicity contour intimate relations, making some relationships flourish while shutting down other possibilities. Gay, disabled, and single mothers face particular challenges as they construct families by calling on unusual amounts of initiative and energy. The clash between traditional and postmodern marital scripts, along with the corresponding competing demands of work and family, affect how women accomplish families. Finally, midlife women grapple with connection, loneliness, and regrets as they reflect on their choices. Using questions of control, compromise, and connection, we examine all the ways in which midlife women become enmeshed in intimate relations that are inherently contradictory. In discussing each of these themes, we employ the concepts of shared story lines, gendered accountability, women's agency, and resistance.

Shared Story Lines

The self in narrative is a standpoint from which to interpret one's life (Spencer, 1993). In the telling, the specifics of stories are less important than how the entire tale is acquired and woven together to construct a life narrative (Nouri and Helterline, 2000). We were curious about how midlife women would tell the story of their lives. Would they begin with themselves or with themselves in connection to others?

Invariably, midlife women began their accounts with **shared story lines** (Mackin, 1995). Their stories are full of intimate connections that have defined their lives. Children, partners, parents, siblings, friends, and co-workers give shape and meaning to their accounts: children return or leave home; marriages break up or endure; friends and parents become frail, ill, or die (ibid.). Whether connections whither or endure, midlife women cannot separate their story lines from those of intimate others (Nouri and Helterline, 2000).

So strong was this tendency that attempts by interviewers to shift the story line to 'me' rather than 'we' often met with confusion. As researchers, we came to understand that it is only from shared story lines that midlife women develop their sense of who they are and who they might become (ibid.). Midlife women see their fate and their character development as tied to the fortunes and growth of others. They feel liable for intimate connections and their outcomes. As a consequence, what we are calling **gendered accountability**, that is, feelings of responsibility women take on for the welfare of family members, represents a series of largely unarticulated norms that place considerable weight on intimacy, and on its moral agents, women, to deliver things the discourse may not be well served to deliver.

When telling intimate narratives as opposed to stories about their employment and health, midlife women's accounts were peppered with hesitancies, uncertainties, sadness, and longings. Listening to the tapes, we were struck by how long women took to consider our questions about intimacy, how often they ignored opportunities to elaborate, and how frequent were the silences, gaps, and omissions in their narratives. This pattern was so widespread that we began to investigate their placement in intimacy discourses as a way to explain their responses.

Intimacy Discourses

Intimacy ambivalence is a social and cultural tension occurring at this particular historic moment as a result of the inevitable incommensurability between two dominant discourses[1]: the discourse of intimacy versus the discourse of individualism (Shumway, 2003; Giddens, 1992; Beck-Gernsheim, 2002). Powerful ideologies of romance and intimacy continue to shape women's life choices at the same time as potent discourses of individualism and self-fulfillment pull women away from traditional scripts. These alternatives might be symbolized as 'Barbie dolls' versus 'Bratz dolls'.

Discourses of intimacy promise self-fulfillment by telling women the path to happiness lies in attaching and giving themselves to others. Discourses of individualism promote a different view by exhorting women to find happiness by fashioning biographies from their own interests, talents, and desires. Intimacy demands self-abnegation while the ideology of individualism promotes self-absorption. The two discourses come together in the **ideology of romantic love**. Romance, separate from and often a prelude to intimacy, offers adventure, intense emotion, closeness, security, and the possibility of finding the perfect mate. Together, romantic love and intimacy prop up most modern North American concepts of marriage (Evans, 1998).

Historically, love has been seen as lower-class, irrational, and deeply suspect, both as a 'weapon of the powerless' and a 'vehicle for their oppression' (ibid.). By the nineteenth century, love had been affixed to marriage making it the only acceptable reason for long-term commitment. While ideas of '"love" in both homosexual and heterosexual relations are unstable and as likely to change as any other social ideology, most people now expect to "fall in love" and establish a life-long relationship with another person' (ibid.).

For same- and opposite-sex partnerships, romantic love stories are told repeatedly through television programs (*Desperate Housewives*), self-help books (*Men Are from Mars, Women from Venus*), talk shows (*Oprah*), and movies (*Knocked Up*). By pursuing enduring love, psychological transcendence will be achieved, allowing women to obtain personal closeness, autonomy, and comfort in living with their true soul mates (Shumway, 2003). Yet midlife women resoundingly fail to achieve this ideal, leaving them with 'mixed emotions'.

Noticeably absent from these fairy tales are critiques of the ways in which fundamental social inequities of economics, ethnicity, and disability make it difficult for midlife women to accomplish families. For the focus group women overwhelmingly, marriage was defined as male-dominated:

> Men are in control in my culture and throughout the world. They are taught this in their families and are born with the need to dominate. At least, that's what I think. (Lynn, 2001: 14)

They speak freely of the 'dark side' of patriarchal family life in which they suffer abuse from husbands, theft from children, and ridicule from in-laws, all of which engenders tremendous shame and guilt. Immigrant women feel 'trapped between two worlds', the traditional culture of their host country and the more liberal culture of Canada. One focus group woman told a typical story that demonstrates the power of cultural values across generations. When a man's mother, visiting from India, saw him caring for his children and helping in the kitchen, she ridiculed him and asked if he had become a woman since moving to Canada. In India, men who help out at home are called 'apron-men', a term that implies they are less masculine than other men who do not help out (ibid.).

Women's Agency

Because midlife women experience themselves as morally and culturally responsible for others, their view of agency differs from that of men. For men, agency is synonymous with autonomy and independent action. For women, agency is relational and interdependent. Agency and empowerment are, thus, contextually located relational concepts (Wray, 2004). Women are not moving away from relationships and achieving autonomy by distinguishing themselves from others but rather feel powerful, worthwhile, and more in control in relationships where they exercise autonomy. In other words, women achieve independence in and through relationships with others, not by distancing themselves from others.[2]

According to Wray (ibid.), simply living longer provides women with more opportunities to exercise this type of agency through their intergenerational care work (see Chapter 5). It also provides them with opportunities for resistance, which, not surprisingly, also are framed in terms of consequences for others. If I divorce, what will happen to the children? If I take a full-time job, how will this improve family finances? If I decide to work weekends, how will this affect family dynamics?

Control

Agency and **empowerment** generally are conceptualized as being in control of one's own life (ibid.). According to Ross and Mirowsky (2002), the primary way in which control is exercised is through the choices one makes for and by oneself. Controlling one's life means exercising authority and influence over it by directing and regulating it oneself. Ross and Mirowsky tell us that people vary tremendously in how they define control and empowerment. All midlife women say that having good health and having good friends and contact with family are important for feeling in control. But here the similarities end. Some women feel they can accomplish goals they set and regard themselves as responsible for their own successes and failures. Others feel no control over situations, seeing their fate as being masterminded by forces beyond them. Still others see control as contingent, partial, and unevenly achieved.

Most of our midlife women fell into the latter category, defining control, empowerment, and agency as gendered and relative experiences. They exercise choice, and thus control, in and through their relationships with others. They do not expect to lead independent lives unattached to others but rather to experience satisfaction, a sense of self and identity, and control and power in and through their involvement in relationships.

Amy (#20), a 57-year-old white Canadian, describes escaping parental control only to substitute for it spousal control:

> Amy: When my parents were moving to [another province]—and my husband and I were just dating at the time—I told him I wasn't moving there. I ended up moving in; my husband and I got married. So it's like, I married my husband, four and a half years later I had my first son, then I had my second one.
> Interviewer: And did you marry your husband to escape going to [another province] with your parents?
> Amy: Yes I did. So I tried to take some control over my own life. And then I had my husband and I didn't have any more control again, you know, I mean, because somebody else still was involved in my decision-making.

Marital Scripts

This apparent lack of autonomy reverberates through many focus groups and interviews. What varies is the degree of recognition given to it and the way it is articulated. As we noted in Chapter 1, midlife women represent a transitional generation who have seen the rules of family and career shift over their lifetimes. They grew up in families in which marital roles were closely aligned with family roles. Women were expected to be full-time mothers responsible for providing emotional and caring resources to family members while fathers were expected to be 'good providers' supplying economic and material resources (Bernard, 1972). Sharon (#5) describes her father as like the character of Peter Griffith in the contemporary cartoon sitcom *Family Guy*:

> I was brought up in a culture where women were subservient to men. My mother was a teacher before she got married. Although my father could have

done with a second earning, it was inappropriate for a wife to work. The husband was the provider, and so my mother always stayed at home. It was a tremendous asset to us children, because she assisted us in many aspects of life. As she grew older, because math was her forte, she assisted my father with his accounts. So, she was able to apply her learning to that, but my mother was still subservient to my father. My father was the head of the house, and my mother just followed. If she wanted anything, she had to ask my father.

Sharon's family of origin was typical of the 1950s upbringing when, against a patriarchal background, family and marital roles began to shift. Most fathers found it increasingly difficult to support numerous dependants on their wages—a situation that necessitated the earning of money by women and older children. Midlife women were daughters in families in which their mothers performed not only most of the emotional and caring work but also contributed, in waged and unwaged ways, to total family income. By the 1970s, midlife women entered partnerships expecting to fulfill traditional mothering scripts as well as venturing into paid employment in a 'saddle' pattern: full-time wage work, followed by a period of employment withdrawal until children were graduated from high school, followed by re-entry into full-time employment. Instead, the majority of these midlife women found their original expectations demolished by the growing economic pressure for two incomes to support one family unit (see Chapter 6).

Many midlife women did not enter marriage intending to work full-time, but found their income necessary to keep families above the poverty line. Being employed means putting in long hours but being a mother also requires lots of time, attention, and investment of social capital to secure children's futures (Sweet and Mandell, 2004). One way to resolve the dilemmas lies in redistributing family work, but very little redistribution seems to have occurred for midlife women.

Before 1970 the family lives of gays and lesbians were largely invisible. When gay liberation activists joined second-wave feminists in protest, they both tended to be stridently anti-family (Stacey, 1996: 106). According to Stacey (ibid., 143), 'Self-identified queer families serve on the pioneer outpost of the postmodern family condition, confronting most directly its features of improvisation, ambiguity, diversity, contradiction, self-reflection and flux.' As Sally (#65), a 63-year-old white American Canadian, jokes, 'for some odd reason, same-sex partnerships have not avoided but rather embraced "the marriage Titanic!"' Issues of negotiating competing demands from home and work, undertaking care work, and searching for and maintaining romance in intimacy all represent concerns same-sex partners as well as opposite-sex partners face in relationships.

Misplacing the Self

In keeping with Canadian trends, midlife women talk a lot about changing family forms. Marriage, divorce, and fertility rates all have declined. Marriage rates peaked at the beginning and end of World War II, dropped in the early 1960s, rose again in the 1970s, but have followed a slow, but not steady, decline since 1971. One explanation for declining marriage rates is increased cohabitation. In 2001, 70 per cent of families were married couples and 14 per cent were cohabiting couples. In 1981 the percentages were 83 per cent and 6 per cent, respectively (Statistics Canada, *The Daily*, 22 Oct. 2002). In 1951, the census did not even measure cohabitation.

A second explanation is delayed marriage. In 2002 the average age of first marriage for women was 28. It was 22 in 1971 (Statistics Canada, 2005: 37). Increased age of marriage reflects both the need for more formal education in order to find sustaining work and changing values, including those regarding premarital sexuality. Of course, some people who postpone marriage simply never marry, and marriage today cannot be considered a universal goal. Some people stay single because that is the way they prefer to live. Others may wish to marry, but for one reason or another never do.

Most of our midlife women had been or were currently in long-term relationships. Gendered accountability is a central assumption with which they entered partnerships and parenting. Even though midlife women have witnessed the demise of the traditional marriage of 'stay-at-home' mothers and 'wage-earning' fathers, they nonetheless carry traditional assumptions with them into contemporary relationships. First, they tend to fashion partnerships, both same and opposite sex, around romantic love, which promises them 'deep communication, friendship and sharing that will last beyond the passion of new love' (Shumway, 2003: 17). Next, most had children, an enterprise that demands putting children's need ahead of their own. Finally, the need to care for aging parents and relatives often arises in midlife. It is, thus, understandably tough for midlife women to keep in touch with themselves with so many responsibilities appearing from all sides of intimacy.

It is no wonder that in pursuing intimacy through family, midlife women describe 'losing themselves'. Malina (#15), a 55-year-old South Asian woman, tells us how this misplacement occurs:

> My husband is my best friend. I struggled with the fact that here was a human being that could change my life, because suddenly I had to think differently. I had to be part of another human being: our wishes had to be balanced; our hopes and dreams had to be balanced. I couldn't just be my own person any more, I had to share myself. So I'd say he was the most important focal point in my life.

Not only does partnering precipitate self-loss, so does raising children. When asked about major turning points in their lives, midlife women report that becoming mothers was one of their most important transitions. But clearly, raising children necessitates compromise and some loss of control. Malina says she 'doesn't even remember who she was before she had children.'

How, we wondered, did she misplace herself? Upon further questioning, we see the answer lies in her description of herself as tied to the lives of others. When asked about life situations in which she exercised control and compromise, Donna (#76) returns to her theme of marriage and mothering as entrapment: 'I think once I was married, I didn't feel like I had hardly any choices and the same with being a mother.'

Misplacing oneself as a woman, and particularly as a mother, is a common theme in our interviews. Misplacement arises out of contemporary moral scripts, which still see women as accountable for intimate relations. Primary among these is responsibility for the growth, development, and protection of children. This task sits squarely on the shoulders of mothers, as one 50-year-old Iranian woman tells us:

> For me, the most important relationship is with my children; because I moved to Canada because of them, for them. . . . I told my husband, I told my kids, '[I am] not going for any job, not going for any classes, just stay at home and look after the kids.' How they go to the school, how they come back, how they choose their friends. And now I can say that I am very proud of my daughter, because everybody looking at her can understand that there is something else. She is not like the others. (Amina, #9)

Focus group participants describe patriarchal social values and cultural norms as pressuring women to become submissive and pleasing to their male partners. Being treated like sex objects, a continuing component of gender traditionalism, represents one condition Anita (#12) discards in middle age:

> . . . the sex object thing. That you're supposed to, as a woman, behave and conform and act a certain way and be subordinate to men. And I've learned in my family the way I was raised; I've learned really well. And I just am not prepared to do it any more.

The combination of objectification and submission to patriarchy leaves some midlife women feeling 'enraged' over decisions they feel they have been forced to undertake. When a focus group participant expressed her anger towards family members who 'demand so much and give so little', the entire group resoundingly agreed (Lynn, 2001: 8).

Given unequal marital roles, midlife women search for ways to describe their situations. Some chronicle their attempts to achieve equitable relationships, or leave those they find completely inequitable; others seem to infantilize male partners, describing them as 'childish', 'obstinate', and 'highly strung'. Here, Brenda (#51), a 56-year-old white woman, describes her partner as 'moody', providing her with a biological justification for being socially subservient:

> With my husband, he was a moody person. At times, I felt I had to do what he wanted regardless of what I wanted. Going back to my background, and thinking about my parents and how I was brought up, I had to be married and be subservient.

Another 52-year-old white woman describes her husband as 'spoiled', someone who needs to be 'coaxed' into doing things, again providing a 'justification' for wrapping her life around his needs:

Well, my husband gets his own way in some things. . . .We generally do things his way, it's easier for me. Sometimes I put my foot down and do it my way, or I can coax him into doing it my way. I do a lot of compromising day-to-day with my husband; he's dominant; he likes his own way. I think he was very spoiled as a child. (Vera, #8)

While we certainly do not think the men in midlife women's lives are childish, we do see their wives' descriptions as ways women reconcile their awareness of their inequitable relationships. A recent study by American sociologist Stephen Nock reveals that, over the past 17 years, equity in domestic labour has superseded shared religious beliefs, good housing, adequate income, and faithfulness as a key factor contributing to marital satisfaction. Men don't have to actually do equal amounts of domestic labour as women, but they have to acknowledge and appreciate the work that women do in order for women to feel satisfied. As Nock says, 'It's not about equity. It's about acknowledgement' (*Globe and Mail*, 2007).

Structured Inequity

Midlife women's experiences are linked to their life choices and to the contingencies of other family members (Mackin, 1995). But control is also related to structured inequality. Class, family support, and local cultural circumstances shape midlife women's notions of coercion versus consent just as firmly as do conditions of social class and religion.

Living on the margins of society, whether due to economics, disability, or ethnicity, makes accomplishing family a more difficult, if not, sometimes, an impossible task. As one focus group participant put it: 'Life is always more difficult when you feel as though you are living on the margins of society' (Lynn, 2001: 13).

Managing on very little income, often alone, means midlife women spend their lives weighing tough choices and putting the financial needs of other family members above their own. Control increases with education, employment, earnings, income, occupational status, work autonomy, work fulfillment, and status of origin. It declines with a heavy burden of domestic work, economic hardship, job loss, poor health, and physical impairment (Ross and Mirowsky, 2002).

Globalization and ethnicity also shape gendered accountability. Racialized focus group women believe their entire lives have been determined by responsibility to family; it is impossible for them to separate their concerns and needs from those of family members both locally and from around the world. Global families place particular demands on midlife women. It is not that they have left anyone 'back home', but in fact that they have carried them with them into a new country. According to focus groups, transnational families are actively maintained through sharing of resources, caring for relatives, visiting during holidays, and communicating through phones and e-mails. A high percentage of the earnings of Filipina women working in Toronto as domestics is sent to their families in the Philippines. Many Jamaican and African women have left children 'at home' to be cared for by extended family

(Lynn, 2001: 15). Often, these women maintain two families: the Canadian one and the international one, giving them additional burdens that are often unacknowledged.

Raising Children

Each year in Canada it is said that the current fertility rate is at a historical low. At 1.49, the Canadian rate is lower than in the United States, where the fertility rate is 2.1 (Statistics Canada, 2003). Over the twentieth century, fertility declined in the Great Depression, peaked during the baby boom, and began to decline in 1960. The drop in birth rate between 1960 and 1970 was particularly dramatic. Widespread availability of birth control in the late 1960s allowed women a far greater measure of fertility control than they had ever experienced. Today, more women have their first child at what once would have been thought of as middle age. Births to women in their forties are no longer unusual.

Most midlife women define having children as a major turning point in their lives, asserting that they 'fully chose to have children'. No one said they 'regretted' having children, but many are disgruntled with the conditions within which they have raised their children. Insufficient help at home, lack of money, little child care, conflicts with paid labour, and a crushing dual workload all were situations women would have altered had they been able to do so. Susan (#16), a 53-year-old white Canadian, tells a familiar story explaining how in her marriage, she and her partner compromise, but that when children came along, she capitulated almost completely:

> I started out only doing things my husband thought it was okay to do, and he had some traditional views about that long ago, and so in order to keep the marriage bearable, I didn't always do what I wanted. Then, we had children . . . well . . . that's what you do when you have babies that [you] need to look after every second of the day. Well, I gave up almost every idea of doing my own work, in order to mother.

Coping with competing demands from partners, work, and raising children means that compromises get made that otherwise might not. Esther (#7), a 45-year-old Jewish woman, believes that if she hadn't compromised, her relationship would have ended:

> I compromise, probably more than I should, in my relationship with [partner] and the girls. I let them lead. I think kids being brought up are so important. I do a lot of fitting my life, my schedule into their life . . . to the point that I'm not really happy with it.

Many midlife women put up with years of personal inequality while raising children for the sake of economic and family security. When asked why they have pursued strategies of appeasement, many, like Joanne (#53), a 61-year-old British woman, explain that it was simply easier and safer to put family needs ahead of their own and that they do not regret the decision:

> I have no regrets, my son has top priority. I have no regrets to the compromises made on his behalf at that age. I regret that the government didn't recognize part-time work at that time, as for CPP the way it does. It's changed the rules. My CPP would be much better if, at that point in time when I was earning part-time, they had taken CPP off. I'm annoyed at the government, most annoyed . . . many other women would be in a better position today had the government realized Canada Pension Plan, we should be able to contribute [to] it.

Many midlife women define their relationships with children in terms of their children's success or failure. Success of children—financial independence, secure jobs, decent partners—becomes a symbol of women's family work that make women feel powerful and worthwhile. Failure of children—financial dependence, insecure employment, incomplete partnerships—leaves women feeling defeated and regretful.

When discussing their early parenting years, women talk about having 'no control' over family responsibilities, which are often intense, and interactions, which are often strained as both are 'thrust upon them'. Many women report feeling they had the least amount of control over their lives when children were young. Mia (#10), a 53-year-old white Canadian, describes this situation:

> When I was raising my children and my ex-husband kept me quite isolated . . . I wasn't a part of any community per se anyway, I was just sort of—everything was my kids and that was it. I just didn't even pay attention to anything that was happening in the community.

Finding Peace: Finding Oneself

One of the strongest findings from both our interviews and our focus groups is the change in sense of control midlife women experience as they age. While many remain responsible for supporting households, taking care of domestic chores, and dealing with adult children, these chores are somehow far less onerous even when they appear heavy.

An emerging literature on long-term relationships indicates that marital satisfaction dips when children are young and increases once the children leave home. Gender roles tend to blur with age, particularly with older men who tend to carry out more care work for female partners. Even though midlife men still retain power within caring relationships, midlife women achieve new degrees of personal freedom (Arber et al., 2005). Many heterosexual midlife women talk of 'satisfactory' partnerships based on long-standing commitment, shared biographies, and shared interests in child-rearing. For those who stick with the same partners, age brings increased feelings of power and marital satisfaction. Lesbian partnerships, even if they report some inequity in care work, report much higher levels of partnership satisfaction throughout their lives.

Having spent years putting the needs of others before their own, midlife women finally are able to pursue goals and activities that bring them pleasure and satisfaction, ones they may have formerly repressed, denied, or neglected, without feeling particularly guilty about excluding partners or giving undue weight to their preferences. Farah (#34), a 59-year-old Indo-Canadian, talks about learning to accept and like herself:

> I guess I'm gaining more control in accepting myself, which I've never done before. And I'm finally starting to accept myself for what I am, instead of having other people's opinions control what I do. . . . Well, like everything, at one time I had my ex-husband, and he was in control, and my kids, when they were with me, they were basically in control, because I had to support them no matter what and so their needs were more than mine. And now, I just, I can't even explain it. . . . if I want to do something, I'll do it, and to hell with everybody else. That's the way I feel.

In giving up control—in no longer attempting to manage the daily lives of adult children, of no longer looking only to partners for fulfillment through intimacy— midlife women feel a sense of freedom and personal control. Anita (#12) reveals how in giving up her false sense of control, she regained her sense of inner peace:

> I don't think I like to control everything. I think life is a roller coaster. And the only thing you can control is yourself. And how you react to, how you decide you're going to live with and feel . . . sometimes I feel like life is like Alice in Wonderland, that chess game. You know you can't control it, what you can control is your spirit and your soul and your value system, and your attitudes when that happens. I think I can really, I've learned to have more of a positive attitude. In the course of the bad stuff that was happening, I took all these courses . . . . I did yoga, and I did a retreat where they talk about your spirit of being and how you communicate, and I read a lot of spiritual texts. And I think it grounded me. And I now work really hard at staying grounded.

Marginalized women also describe achieving greater peace in midlife as some of their huge burdens are lifted. Saroj, a 52-year-old South Asian woman, describes a lifetime of struggles—being forced to marry her deceased husband's cousin who refused to have anything to do with her child from her first marriage; being forced to leave the child in India when immigrating to Canada; overcoming poor health, long hours of work in a factory, and challenging in-laws—only to reach her spiritual centre at midlife. Another woman describes her life as 'walking through a labyrinth, a process of long stretches of sameness, sharp turns and rapid changes and finally leaving behind material well-being for a more authentic, exciting and searching self' (Lynn, 2001: 22). Resilience, strength, and forbearance allow many midlife women who have overcome hurdles to reach a space of serenity and calm.

Divorce

Until 1968 when federal legislation liberalized divorce, divorce rates in Canada were very low. Since divorce was difficult to obtain, many 'broken' marriages ended in desertion or lasted until death. Once divorce laws were relaxed, the divorce rate rose dramatically and remained high until the backlog of persons seeking divorce had received their divorces. When divorce legislation changed again in 1985, there was another rise in the number of divorces. With fewer couples seeking marriage, more cohabiting, and more individuals staying single, the number of divorces has been decreasing since the late 1980s. Thus, midlife women have seen the nature of intimate partnerships move away from a linear, fixed model to a plurality of choices with fewer permanent forms, different living arrangements, more beginnings, and more farewells (Beck-Gernsheim, 2002: 41). Mothers of midlife women for the most part married young and stayed married whatever the quality of their partnerships.

In contrast, their daughters (our participants) know that intimate partnerships are just as likely to dissolve as new arrangements are to emerge. As Louisa (#23), a 46-year-old black Caribbean Canadian, says, the best day of her life was the day she left her husband. It is tough to imagine her mother making the same statement!

It was the best day of my life. I felt empowered, I mean I was terrified, I had two kids. I borrowed a thousand dollars off my grandmother; two kids, three suitcases and a thousand dollars, and I took off and I've never looked back. To me, it was the day that I finally became an adult. I was a child up until then even though I was 30, I was still a child... I [had] lived with him for 13 years.

Once divorced, single mothers face acute demands. After a tumultuous 12-year marriage, Lynette's husband left. He saw neither her nor the children again, nor did he pay child support. The stress and subsequent depression involved in raising two bi-racial daughters, where racialization is yet another factor to try to cope with, eventually resulted in her being fired from a well-paying job, plunging her and the children into poverty. At the time of the interview, at age 59, Lynette (#27) finally was living alone, in shared accommodation, after living for the previous three years with her adult daughter and three grandchildren.

The longevity revolution means that a partnership now has the potential to last much longer than most marriages did a couple of generations earlier. According to Oppenheimer (1988), there is a polarization between increasing numbers of very high-quality, long-lasting marriages (40 years or more) and increasing numbers of low-quality, short-lived, 'starter' marriages. The majority of relationships fall somewhere in the middle, being of medium duration and medium quality.

Some midlife women simply divorced their partners feeling they could not find acceptable compromises. Other women say that while they do not regret getting married, nonetheless they cannot imagine staying in the relationship once the children leave home, suggesting the purpose of family units is to raise children, not to provide a site for personal actualization. Nicole (#45), a 52-year-old French-Canadian woman, talks about deciding to leave her partner:

> Before he [my ex-husband] and I married, we travelled in Europe for three months. I was 25 at that time. It was fun. My ex-husband and I are still friends. We were together for seven years, two of them married. . . . That turning point lasted a couple of years. It didn't feel traumatic, but I knew my marriage was bad and we just didn't belong together. We married to try and make it work, which is not a good reason to marry.

Intimate Connections: Female Friendships

Female friendships take two forms: relations of attachment and relations of community (de Vries and Johnson, 2002). According to de Vries and Johnson, relationships of attachment include the more intimate category, which describes relationships between romantic partners, parent–child relationships, and transference relationships that characterize the bonds between patient and therapist. Relationships of community include friendships, co-workers and colleagues, adult sibling relationships, and other non-household familial relationships. Both types of friends represent yardsticks against which self-development may be assessed, addressing tasks of socialization, maintaining role continuity, and assisting in managing life's challenges (de Vries, 1996).

Among all their social sources of support, many midlife women name female friends as their most enduring and nurturing contacts. In her work with older females, Rind (2002) highlights the link between quality of life and family and friendship networks for older women. Friendships promote the type of autonomy that women value as they grow older: independence with others as opposed to independence from others. When linked to midlife women's feelings about control rising as they age, the significance of freely formed friendships as vehicles to promote independence is obvious.

A common theme in interviews and focus groups was the extent to which many women celebrate the virtues of female friendship as long-lasting, enduring, and sustaining. Martha (#49), a 50-year-old white English Canadian, describes the nourishment female friends bring:

> I have these wonderful women friends that validate my existence and I validate theirs. And we giggle because we don't have the opportunity to spend lots of time. I have a friend who lives across the way here, not even a five-minute walk, but we're lucky if we see each other every six months. But we

talk and e-mail, and I have a cottage of my own now; we have a cottage. And we go up there and have a girls' week. And it's absolutely spectacular.

With friends, midlife women discuss many of the things they cannot discuss in families. One of the central reasons midlife women cherish their female friends lies in their ability to communicate with them about anything, at any time. Shana (#63), a black Jamaican Canadian, talks about the joy of female friends:

I think that the joy of conversation among women is so much better as you get older. And because you can talk about absolutely nothing for hours and that's so great. You know, you can talk about the garden or you can walk along the beach or you can go to a movie. My aunt once told me that she didn't want to be here any more '(if) all my friends are gone'. And I can totally understand that . . . if I live that long, I'll get there to that view.

Community Ties as Friendships

Our participants engaged in a great deal of self-silencing. According to White and Sherman (2002), self-silencing is alternatively seen as a strategy adopted by midlife women to decrease intimate conflict, as a means of evaluating oneself by external standards, and as way of fulfilling traditional feminine role proscriptions. It is usually viewed negatively as passive acceptance of gender roles and linked psychologically to female depression (ibid.).

We solicited study participants through community groups and, thus, were in a unique position to witness the tremendous power of communities to break self-silencing. Community groups allow women to negotiate cultural clashes. Some of these groups were religious organizations while others were neighbourhood or interest groups. Professional women relate to their work communities. Stay-at-home moms relate to their neighbourhoods, community centres, and schools. Immigrant women and those with strong cultural or religious ties describe their communities as being very important, as being the primary way in which they structure work and family life. These groups offer women a safe place in which to discuss openly their innermost feelings.

For women continents away from family networks and who are mistrusting of public agencies, community groups offer buffers against social isolation. Paloma (#40), a 59-year-old black Central American woman, Shoshana (#60), a 50-year-old Jewish woman, and Yagana (#39), a 49-year-old Arab woman, each use different religions and prayers to help cope with life and its troubles.

Communities mitigate the intense loneliness that accompanies a lack of emotional intimacy. Loneliness has been described as 'perceived absence of satisfying social relationships, accompanied by symptoms of psychological distress that are related to the perceived absence' (Young, 1982: 380). Social-cognitive psychologists define loneliness as an experienced discrepancy between the kinds of interpersonal relationships that individuals perceive themselves as having and the kind of relationships they would like to have (Sermat, 1978: 274).

According to social psychologists, the main cause of loneliness is lack of social integration and social support (Pinquart, 2003). Social integration is defined by the amount of time individuals spend alone and loneliness is a result of a lack of involvement and integration into a social network (ibid.). Emotional isolation refers to a perceived lack of close personal relationships because of deficits in social interaction (ibid.).

Structural factors also may promote emotional isolation. The most common variables include marital status and other social ties, socio-demographic variables, health/functional status, and personality (shyness and introversion) (ibid.). Economic security protects against loneliness, as does having a marital partner, good health, and an extroverted personality. Age-associated losses such as death and widowhood reduce the available levels of quantity and quality of social relationships and may trigger loneliness in older adults (ibid.).

Many of the focus group women, but few of the interviewees, report intense feelings of loneliness. We attribute this difference to both economics and ethnicity. The different field research methodologies would also account for this difference, probably significantly. Most of the focus group women are racialized, low-income, older immigrant women who have struggled against state and family patriarchal discrimination their entire lives. Loneliness is correlated with lack of power and loss of control. One Chinese-Canadian woman spoke for her focus group cohort when she outlined how pervasive loneliness is among immigrant women, defining it as a severe health hazard:

All over Toronto women our age are dying of loneliness and isolation and nobody cares. They do not speak English and are not allowed out of the house, kept in by controlling husbands. They have no access to money. Others live alone, eat very little, eat the wrong food and are just depressed by the loneliness of their lives. Companionship is so important to women and they just don't have it.

In contrast, few of our midlife interviewees report intense loneliness although many report frequently feeling lonely compared to their earlier lives when they were surrounded by small children and their friends. This finding fits with American studies that suggest only about 5–15 per cent of seniors report feeling lonely frequently and an additional 20–40 per cent report occasional feelings of loneliness (Prince et al., 1997). According to Pinquart (2003), about 50 per cent of adults over age 80 often feel lonely, so finding activities and new friendships in midlife possibly offers a protective effect in later old age.

Contacts provide both support and anxiety (ibid.). In the literature on loneliness, the assumption is that quality of contact is more important than quantity for well-being. Whom do midlife women report as providing support? Overwhelmingly, they mention three sources: family, including children and siblings, friends, and community affiliations. The latter two often overlap.

Women report partners and children as their first sources of social support. Marriage exerts a protective effect on men's well-being as women take primary responsibility for maintaining social networks (Arber et al., 2003). Men are more likely to name female partners as their 'best friends' while women are more likely to name female friends. For midlife women, men provide economic more than social support. Friendships and community links are the social locations in which women pour out their hearts and find solace and encouragement against the daily grind of putting others' needs ahead of their own.

Marginalization seems to promote community involvement. Many lesbian midlife women seem connected to a larger lesbian community from which they derive friendship and support. In answer to the question of what community involvement has brought them, a 56-year-old white lesbian describes both the costs and benefits:

It takes away in terms of time commitment. It adds back in terms of what it does for me mentally and/or spiritually, whatever the right language is there. And it has also created a whole new ring of friendships. (Gail, #14)

Communities can also be sources of tension, bringing feminist midlife women into direct conflict with more traditional ethno-cultural norms that may be extolled by agencies. Malina (#15) does not describe herself as a feminist but she has always maintained that women should have equal rights. She belongs to a Muslim sect—Ismaili—and so follows some of the teachings, but says:

I really feel angry when I see a woman that has not been given her rights . . . I don't believe in some of the way the Muslim men [get their wives to behave] . . . keeping the women in purdah, getting the women to cover their heads, not letting the women show the ankle. The only thing I have insisted as far as my daughter is concerned, we do not flaunt our bodies, so you are not going out in a blouse that is showing your cleavage or short shorts, but you want to wear shorts, that is fine. You want to wear a tight skirt, that's up to you. It is your body. They are liberated. I'm very proud of my daughter.

Even if some disputes take place, on the whole midlife women remain extremely grateful for, and depend on, the various community agencies that allow them spaces to speak freely with others who understand their culture, religion, and lifestyle (Lynn, 2001: 20–1).

Taking Stock: Midlife Evaluation

Stock-taking involves self-evaluation when women question every aspect of their lives and often seem surprised by much of what is revealed. Regrets, defined as unfulfilled or unattainable intentions or goals, include all the missed opportunities that bring midlife women feelings of shame and sadness (Stewart and Vandwater,

1999). Feelings of regret invoke emotions ranging from intense to mild, from anger to helplessness to wistfulness. All midlife women report regrets, and neither their marital status nor their education affects the intensity of their regret or the experience of intrusive thoughts (Wrosch and Hechausen, 2002). But intense regret verging on despair emerges only when women talk about intimacy or family regrets.

When Stewart and Vandwater (1999) asked midlife women about their regrets, women said they would have married someone who shared equally in domestic labour; they would not have put their husbands' needs before their own; they would not have had children. There is some evidence that midlife women who pursued a traditional role of homemaker are more likely to see the marriage enterprise as a massive or partial failure and either want out or hope for a new marriage (ibid.).

When we asked midlife women about 'things they would do differently', talk about compromise and agency emerged. Many of our midlife women report dissatisfaction at some point in their partnerships. Juggling the demands of home and work exhausts many midlife women, but it also brings them enormous self-respect, a sense of efficacy, and spheres of autonomy, none of which they would trade.

As we explore these themes more fully in Chapter 6, we see that the most frequently cited long-term regrets involve work and education. When asked what they would have done differently, the women in our study replied that they would have thought more seriously about a career, chosen a career over homemaking, gone to graduate school, gone earlier to graduate school, chosen a career in a traditionally male-dominated field, gone back to work earlier, or put their career before their children. Most midlife women are aware of their contingent choices and potentially missed opportunities in work, education, and family. As Dorothy (#22), a 59-year-old white British woman, says:

> I think if I hadn't had to compromise certain things when I was younger and married, then I certainly would be doing different things. It's difficult to look back and say, well, if you would have gone to law school, this is what would have happened.

This observation confirms the findings of Wrosch and Hechausen (2002) that the most frequently expressed regrets were related to work–education (32 per cent), family–partnership (24 per cent), and self-development (15.5 per cent). According to Landman (1993), two-thirds of women surveyed in the early 1980s stated that missed opportunities for education and career development were their biggest regrets.

Midlife women are part of the first generation to come of age as new opportunities for education and careers were opening up, so they are particularly vulnerable to regrets about choices made under one set of social pressures when, later in life, they are subject to a different set (Hulbert and Schuster, 1993). Midlife acknowledgement of missed opportunities for career and education is associated with higher levels of concurrent depression and anxiety among college-educated women who put aside their training to become stay-at-home moms. These women, Landman (1993) found, were more prone to emotional difficulty. Yvonne (#32), a 56-year-old Chinese-Canadian woman, says:

I regret I wasn't able to get more of an education, and that had to do with compromise, because we were never able to afford it. Even now, thinking about going back and doing a full training in psychotherapy cannot be done because I have a son I'm putting through university and a daughter that I hope will go on to college in the next year. We need money to put them through.

If regrets spark self-evaluation, do they precipitate change? The answer is complicated, because an acknowledgement of regrets is insufficient to bring about personal change, just as external barriers are insufficient to prevent them (Stewart and Vandwater, 1999). For example, many midlife women who live traditional lives did not make changes even though they said they wanted to. These women seem to have adapted internally to regrettable behaviour by adjusting their perceptions about their personal responsibility and control for the regret (Wrosch and Hechausen, 2002). Structures, they say, made it impossible for them to act in ways other than the ones they pursued. Other midlife women used self-examination, anger, and despair as catalysts for personal change. Helene (#36), a 53-year-old Polish woman, explains:

Now it's interesting, it just started a few years ago, my husband would say, 'Oh you know so-and-so, we are going to go for dinner.' And I would say, 'And you answered for both of us and you didn't run it by me? Oh, no; that's not acceptable.' And he would just do it in little situations. And now none of that goes on, it's always, 'I have to check with . . . .' And I do the same thing with him. But I think as the woman, because it wasn't important to me, I would just go along and do everything, 'Sure, that's great.' And then all of a sudden it's like, 'Uh-uh, not unless you ask me and not unless I want to do it.' I find I'm very strong there.

Regrets represent a fascinating and complicated aspect of the feelings and actions of midlife women. Perhaps, as the playwright Arthur Miller advised, 'all one can do is hope to end up with the right regrets' (Miller, 1991: Act I, 20).

Conclusion

Constructing family remains a central life project for most contemporary midlife women. From intimacy, women gain love, happiness, and profound satisfaction, which sustain them through the inevitable disappointments and setbacks that characterize a life. From intimacy, midlife women also suffer betrayal, setbacks, and, sometimes, abuse. Finding a balance between these two sets of extremes becomes the central goal of accomplishing families and intimate relations. Achieving intimacy also is synonymous with success for many midlife women, a concrete marker that tells them that the significant effort, time, and thought they have put into fashioning intimate attachments has been worth their effort. But love and intimacy are greedy. Finding partners, maintaining good family relations, nurturing friendships, and raising children take tremendous time and energy and necessarily limit women's ventures into work and leisure.

The central bind that midlife women recount as they tell the stories of their lives is that if they eschew or miss out on intimacy, they open themselves to considering their lives unsuccessful. Yet, if they throw all their effort into achieving intimacy, they may fail to find economic security or personal gratification through engagement in the worlds of work or community.

Ambivalence—structured, gendered, and interpersonal—emerges from our discussions with midlife women as they put into words what goes on in their families and in their intimate relationships. Specifically, it reverberates through their narratives of control, compromise, and community. Ambivalence may be structurally, culturally, and historically induced, but it is acted out on the level of institutional practices and individual behaviour. As such, it forms a bridging concept between our analysis of social structures and individual action. As Connidis and McMullin (2002a, 2002b) tell us, ambivalence reflects the contradictions and paradoxes characteristic of social experience. In the next chapter, on caring activities, this theme is explored as we examine the interface between home and work.

Key Concepts

Agency The capacity of an agent or individual to act in the world. Human agency is the capacity for human beings to make choices and to impose those choices on the world.

Empowerment An increase in the social, political, spiritual, and economic strength of individuals and communities, usually referring to being in control of one's life and involving the development of confidence in one's abilities. Both agency and empowerment are contextually located relational concepts (Wray, 2004).

Gendered accountability The ways in which accountability is invoked and anticipated through gendered socialization (Curran, 2002). An example would be the assumption that women are more likely to experience, or to expect to experience, being held responsible for relationships. It then follows that it is the moral responsibility of women to take care of the emotional needs of family members.

Ideology of romantic love An idea that 'promises' women happiness, satisfaction, affection, closeness, and security through their mates.

Shared story lines Narrative descriptions of life experience that explain, justify, rationalize, and classify one's own life course principally in terms of the intimate others (parents, siblings, partners, children, friends) with whom those experiences were shared.

Questions for Critical Discussion

1. Does the ideology of romantic love direct women's intimate attachments? If so, how?
2. How and why do midlife women develop shared story lines?
3. In what ways do family ties both empower and restrain midlife women?
4. How do community ties help midlife women negotiate the demands of family?
5. Describe how control and compromise by women make them, at midlife, ambivalent about intimacy.

Chapter 5

Caregiving: The Lifelong Compromise

By midlife, most women have learned that being female can often mean a lifelong commitment to caring for others. Typically, midlife women have spent their adult lives in one or more caregiving roles. Almost without exception, they have been partners, parents, daughters, or siblings with caregiving responsibilities. This generation had children later in life than their mothers and, for economic reasons, these children are more likely to remain in or return to the family home. The period between children establishing their own homes and aging parents requiring care may be brief or non-existent for midlife women. Clearly, caregiving is a role one is likely to enter and exit more than once in the life course (Moen et al., 1994). In addition, many midlife women have worked in the helping professions as nurses, social workers, midwives, or primary-level teachers where caregiving is a fundamental aspect of the work.

While care work has long been part of women's family responsibilities, increased involvement in paid work, increased longevity, and decreased fertility have dramatically changed its context. In this chapter, our focus is on family or 'informal' care. **Informal care** includes the help and care provided to family members of all ages who may or may not live in the same household. Based on the 1998 General Social Survey, about one-third of Canadian women and one-quarter of Canadian men provide informal care (Zukewich, 2003: 16). Men are more actively involved in parent than child care, although, as we would expect, women caregivers devote more time to informal caregiving than do men (ibid). More recent estimates of care work are available from the 2002 General Social Survey on Aging and Social Support. This survey focused on care provided to seniors by midlife Canadians. 'Over 1.7 million Canadian adults aged 45–64—16 per cent of this age group—are providing informal care to almost 2.3 million seniors with a long-term disability or physical limitation' (Stobart and Cranswick, 2004: 2).

The caregiving demands on midlife women are particularly acute at this historical moment because of the conjunction of longevity and fertility trends. While the number of children in a family has shrunk, senior members of the family now live longer. As a result, in most developed countries the family looks less like a pyramid— lots of children at the bottom of the pyramid, a parental generation, and then a smattering of seniors—and more like a pillar—similar numbers of elderly seniors relying on seniors who are relying on midlifers who are also engaged with their children (Barnett, 2005). The net result is that a 60-year-old woman may have few siblings or in-laws to turn to when her 85-year-old mother or mother-in-law needs care.

This phenomenon has been referred to as the 'second work–family incompatibility' (Perrig-Chiello and Höpflinger, 2005: 185), describing the conflicting demands of later-stage career and caring responsibilities for aging parents. The first work–family incompatibility was, of course, between paid work and the care of young children. As was true for mothers of young children, women manage to care for their ailing parents through a number of personally negotiated strategies. Depending on the nature of the responsibilities, some will reduce working hours or retire; others will hire professional care or try to solicit help from other relatives (ibid.).

Although household and caregiving obligations show signs of some gender 'convergence' (Marshall, 2006), a significant gap still remains, so that we can speak of **gendered care** as being the reality for many women. It is not surprising that except for families in which husbands are the sole earner, women reported being significantly more stressed for time than men, regardless of length of workday or presence of children (ibid.). Mothers spend more hours in a week caring for children, and daughters are more likely than sons to provide care for their parents. While both middle-aged men and women are engaged in parental elder care, the amount of time they spend and the activities in which they engage differ. Women dedicate almost twice as much time as men, contributing 29.6 hours/month versus 16.1 hours/month for men (Williams, 2005; Stobart and Cranswick, 2004). When family members become ill or frail or disabled, care can become intense. In those cases so-called informal care becomes a mainstay of our health and continuing care system (Fast, 2005). Typically, wives, mothers, and daughters are expected to step up.

In her book *In a Different Voice* (1982), psychologist Carol Gilligan identified a gender difference in the ethics of justice and care. She argued that men favour the ethic of justice and women the **ethic of care**. In other words, women are more concerned about others and maintaining relationships. Evidence to support the gender distinction is inconclusive, and there are many who disagree with Gilligan's fundamental distinction (Brabeck, 1989; Hurd and Brabeck, 1997). Nevertheless, the concept and the distinction have wide appeal, and have been used to explain gender differences in both public and private caregiving.

Social expectations that care work is gendered guide behaviour at both the structural and individual levels. Women's 'private' care work supplements the 'public' health-care system. It also frames women's choices regarding paid work, leisure, intimacy—indeed, all aspects of their lives (Hooyman and Gonyea, 1999; Lee and Porteous, 2002).

When added to paid employment, informal care work is stressful. Canadian workers experienced increased difficulty balancing work and family responsibilities through the 1990s (Duxbury and Higgins, 2001). Women are particularly vulnerable to the repercussions of stress. In 1994 and 2000 the General Social Survey (GSS) asked a representative number of Canadians about workplace stress (Williams and Normand, 2003: 8). In both years the most significant source of job stress was 'too many demands or too many hours'. Regardless of age, women were more likely to report feeling stressed by time pressures. Midlife women (aged 45–64) experienced greatest stress as a result of too many demands or too many hours (ibid.).

Despite the changes in participation rates, work structures and work cultures have been largely unresponsive to family care issues. Hochschild's (1989: 267) comment of nearly 20 years ago remains true today: 'Corporations have done little to accommodate the needs of working parents and government has done little to prod them.' As a result, many individuals and couples continue to struggle to find balance in their complicated family and work lives. The search for balance is particularly elusive for women who continue to shoulder the lion's share of family responsibilities. As women in this study argued, the stress of trying to manage can be detrimental to their health and sense of well-being.

The stress experienced by middle-aged women is the result of 30 years of trying to balance paid work and family care. This is especially true for women with children, but also remains the case for women caring for older relatives. Women have been socialized to nurture others; they are not as good at taking care of themselves. As Kendra (#77) said: 'I learned from my mother. She waited on my father, so I did the same thing.' Women also have high expectations of themselves for maintaining both home and work despite other demands on their time.

For many years, care responsibilities were described in the literature as more onerous than not, focusing on the emotional, physical, and economic costs to caregivers (Moen et al., 1995). A life course approach, in contrast, sees the caregiver–care receiver relationship as more fluid and complex than either benefit or burden. In Chapter 1 we referred to the concept of structured ambivalence suggested by Connidis and McMullin (2002a). This pattern of structured ambivalence often exists. While individuals may seek to exercise agency and negotiate relationships in terms of their wants and desires, they also run up against the limitations imposed by the social structure. For example, in the absence of social structures that facilitate the integration of all parenting partners into child care, while also allowing opportunities for education and paid employment, individuals' alternatives are restricted. However, the compromises necessitated by these structures are not necessarily validated. Mothers, for example, may express guilt at their absence from their children's lives at the same time as they express frustration at their lack of advancement, security, and recognition in their paid employment. Struggling with these contradictions emerges as a recurrent feature of their interpersonal lives.

It is enormously difficult to generalize about women's caregiving responsibilities. In some cases, the pressures on individual women seem impossible to bear. Other women not only have less intense and shorter periods of caregiving but also more extensive support systems, including not only supportive husbands/partners but also siblings, friends, and communities that directly or indirectly assist with the caregiving. Care work is both layered and reciprocal. Women in this study were caregivers, but they have also been cared for at different points in time. Children and adults of all ages are both cared for and caregivers—sometimes simultaneously. Furthermore, increased evidence indicates that men have taken greater responsibility in informal family care, particularly parent and spousal care (Calasanti, 2006; Campbell and Carroll, 2007). Sometimes the roles of caregivers and care receivers are blurred, and in either role there will be a degree of resistance and a degree of acceptance. While recognizing the varied and reciprocal nature of family care, this study focused on ways midlife women reflect on their past, present, and future caregiving.

Looking Back on the Child-Care Years

In the interviews we asked women about their past and current family relationships and their paid and unpaid work. We also asked if they felt they had made compromises in their work and family lives. Eighty per cent of the women in the study had children and one-quarter of these had grandchildren. Typical of their generation, the average number of children was 2.4. In most cases, these children are now adults, although some are teenagers. Most midlife women readily agreed that they made compromises, but they did not expect family life to be otherwise. Embedded in many of the respondents' comments about their efforts to balance caregiving, personal life, and paid employment is a sense of the inevitable. The need to make sacrifices is a personal and social expectation—particularly for women.

Some women in the study looked back at the early stages of mothering with pure joy. Susan (#16) said, 'I don't remember who I was before I had children and I think they became the centre of my life, much more than my marriage. It's a much more primal relationship and continues to be.' Not surprisingly, Susan now considers her adult daughters as close friends.

While some women speak of the day-to-day satisfaction of being involved in their children's discovery of the world, they also comment on missing the adult world and on the sense of economic independence or growth that went along with full-time education or employment. Malina (#15), a 57-year-old health-care worker, regards her children as a blessing and comments: 'My children have meant a great, great deal. I can still remember the first fluttering, the first time I felt the baby move when I was pregnant.' But she also acknowledges that since she was an immigrant to Canada she undertook most of her education after she married and had children. As a result of these caregiving responsibilities, education was by necessity truncated and 'very difficult', and opportunities were lost.

Some women stayed home with their young children; others returned to paid employment. Then as now, neither path is wholly satisfactory. Women who stayed home with young children felt that they gave up opportunities for paid work. Women who returned to work described a feeling of loss. Susan (#16) stayed home with her children, but as she said, 'I gave up almost every idea of doing my own work in order to mother.'

Miriam and Tamika seem content to have made certain sacrifices in order to focus on mothering. They saw these as investments in the future, a type of insurance policy, guarding against future damages.

As a mom, I think I made a HUGE . . . I don't like the word compromise . . . I've made a huge commitment which meant to me, their needs as I saw them, as best I could, had priority over some of my desires and choices, so it might have meant I had to give a lot more time and a lot more years. (Miriam, #44)

Professionally, I could have advanced. I could have gone off to do a master's. Let's face it . . . at what cost? You see the choices I would have had to make would be—not neglect—but to become so selfish that my son might have been walking the streets or on drugs today. Or, my husband might have gone off with some other lady, 'cause I'm in the halls of some university. (Tamika, #58)

Janet (#72), Kendra (#77), and Karen (#88) would have preferred to stay home with their young children, were it not for financial considerations.

I've had to compromise the ability to stay home and watch my child grow. I was never able to do that. I've always had to work. Three months after I gave birth to her I had to go back to work. (Janet, #72)

Well, I think it was a compromise to take my kids to daycare. That really bothered me. When I was working, I can remember them standing in the front window of the daycare just crying their eyes out as I was leaving to go to work. (Kendra, #77)

When you have children, as a woman, I think you're torn between whether you go back to work or whether you stay at home, and for me going back to work was an issue 'cause it's not what I wanted to do. I wanted to stay home, but financially I had to go back to work. (Karen, #88)

Sophia's (#74) ambivalence about managing her work–family imbalance is reflected in a longing for the good old days when mothers stayed home with the children.

Sometimes I think that it was better in the old days when the mother stayed home with the children. I think it was to the children's benefit. But these days and in my past, it seems very difficult for a mother to stay home financially to give her kids the things that they want or need. I would much rather have been in the other generation where the mother stayed home with the children.

Janet, Kendra, Karen, and Sophia returned to work because of financial necessity. While economic considerations are paramount, other factors influence women's decisions about where to focus their energies in the work–family dynamic. Evaluations of early parenting years are hugely dependent on the presence of a support system—typically a supportive partner. Pamela (#11) said she felt grateful to have had a supportive partner: 'I'm very grateful that there's two of us and we have a partnership here and we can try and balance out our work schedules here.'

Paloma (#40), a 50-year-old immigrant who is a single parent of an 18-year-old daughter, experienced marriage and motherhood as unfairly one-sided arrangements:

> In marriage I find that it's all about compromising and it's one-sided and it's the woman that is always expected to compromise so I'm not married and this is why I'm not really in a relationship either. I find that it is hard and unless you're willing to be constantly compromising, it is not going to work.

Considering that she presents herself as completely devoted to her daughter and her pursuits, it would seem that leaving her marriage and focusing on 'mothering' was a strategy for managing the competing demands of home and paid work.

Mia (#10) did not have anyone to count on when her young child was ill. As she explained: 'I got fired from a job because my son had measles and I had to stay home to take care of him. In those days, you didn't show up for work, you just didn't have a job when you came back.'

Rita (#1) started off her caregiving in a very traditional manner. She was able to shift the balance with the help of a supportive partner. As the young mother of three small children, she assumed complete responsibility for their care 'in a town where I knew nobody, isolated completely, living in the married students' quarters, with no money, living with nothing.' Meanwhile, her husband 'would walk out each day at 8 a.m. and come back at 10 p.m., was part of the drama club and the whole university scene.' After the addition of two more children to her family, Rita grew increasingly involved with her work and pursuing her education. The couple simply switched roles:

> In many ways, in our household there has been a role reversal, where my husband has been the one who has made the dinner the last 15 years. Twenty years ago, ever since I started off as a new mother, I was making everything that went into my children's mouths . . . there was not anything that they touched that was not made by me. And I, you know, six or seven years into that . . . I just looked up one day and said I am finished and my husband started cooking and he has been cooking ever since.

Further along in the interview it is clear that this role reversal involved a process of intense struggle and conflict:

> . . . when I became a midwife and started doing my work and he would complain about me not being there, my response would be, 'I was with the kids when you were at work . . . year after year after year. It is your turn now; what do you mean I should be at home.' I didn't want to come to Toronto in the first place.

Today, Rita's dramatically reduced role as caregiver is explained in positive terms, but the switch was neither easy nor uncontested. She explains the current arrangements as follows:

> My work life was basically able to be what it was, because I have a very sup-
> portive husband and he would be able to pick up the role of parent and
> provider in the family for the children.

From her contemporary vantage point, her attention focuses on what she has lost
rather than on what she gained by restricting her caregiving role. 'I essentially sacrificed my role as mother in order to do my work.'

She points out that even when she is at home, her school work, political work,
and organization work mean that she is not available even when she is around. This
eclipsing of so many caregiving responsibilities as mother is not entirely comfortable. In the interview Rita catches herself complaining about what her husband is
serving for dinner and considers what she, as a feminist, would say if a husband were
complaining to his wife. She also worries that she '[has] negotiated motherhood to
the point where I am missing something', and she is certainly aware that her children
and husband feel angry at all that they have sacrificed for her work. Once again, the
socially constructed ambivalence and conflict are glaring features of her account.

Vivian (#17) reflects this kind of ambivalence even though she is a member of a
long-term same-sex couple. She and her partner are both well-educated professionals. However, when they started a family, her partner gave up her career and became
a stay-at-home parent to their two children. Given the primary role played by her
partner, Vivian has not felt torn between work and home, although she does feel an
obligation to be home by 5:30 p.m. since she knows her partner will probably be
'tearing her hair out by then'. She also describes herself as a more detached parent,
who leaves in the morning before anyone is awake and often forgets to say good
night to her son. On her weekly day off, she indulges in yoga and baking bread. As
she comments, 'if I was a more attached parent I would feel like I was making big
compromises for work.' As she points out, her partner 'certainly has to make compromises because of my job and my not being around and available and stuff.' In a
telling comparison to the role of her partner, she acknowledges that 'I don't feel kind
of conflicted about "oh, my gosh, I could be doing this or that." I feel like I definitely
have the good end of the stick in our family.'

Women who live with poverty face far greater challenges. Lynette (#27) has been
providing care for or receiving care from her family all her life. As she approaches 60,
she lives alone, in a room, earning enough to support herself by working as a nanny,
caring for young children she has raised from infancy. She had been very young when
her children were born and is now a grandmother. She has never experienced economic security, but describes her experience as a nanny as a second chance at mothering. Reflecting on her experience as a young mother, she comments:

> I didn't have the skills and I didn't have the temperament, I didn't have any-
> thing, I didn't have the money, food, I didn't have the things that I needed to
> be a good mother, I mean I was a good mother, I never hit my children or neg-
> lected them in any way, but sometimes when there isn't enough food around
> and you have this epilepsy, and you know it's just a struggle because you know
> sometimes, you're there but you are not listening to your kids sometimes, you

know, you can't be there, sometimes I would have these seizures where things would go blank and I didn't hear everything they said, you know . . . .

While she is conflicted about her past mothering, Lynette feels she does a very good job as a nanny—in fact, she describes the opportunity to work as a nanny as her having been given a second chance. Her comments speak to the importance that many women of her generation attach to seeing themselves (and being seen by others) as a 'good mother':

> I learned a lot from raising those children. I learned how wonderful a mother I would have been had I been older, and it gave a second chance at sort of having my own kids. Without that I probably would have never known how great a woman I could be.

As a midlife woman Lynette's life course reflects a complex web of caregiving relationships. In the period between caring for her own children as a very young mother and her current job as a nanny, Lynette cared for her dying mother, and in turn received support and care from her own daughter. When she talks about attending her mother in hospital it is clear that she saw this as intrinsic to her role as a woman:

> I gave up my social life because women, we really are caregivers, and I think I was born to be a caregiver. . . . I spent about 10 hours a day at the hospital, not even wanting to go home, just wanting to be with her as much as I could. And after she died, I still miss her. I miss her more than I ever thought was possible. . . . I don't have that dear woman to take care of any more.

However, a life of caregiving and self-denial can have significant economic impacts. In Lynette's case, when her job went from full-time to part-time, she was no longer able to afford to live independently, and so moved in with her daughter. Three years later, as her grandchildren began to grow up, she reluctantly accepted the inevitable move to a rented room.

> So I lived with my daughter for three years on the chesterfield. I had to leave there because she has three children and the kids wanting to use the couch at some point, you know. I was very sad about that, but it was somehow very necessary, I had to let them have their life. (Lynette, #27)

Lynette's experience shows the reciprocal nature of care and the added burden for women who live in poverty. Several women in the study had children who lived with disability, and these parenting experiences are described as emotionally demanding.

Importantly, even women who opted not to have children, and who devoted much of their energies to their education and career, speak of the pressures to juggle their career with: 'my obligations to my marriage, to my extended family . . . I've always had to juggle . . . I've probably compromised on the career side in the sense of maybe not taking on [being] chair of a committee [or] taking on extra work' (Margaret, #4). She elaborates on the current tensions:

> . . . my marriage and beyond that to my aging father . . . we're in touch a lot. I assist him with medical problems . . . he has expectations, my board chairman has expectations, my husband has expectations. I've got a lot of people expecting things from me. I would say that has been a constant tension throughout my career—to determine the appropriate balance.

Interestingly, Margaret consciously elected not to have children so that she would have a more manageable life.

> An interesting thing for me, and something that Lorna Marsden [sociologist and former president of York University] said 20 years ago . . . 'Marriage, career, children . . . pick two'.

Anticipating Grandparenting

As our interviewees move into middle age they reflect a complex variety of living arrangements. Mothers of teenagers are in their final years of child-rearing. Others have seen their 20-something children launched, and are anticipating or experiencing the joys of grandparenting. They see being a grandmother as a less complicated and easier responsibility than being a mother. Assuming that they will never be required to take on a parental role with their grandchildren, their anticipation is for a relationship premised on choice and flexibility. They have little sense that grandchildren will impose on their other plans, such as to travel, to pursue education, or to focus on a career. Women who currently have grandchildren point out that they visit or talk 'regularly' with them. The word 'regularly' appears so frequently in conjunction with any mention of grandchildren that it seems key to these relationships. Women fulfill this relationship by attending to it 'regularly': it does not overwhelm their lives. Beyond this regularity, interviewees make scant mention of grandchildren as they go on to talk about their work, communities, and future. The intense and challenging relationships are with children—spouses, parents, and grandchildren typically appear on the periphery—as a source of pleasure and familial continuity but not of obligation and constriction.

In Canada, approximately two-thirds of Canadian women aged 55–64 are grandparents (Milan and Hamm, 2003). Only 18 per cent of the midlife women in this study had grandchildren. Demographically, they are at the young end of the grandparenting group when compared to the country as a whole. At this stage both their experience and anticipation of grandparenting are positive. Women like Lenora (#41) 'would love to be a gramma'.

Kemp (2004) has studied the relatively new (demographically speaking) relationships between Canadian grandparents and their adult grandchildren. She found that because grandchildren and grandparents can define their relationship 'based on personal need and personal history' (ibid., 520), these relationships are character-ized by a combination of tradition and obligation; choice and freedom.

Empty Nests and Boomerang Kids

For many years, analysts spoke of the sadness (and loss of role) that women encoun-tered when their children 'flew the nest'. Some women we interviewed are in the '**empty nest**' stage, and for many this 'freer' period allows them to be intensely and happily engaged with their careers, extended families, marital relationships, or leisure activities. While they may feel a pang of sadness at the absence of children who were once such an intense presence in the family and glue in the marital rela-tionship, they also sense adventure and new beginnings. Although we did not specifically ask women in the study to talk about their experiences of empty nests or boomerang children, Nancy (#2) raised these topics when asked about family relationships, and Gail (#14), in alluding to her boomerang kids, talked about her home as a revolving door. Nancy, a 55-year-old professional, remarks:

> We have been empty-nesting—[daughter] moved out about a year ago, last September—so a year and a half ago, I guess, for 18 months . . . almost two years. We have been empty-nesting and firstly we thought we'd miss her, but we have tried to find things to do together and keep our relationship . . . dynamic, I guess is the word I want. And, we have also started to do more things [together].

Gail has two daughters, one of whom is married and was living with her at the time of the interview. According to Gail: 'we're in the revolving door. They've both been out and we've been by ourselves, but they are in and out.' Gail does not look forward to an empty nest. 'Emotionally, I think I will get through it, but I feel a lit-tle fragile when I think of them both being away because they are very dear to me.'

For those midlife women whose adult children, members of the boomerang gen-eration, have returned home, the empty nest remains an illusion. More and more Canadians in their twenties, especially young men, are remaining in or returning to their familial homes because of employment uncertainty and rising housing and educational costs (Beaupre et al., 2003). Indeed, leaving and returning home may occur several times before their final launch (ibid.; Milan and Hamm, 2003), sug-gesting to Dennerstein et al. (2002) that the more appropriate term is 'revolving door'. In 2001 in Canada, 57 per cent of 20–4-year-olds were living with their par-ents. One-quarter of these were **boomerang kids** (Turcotte, 2006). Culture is an important determinant. Parents born in Asia and Central and South America were far more likely to live with their adult children (ibid.). Because it is increasingly the norm, there is little stigma associated with 'living with my parents'. 'An adult child returning home has become a fairly common, predictable event in family life' (Beaupre et al., 2003: 28). Even when there are no or few 'mothering' activities involved with these arrangements, educational and living costs continue to impact on the family and, as a result, on midlife women's economic well-being.

Holdsworth's research on mother–adult co-resident daughter relationships helps illuminate the complexity and reciprocity that can be part of these relationships. Based on interviews with mothers and daughters in three European cities, Holdsworth (2007: 66) argues that both the identities of mothers and daughters and their interdependencies are continually constructed. She describes in detail three case studies that illustrate a sense of mutual dependence and independence—very different from patterns observed in dyads involving sons or fathers. 'The mutuality of the women's relationship is what stands out most' (ibid., 68). This sense of reciprocity, and a balance between autonomy and connection (McGraw and Walker 2004), dependence and independence (Spitz and Gallant, 2004), characterizes caring relationships in midlife and older families: caring relationships involving adults, from their twenties through dependent aging.

The Sandwich Generation

The **sandwich generation** consists of those midlife adults who care for both their parents and their children. The term has been used to refer to social as well as familial responsibilities (see Arber and Attias-Donfut, 2000). Social responsibilities are reflected in the tax burden of the gainfully employed to support older and younger dependent citizens. When referring to familial responsibilities, 'sandwich generation' has been used broadly to include midlife adults with living parents and dependent adult children. More customarily, the reference is limited to adults with dependent children at home who at the same time have caregiving responsibilities for dependent parents (see Perrig-Chiello and Höpflinger, 2005).

Although many middle-aged adults provide care for their parents or other older family members, relatively few Canadian men or women care for children and aging parents *at the same time*. Less than a million Canadians in their forties, fifties, or sixties had children under 25 living at home *and* provided some kind of elder care for at least one senior. Most (80 per cent) of this sandwich generation were employed, although some had reduced their work hours so that they could manage their care responsibilities (Williams, 2005). Typically, caregivers had ambivalent feelings about their responsibilities. They experienced loss of sleep and had other health concerns, as well as curtailed social activities. However, they said that the caregiving experience strengthened their relationship with their parent, and that they felt good about giving back (ibid.).

The situation for all those caring for dependent adults is exacerbated by the aging of the population and cutbacks in social service supports. Given longevity and smaller family size, we can expect that this kind of care will fall on fewer shoulders in the future. As state-funded formal support continues to erode, caregiving increasingly falls on women family members. The role of caregiving for elderly parents 'naturally' falls more on daughters than on sons. It is a logical extension of their parenting, partnering, and, in some cases, paid work.

There are two predominant forms of elder care: that provided by middle-aged adults between the ages of 45 and 64 to seniors and that provided by seniors over age 65 to other seniors. In the first instance, over 1.7 million midlife Canadians (16 per cent of this age group) care for almost 2.3 million seniors (Stobart and Cranswick, 2004). As expected, most (67 per cent) are providing care for their own parents while a significant minority are looking after their spouse's parents (24 per cent) or close friends and neighbours (24 per cent) (ibid.).

Not surprisingly, the women we found who were currently caring for aging parents frequently voiced their frustrations and exhaustion. Phyllis (#3), who has a severely disabled brother and aging mother, speaks, for example, of talking with her mother five or six times a day and finding it 'exhausting, it's draining, it's debilitating.' She makes the point that it is not the time demanded so much as the emotional pressure of being constantly concerned about both her brother's prospects and her mother's declining health. 'It occupies my psyche and my heart more than anything else.' The ambivalence Phyllis feels is clear in the following comment:

> I care deeply about them and I love them, but I have more mixed emotions about it. There's much more feeling of obligation. When I meet the obligation I feel satisfied but I don't feel ecstatic. I don't feel very nurtured. I don't necessarily look forward to it . . . or replenished. . . . My brother's disability had depleted a lot of hope in our family and a lot of sort of reserve. There's not much happiness or joy.

A number of the women in the focus groups were highly involved in family care of several generations—dealing with the difficulties of adult children, or of grandchildren, or caring for a disabled spouse or elderly parents at the same time as they are caring for young children and working or going to school. One focus group woman said she lives on a treadmill in order to survive. She is working, going to school to finish a professional degree, and caring for two children as a single parent. At the same time, she is engaged in an ongoing battle over child custody with her exhusband. Some women spoke of their feelings of failure because of their inability to carry on multiple family duties. Others spoke of their anger towards family members who demand so much and give so little, thus contributing further to the woman's own ill health (Lynn et al., 2001: 8).

Caregiving is a complex activity. It can be physically, financially, and emotionally demanding. Mary (#24) was the only woman we interviewed to describe herself as 'sandwiched'. Time conflicts were her biggest pressure: 'time you think is required to your career, to your own family, to your husband, child, to your parents, to your friends . . . it's very difficult.' Yet, clearly, her greatest feelings were of love for her parents. Her father died three years ago and her mother was 80 at the time of the interviews. 'I love my parents dearly. I just look at my mother now and I know I'm going to lose her someday and that's very hard.' Dorothy (#22) expressed a similar sense of loss in her fifties after her parents had died. With no siblings, she describes experiencing a period of 'profound loneliness'.

Lenora (#41), a 55-year-old immigrant to Canada, refers to the very difficult time when her suddenly widowed elderly father came to live with her, her husband, and their two teenage children. She felt that the decision was 'out of her control', since her siblings 'chose' her home as the most accessible and appropriate for their aging and ill father:

> And, for me, that was really traumatic, [it] being a lot of work to look after a diabetic and an elderly man. He was used to my mother. So I had to sort of take over where she left off and that was quite traumatic for me . . . and traumatic for my children.

Although Lenora felt her husband was, in fact, more patient and 'better' in dealing with this sudden responsibility, there is an undertone of resentment:

> He [husband] could afford to be [patient] . . . because I was doing all the . . . check with the needle, with the meals, which I had to learn . . . if he had a reaction . . . quite a strain if you don't have any medical background.

The physical work of caregiving was only the most obvious part of the stress. She felt called upon to negotiate complex emotional terrain in which her father wanted to take on the role of parent with her teenage girls and in which her daughters were resentful if they felt their mother wasn't defending them:

> . . . he [elderly father] would go up and go to his room and close the door and say, 'Oh, I can't tell you anything about your kids'. . . . And, I said, 'Fine. Okay, feel that way' . . . but I didn't want my kids to suffer.

In this instance, after briefly trying part-time work, Lenora returned full-time to her work as a department head at a department store in order to get relief from the caregiving pressures, 'I went back full-time . . . mainly because otherwise I'd go crazy.'

Amy (#20), a 58-year-old mother of two sons who has been widowed for 22 years, is ambivalent about this implicit family division of labour:

> Well, I have a feeling that with me being the oldest and their daughter, that my responsibility . . . well, my brother told me, 'You have to deal with them.' My brother will come every couple of weeks, where I basically see them every single week. If they need anything I will go and get it for them and as their needs increase or change I will have to see what I am prepared to do within the boundaries of myself. . . . So, if they end up in a home, in a senior's place, you know, it'll be my fault; [as if] I didn't want to look after them. If I move in with them, it will be me that will live in hell, because that's what it will be, total abuse.

Later in the interview, she explains how she sees the health implications of the responsibilities that fall on women's shoulders.

Trying to work and look after children and to do all of that leaves an enormous strain on that one individual and I think that's where health comes in. I think that's where it's just too hard to keep all of those things going. And I think there are so many women that have been mistreated. Well, myself included, actually; I have been quite . . . [trails off], now that I think about it. I don't like to say that, but it is the truth.

Barbara (#78), who has undertaken considerable caregiving responsibilities for her aged parents (one of whom has died), reflects this complex interplay between choice and obligation; agency and structure:

It didn't bother me [caring for my parents] because I felt it was my duty to look after my parents because they raised me and they were always good to me, so I had to do it. There was no question about it.

Ageism depicts elder care as unpleasant at best. However, this stereotype is not borne out by Canadian statistics. Only a small minority—13 per cent—of Canadians providing informal elder care describe their lives as very stressful, while 49 per cent find their lives somewhat stressful (Stobart and Cranswick, 2004). As Stobart and Cranswick note, these rates of life satisfaction are the same as rates found among adult Canadians who are not providing elder care. Does this imply that satisfaction rates are generally unreliable or that Canadians are, on balance, a fairly satisfied lot? In either case, it does not suggest that providing elder care is a negative experience for people. In fact, quite the opposite seems to be true. When asked to evaluate their experiences, both middle-aged elder caregivers and senior caregivers rate their elder care positively. Between 80 and 90 per cent feel that helping others strengthens their relationships with the care receivers and repays some of what they themselves have received from others and from life (ibid.).

Other studies suggest that caregiving is neither simply onerous nor fulfilling. Understandably, most daughters caring for their mothers find the experience both rewarding and trying, and experience the kind of ambivalence discussed earlier in the chapter as they negotiate this terrain. According to McGraw and Walker (2004: S324), women are both burdened and enriched by family care as they struggle to find a balance between connection and autonomy.

Lee and Porteous (2002: 90) found that some Australian women who were involved in caregiving internalized an ethic of care while others perceived it as imposed. Some women in the Australian study referred to their *valuable but unappreciated contribution to the country's health-care system*. While they recognized the way care is gendered, many women saw no choice—regardless of the cost to themselves. Some accepted or were resigned to their situations. Others were angry about the compromises they were required to make. Whether 'true believers' or resentful skeptics, these women still accepted their obligation to provide care.

'Experiencing a frail and dependent parent is in many cases associated with the fear of having to confront the same fate themselves at a later stage' (Perrig-Chiello and Höpflinger, 2005: 186). Many midlife women talked about their worry about inheriting the health problems that plague their parents. An air of resignation in their comments often suggests an inevitable health outcome of their own. Paloma (#40) described her health heritage as follows: 'my father's side of the family is heart and my mother's side of the family is stroke. My grandmother died from a stroke, and I had a stroke when I was 25.' Amy (#20) notes:

> The history in my family has been heart, cancer, and my mother has rheuma-toid arthritis. I would think that one or some of that will happen to me even-tually. I mean, I'm not naive enough to think it will bypass me. What I think that you have to do is take as good care of yourself as possible and that's what I try and do in order to hold off from that.

Worries about health uncertainties in the future leave many, like 54-year-old Ruth (#6), feeling vulnerable about their own future health, on one hand, and pres-sured to take action to forestall ill health, on the other. She worries because when she was a teenager her mother died with multiple sclerosis at age 57, and also because she has the beginnings of high blood pressure and osteoarthritis. She says:

> I have to begin to really focus on a program of physical fitness of running, weightlifting . . . as much as possible to alter the aging process. So I have con-cerns because I do not wish to end up being debilitated because of heart attack or stroke. . . . I can make changes . . . [but I could still] wake up tomor-row with cancer.

In short, when midlife women talk about the prospects or realities of caring for aged parents, practical considerations of finding the time, energy, and funds are complexly intermixed not only with conflicting feelings of resentment, guilt, and obligation but also with concerns about their own health practices and the implica-tions of current caregiving stresses for their future personal health.

Elaine Brody's study of the sandwich generation, *Women in the Middle*, points to both the life stage and the shared experience of competing demands. 'What parent-caring women have in common is that they are feeling the stunning impact of mas-sive demographic and socioeconomic trends that have converged to place them in the middle' (Brody, 2004: 7). Brody argues that despite these changes, women accept parental care as their responsibility, and they set high standards for themselves in trying to meet those responsibilities (ibid., 335). 'In the middle generationally, in the middle years, in the middle of competing responsibilities to various people in their families and to their jobs, and in the middle between values that compete, they often ignore their responsibilities to themselves' (ibid., 336).

In their interviews, women clearly anticipated that parental caregiving will emerge as a growing demand. They recognize, too, that other caregiving responsi-bilities may conflict and that there will be lots of juggling. The overall impression is not of their being overwhelmed at the prospect of these demands. Possibly, the underlying feeling at this point in the life course is that conflicting and intense care-giving demands have already been survived. Whatever the future holds, they have this experience to draw on. The fear may be more in terms of future personal implications.

In Sickness and in Health: Caring for Partners

Since women still tend to marry older men and since men may reasonably expect to live into old age, many women will spend a portion of their lives caring for an ailing partner. As Calasanti (2006) suggests, a significant number of older women will also be cared for by their partners. As midlife women, our participants have not reached this life stage. However, a handful, including eight widows, have cared for their partners through illness.

Dalia (#56), a 53-year-old mother of three, talks about trying to help her husband live a less stressful life. Even her concerns for her own health are completely interwoven with her caring obligations to her husband.

> So you know I worry, and my concern is keeping my stress level down. Because I think stress is a killer, you know, you get heart disease, and I think sometimes it is stress-related. And I have seen friends who have been under lots of stress developing cancers, so that is one reason why I am very insistent that my husband and I do something, because he's been under so much stress, and he says it's been no problem, it's their problem, and it's been going on for so many years, and this year he's suddenly, he's off on sick leave. He's actually having physical symptoms. So there I worry about levels of stress, so that's why I want to reduce it, and that's why I'm thinking more about retirement and seeing how we can manage to survive.

Tracy (#35), a 51-year-old married and childless woman employed full-time as a community service co-ordinator, was 46 years old when her husband was diagnosed with cancer. As a result, in midlife she experienced an extremely intense period of needing and wanting to provide support and care to her ailing spouse. Significantly, she starts to describe the progress through his cancer treatment in terms of 'we':

> So when we were accepted into the [stem cell] program, we were really delighted. It gave a possibility for a cure . . . . So we went through in 1999 the stem cell transplant . . . .

It is apparent that her daily life became deeply entwined with providing for his care, to the point that three years later, when his condition stabilized, she took a job with a non-profit organization that would allow her time with her spouse:

> I wanted a job that took away that firm line of responsibility so I could have the freedom to enjoy my relationship with my husband or, if something does happen to him, to be able to respond to it.

Later she adds:

> I think what I would want to be able to do is enjoy the time with my husband, whether it's two years or 20 years. What I want out of my work relationship is to find something that is satisfying but not so engulfing that I don't have time for the other.

Amanda (#87) talked about the care work involved in living with her husband, who is a 'recovering alcoholic':

> I had to deal with his absences, both physical and emotional, and I kind of put my life on hold sometimes to keep things going and provide some sort of stable family life. It's been up and down since he was in treatment centres and would relapse.

Amanda learned caregiving lessons from both her grandmother and her mother. 'Caring for my grandmother and aunt helped me to reach out and realize we all need the support of someone sometimes.' Amanda explained that since her grandmother's death, her mother has taken over as 'matriarch of the family'. 'I don't think I want to inherit that role. Also, I don't want to repeat the pattern, although I'm afraid I am, of caring for a partner.'

Social and demographic trends predict that, like Amanda, as midlife women age, they will 'inherit' the role of caregiver to a partner.

Stressed Out and 'Downright Tired'

Much of a midlife woman's caregiving is beyond her control to manage because it involves the onset of illness or disability of an adult child, a parent, or a partner in a culture that has limited the size of its families (the old social support network) and in a society that has failed to provide public community resources (the contemporary social support network in socialist societies). Caregiving needs also change as households expand or contract. Young adults leave home for education or work and return when emotional or economic relationships change. One of our respondents talked about the sheer impossibility of giving time to her career, her family, her husband, her child, her friends, and her parents. Just the thought of it was overwhelming. Many talked about how it was unrealistic to continue to work long hours and care for their family and home—yet they do continue, because they don't see an alternative.

For many people, tiredness, like stress, is chronic. Popay (1992) interviewed British men and women to try to better understand the ways the experience of tiredness differs for men and women. She found that men (and some women) were more likely to report episodic tiredness, while women (and some men) were more likely to report chronic tiredness. Women 'normalized' chronic stress. It was simply the result of the way they lived (ibid., 108). Although one of the reasons for extreme tiredness was interrupted sleep and the demands of young children, it wasn't only parents of young children who were exhausted, according to Popay's findings. Extreme tiredness was intrinsic to combining paid and unpaid work and affected both men and women.

Although most adults experience occasional sleep problems, midlife women may be more susceptible. The gendered nature of family responsibilities means that women normally respond to nighttime disturbances (Hislop and Arber, 2003), but in addition to being awakened by family members' or young children's nighttime needs, adolescents' and older children's late-night return home, partners' snoring, work worries, and elder care, midlife women may experience night sweats and other sleep-disrupting symptoms of menopause. Sophia (#74), a 53-year-old married mother of two daughters, captures the depth of feelings of chronic tiredness:

> Sometimes you're just downright tired. And I don't mean you're going to get a good night sleep and feel refreshed tomorrow. I mean the other kind of tired where you feel that you are pulled into so many different directions and sometimes you just feel totally mentally and physically exhausted. It's very hard for a working mother to raise children in this day.

As a culture, we neither acknowledge how stressful it is for women to try to manage paid employment, housework, child care, and elder care, nor do we acknowledge the cumulative effect. Studies of stress over the life course often argue that employed mothers of young children suffer greatest stress. When midlife stress becomes part of the discourse of decline, it is easy for women and their doctors to associate stress with menopause, and hormone replacement therapy or anti-depressants become 'easy' medical solutions. This ignores the underlying causes—years of working a double shift. Systemic inequities created by the burden of the double day are far more difficult problems to address. The medicalization of menopause further overlooks the real problems of stress and overload for midlife women (Cousins and Edwards, 2002: 326).

Stress is part of the taken-for-granted reality of Canadian women's lives. Because we accept that stress is an individual's responsibility to manage, there are few structural supports to relieve it. The media reinforce that individuals are responsible for resolving their stress. When Kranz and Long (2002: 526) looked at articles on stress in *Chatelaine* and *Cosmopolitan* magazines they found that two messages stood out: 'First, stress is pervasive and unavoidable in women's lives. Second, women are responsible for managing their stress by shopping (that is, consumerism), consulting experts and changing how they think, feel and behave.' This view both normalizes and individualizes the experience of stress. 'Thus, women are not encouraged to use their dis/stress as indicators of legitimate grievances' (ibid., 528) or to seek change in the structural factors that help create their stress, such as poverty, sexism, ageism, racism, and so on.

Survey results confirm the endemic nature of stress. Stress was the most frequently mentioned health problem in the 1997 study by Walters and Denton of Canadian women. Williams and Normand (2003) found that the most significant source of job stress was 'too many demands or too many hours'. Midlife women (aged 45–64) experienced greatest stress in this regard.

Caught at the nexus of greedy social demands and inadequate social resources, midlife women's engagement with stress may verge on desperation. Rita (#1), who is 50 years old and the mother of five children, worries about the effect on her children and herself of living with a pager for 20 years: her health breaking point (is she at risk for a stroke or heart disease?) and her emotional breaking point. She talked about the difficulty of finding balance.

> Doing, doing, I have to move. I mean, I literally feel that exercise is so essential to my life from here on now and I still don't do it. I don't get enough sleep, don't get enough exercise, don't have enough of a social life, don't manage my time well enough to give my priorities their due. . . . .The huge issue for me right now is balance. How do I begin to get an equilibrium of balance? How do I begin to care for myself and still continue to do the work I do? How do I begin to have mercy on myself, in order that I can continue over these next 10 to 20 years?

For many midlife women the twinges and aches of midlife are persistent reminders of aging, and there is a strong connection between aging and declining health. Women worry because they feel less energetic and because they see their aging selves reflected in their parents' health experiences. Most of all, they worry about the consequences of a lifetime of juggling. They talk repeatedly about the difficulty of finding balance. They are exhausted and feel guilty about not giving enough time to work or family. Mary (#24) talked about 'carving herself into pieces'. Gail (#14) asks, 'how do you have the family time and the work time and the social time and the just-getting-in-bed-and-doing-nothing time?'

Although we can assume that this generation did not invent the notion of stress, it seems that stress is more widespread now. Perhaps every generation has had this reaction to the pace of life they experience compared to a calmer, more fulfilling ideal. Certainly, it would be hard to argue against the notion that the pace of change has accelerated. According to Statistics Canada, one-quarter of Canadians describe their days as 'quite' or 'extremely' stressful (Shields, 2004: 9). When Walters and Denton (1997) asked a sample of Canadian women about their health concerns they were curious to know whether women would focus on reproductive issues, since much of the research on women's health has concentrated on reproductive health, particularly menopause. Their findings suggest not. Stress was found to be the most significant issue. The health problems that had been *most often experienced* in the last six months prior to the survey were tiredness, stress, disturbed sleep, and arthritis.

Overwork, stress, and lack of sleep cut across class and ethnicity. Changes in the structure of work and family life over the past three decades create complex interactions among gender, age, and economic well-being. Certainly, women raising children without partners or without access to secure and reasonable remuneration in exchange for their labour will pay an additional price in terms of health. Currently, the work and family lives of young women and men are similar in part because of educational gains of women as well as later age of marriage, lower rates of marriage, and delayed child-bearing. This is not the case for middle-aged and older women, whose history of labour force participation will have been more intermittent than their male counterparts', a result of the structural barriers to combining paid and unpaid work. We are not suggesting that all women's lives are equally stressful or that women's lives are necessarily more stressful than men's lives. Women's lives are stressful in different ways. Similarly, health challenges are experienced differently. As Lorber (1997: 27) points out, both home and workplace can offer social support; both can have harmful physical impacts, and both can be stressful.

Beginning to Think about Self-Care

Many women in this study talked about beginning to take better care of themselves at this stage of their lives. They described seeing naturopaths, taking vitamins, going to a chiropractor or a massage therapist, doing yoga, walking more, and generally paying attention to their own health in a way that they hadn't in the past. And, as Nancy (#2) said, she doesn't jaywalk as much as she used to! Not everyone felt this way. Clearly, Rita (#1) was not yet ready to go down the path of self-care.

> I don't want my health to take my attention. I don't want to spend time on it, I don't want to do the research, I don't want to go to the health food stores and get my appropriate supplements. I don't want to have to remember to take them.

Women like Valerie (#21) talked about the importance of taking better care of oneself. 'I think as you get older you realize that you have to take care of yourself more, or else you fall apart.' For Valerie, self-care meant facials, manicures, and pedicures as well as that ever-elusive exercise program that we will talk more about in Chapter 7. The midlife women we interviewed seemingly internalized a culture of care and accepted caregiving responsibilities—albeit with ambivalence. For these women self-care was a departure. As Banister found, seeing oneself as a central source of support and strength is a big change for women at midlife (Banister, 1999: 531). The transition to self-care is difficult because it means overcoming cultural messages that require women to put others' needs first (ibid., 532).

We can sense the ambivalence in the self-talk of the women in this study. Although this 56-year-old new grandmother intends to do things she wants to do, 'should' remains part of her discourse.

> At this point at times I feel, you know, I should look after myself, and do things that I want to do and not things that people want to do. But I have that freedom to do what I want to do and buy something for myself if I feel I should [laughs]. (Lenora, #41)

For others, self-care meant asserting their own needs. As Sophia (#74) said:

> Well, there will be a lot less compromise in my future. I have had to compromise my whole life with working and raising children. I am looking forward to not have to compromise. Maybe there will be more relaxation time. Things that I want to do for myself.

And Anna (#73) reflected much the same view:

> I think that the change, if there's any change, it's just doing what's good for me, accepting who I am, not trying to be something for somebody or anybody else.

By midlife, women inevitably have overcome a number of life crises and have learned from their experiences. They have developed large measures of resilience, and this is a resource they draw upon regularly. Esther (#7), a 46-year-old lesbian who has lived with abuse, described her situation as follows:

> I don't know, it's like here I am, and I'm this woman, and I've been through all these things, and people might stop and say, 'oh, what an awful life'; but that's the way it was, and there's no turning back, and there's no getting someone else's life. . . . I try to take away something positive from that, and say 'I won't treat people that way.' . . . At this age, I feel like I have more control of my life, or I'm able to take more control and steer the boat where I want to be, and the rest of my life's up to me.

The topic of self-care speaks once again to the ambivalent relationship between control and compromise that characterizes so much of midlife women's lives. Self-care is experienced as both obligation ('should') and agency ('can'), as caring for self and as satisfying a social requirement. Ironically, the marketing of self-care products and services to midlife women engages this contradiction. Midlife women 'should' enhance their appearance (cosmetics, facial treatments, surgery, and so on) because they 'should' respond to the prevailing standards of female beauty and/or because they will feel better about themselves and therefore be healthier (for example, the campaign to provide cosmetics for female cancer patients). Not surprisingly, the same acts of self-care—putting on lipstick, having a pedicure—may encapsulate contradictory impulses: the desire to indulge oneself as much as the desire to fend off the ravages of time. The midlife runner may want to enjoy her physicality as much as she wants to lose those hated extra pounds. Both empowerment and concession permeate women's conversations about looking after themselves, but at this point in their lives a sense of possibility and freedom appears to prevail in their sense of the 'self' as a personal project.

Conclusions

This generation of midlife women is the first to find themselves in the middle of an intense web of commitments to paid work and family care. They describe the costs in terms of stress and long for a situation that would allow a little time for themselves.

> I feel like I've lived my entire life taking care of other people's needs. . . . I feel there's gotta be more to life than that. I guess I feel somewhat that I still have to experience something where I, as an individual, have done something for myself what would make me feel fulfilled for me. (Maya, #43)

The net result is an often frustrating and unsatisfactory struggle to manage contradictory agendas. Women, in particular, appear to feel themselves called upon to negotiate a path that inevitably involves losses and dissatisfaction. Not surprisingly, as women edge out of their most intensive caregiving responsibilities, many feel freed from the compromises and conflicts of the past.

Even the women who have been able to opt out of sacrificing and compromising themselves for their families are left with profoundly ambivalent feelings about their relationship to their family. The woman who relied on her partner to carry the lion's share of parenting responsibilities worries about how she appears to the interviewer: 'I don't know how to say this without making me sound like a really horrible person but I'm a fairly detached parent.' The midwife who reversed roles with her husband does not express satisfaction with her career path. She questions whether her self-sacrifice was simply displaced into her work so that a puritanical work ethic led her to sacrifice for her career rather than for her family. As she comments, 'What is the difference between sacrifice to the family at the self level and the sacrifice to the career . . . because in both instances, this self is being sacrificed?'

These results, of course, strongly suggest that the women's movement and social change of the 1960s and later, and the movement of women into the paid labour force, did not address the issue of the need for balance between the demands of connection and fulfillment. What is absent from the interviewees is any articulation of an equitable arrangement of familial roles—the 50–50 marriage, for example. There is no sense of who the person is in such a model and no expectation that the social structure could accommodate such familial arrangements. Instead, highly individualized strategies have emerged and have failed to resolve adequately the conflict women (and, to a lesser degree, men) experience between their responsibilities as parents and their role in economic activities.

Those who can negotiate to share family care with partners, siblings, or children are able to find meaningful employment, although this effort often is attached to a profound ambivalence about the sacrifices they have made in terms of personal relationships. As Rita (#1) comments in looking back on her life and the sacrifices she has made to pursue a career:

I am just wondering about balance, about what are we winning . . . what is it . . . where do we spend our time? . . . Because I get paid for what I do, the self-sacrifice of my 'self' . . . is it somehow okay?

Key Concepts

Boomerang kids Adult children who return to their familial homes because of employment uncertainty, rising housing and educational costs, or marital breakdown.

Empty nest That life stage that signals the end of active parenting when young adults leave the familial home to establish independent lives. Popular literature gave support to the idea that this was a particularly stressful time for mothers.

Ethic of care A concept introduced by feminist psychologist Carol Gilligan to characterize what she saw as women's focus on others and on maintaining relationships.

Gendered care According to Statistics Canada, men and women perform different types of care work and devote different amounts of time to performing this work. These differences are documented in the 2002 Statistics Canada General Social Survey, 'Aging and Social Support'.

Informal care The help and care provided to family members of all ages who may or may not live in the same household.

Sandwich generation Midlife men and women who are 'sandwiched' between the demands of their parents and their children as a result of demographic and familial patterns of longevity and later childbirth.

Questions for Critical Discussion

1. What is care work? How is it gendered? How is it distributed differently over the life course?
2. What kinds of self-care do women engage in over the life course? How does self-care vary by class? By sexuality?
3. How is care work portrayed in popular culture?
4. Care work engenders deep ambivalence among women. Why?
5. Caregiving both empowers and constrains women. Explain. Caregiving provides women with their most intimate and their most frustrating experiences. Explain.
6. What particular stresses do those of the sandwich generation face?
7. Both young and middle-aged women report chronic stress and fatigue as a frequent or daily experience. Provide examples and explain how stress and fatigue alter over the life course.

Chapter 6

Women, Work, and Economic Security

A Brave New World of Paid Work

If there is one feature of women's lives that has been transformed in the past 50 years it is their participation in paid employment. Today, young women expect to be employed for most of their adult life and are daunted at the prospect of creating strategies for balancing work and family. In contrast, Canadian women in the 1950s faced a more proscribed but clearer path, since the woman with paid employment was the anomaly among married women with children at home. In 1951, only 24 per cent of all Canadian women 14 years of age and older participated in the paid labour force (in contrast to 84 per cent of comparable Canadian men) and only about 1 in 10 married women was a paid worker. When marriage was combined with motherhood, it was an even stronger obstacle to paid employment. By 1967 only 19 per cent of Canadian women with preschool children and 28 per cent with school-age children were employed (Phillips and Phillips, 1983: 36; Rennie, 1983: 36, 30). In contrast, by 2004, 73 per cent of all women with children under age 16 living at home were part of the paid workforce and 65 per cent of women with children under age 3 were employed (Statistics Canada, 2007: 105). These two scenarios speak to a significant transformation in norms and expectations surrounding many facets of women's lives. Unlike the more typical basic continuity from one generation to the next, many women born between 1946 and 1964 confronted an adult reality that not only had not been modelled for them by their mothers but was contradicted by many societal beliefs and values. They would live through a societal shift in which the iconic Betty Crocker image of wife and mother, apron-clad, proffering food to her loving family, would be eventually supplanted by cultural expectations that women shoulder some or all of the responsibilities of earning a living during their adult lives (Duffy et al., 1989; Wilson, 1996).

Of course, women have always worked for pay, especially young women and girls. Further, married women and women with young children have never been completely absent from paid employment. Even during the best of economic times, working-class women and women who were widowed or deserted often had little choice but to piece together an income, for example, by taking in boarders, providing laundry or sewing services, or working as domestics and cooks. Still, there was often a socially constructed gulf between the worlds of men's and women's paid work (Duffy and Pupo, 1992).

The revolution in these traditional social arrangements commenced for the generation of women born between 1946 and 1960 and continues to reverberate through women's lives today. During this post-World War II period an unusual conjunction of economic and social forces both permitted and encouraged large numbers of women to work exclusively in the home as wives and mothers. Overall economic prosperity, the expansion of the welfare state, the achievement of a family wage by many unionized male wage earners, and the idealization of the family unit (composed of a male breadwinner and female homemaker) resulted in many wives and mothers devoting much of their adult lives to unpaid household work. In this social context, working-class and middle-class women's lives would be comprised of considerable hard work; however, they had much more discretion over how they spent their daily lives—with activities ranging from sewing their children's clothes, making preserves, or volunteering for the local school or church/synagogue women's organizations. Their daughters—the so-called boomer generation—would inherit a markedly different economic and social reality. Although as adults many would shoulder a traditional 'caring' role in the family, by midlife most would have spent a substantial portion of their adult lives in the paid labour force.

In this chapter we examine the employment realities into which midlife women were born, their individual paths through the conjunctions of work and family, and their current relationships to paid employment. In the course of this discussion it becomes apparent that the tentacles of the past reach far into women's adult lives; in particular, for many, youthful decisions about education resonate through a lifetime of employment. However, it is also clear that the past does not necessarily determine the present. Many of the women who grew up in a traditional household with a full-time wife/mother went on to live very non-traditional lives. They moved into traditionally male occupations; they formed non-traditional households as divorced or single women and as lesbian couples (Wright, 2005). Despite the enormous disjunction between their childhood and adult life, many of these women report tremendous personal satisfaction and empowerment through their activities in the paid labour force and articulate extensive plans for continuing their active involvement. Of course, there are also many who are less advantaged and report a working life that is both oppressive and unfulfilling. What remains to be seen is how this generation of women will be able to negotiate their paid employment and financial well-being as they enter the ranks of seniors and the elderly.

Before discussing the specifics of individual women's lives, it is important to acknowledge that it is very easy to become lost in personal narratives. The lesbian employed in the provincial government and supporting a disabled son, the midwife who relies on her husband to keep the household running, and the immigrant woman who finds herself frozen out of meaningful employment all speak to profoundly different personal realities, and their lives must be understood in terms of their distinctive struggles, strategies, and successes. As feminist theorists have long pointed out, women's lives are lived at the intersections of complex interplays between social class, sexual orientation, race/ethnicity, immigrant status, ability, marital status, attractiveness, age, geographic location, and so on (Lorber, 2005). While various diversities are visible in the following accounts, the particular focus here is on 'generation' and the implications of sharing a specific socio-historical context. The baby-boom generation of women who speak here grew to maturity and negotiated their diverse identities while being conditioned by similar societal and historical forces. **Generation** in this context refers to the likelihood that women born during a specific time period will confront many similar issues, concerns, forces, and social movements (McDaniel, 2003). Women who are at midlife today have experienced a remarkable shift in the nature of the economy and of paid employment. The diversity of their personal lives is anchored by these economic realities.

The Grip of the Past

For many contemporary young Canadians, portrayals of women's lives in the 1950s may evoke the nostalgia and sense of quaintness that older Canadians experience when confronted with a horse and buggy or corset and bloomers. It may, however, feel less benign to actually live through this kind of societal transformation. What the tremendous surge of social change between the 1950s and the present means for the women we interviewed is that they were born into the beliefs, values, and norms of an alien script and are now living their adult lives in a society that is often wildly variant from this beginning,

> . . . not that I expected to work my whole work life, because I didn't, to be honest. My mother hadn't worked outside the home. Growing up, I didn't know any women who worked outside the home, [it was] a very middle-class background. Any women I knew were homemakers. (Margaret, #4)

Of course, the authors of this study grew up in these post-war neighbourhoods. We know from personal experience that the majority of the mothers in working-class and middle-class residential areas were mostly at home. Certainly, some women had regular paid jobs, but this was an exception that needed to be explained—she was a widow or her husband was a drunk or he had some illness. We knew that 'average' mothers stayed home.

The nature and intensity of this traditional background varied. Reflecting Canada's increasingly diverse population, some women report intensely patriarchal family origins. A Muslim woman who emigrated from Africa comments:

> I was brought up in a culture where women were subservient to men. My mother was a teacher before she got married. Although my father could have done with a second earning, it was inappropriate for a wife to work. The

husband was the provider, and so my mother always stayed at home. . . . My father was the head of the house and my mother just followed. If she wanted anything, she had to ask my father. (Malina, #15)

Despite the very traditional role played by her mother and her own personal aversion to calling herself a feminist, our respondent went on to lead a much less traditional life. Over her husband's protests she continued to work once she married and even after she had a child. Now, although her husband resents the importance she gives to her career, she reports that he understands it. Further, she describes her daughters—daughters she is 'very proud of'—as 'liberated'.

Another respondent, who emigrated from Singapore, clearly resents the constraints imposed by a deeply **patriarchal culture**. In her very traditional family, sons were the priority. Her mother was bitterly disappointed when she was the first-born and this was only compounded when the next child was also a daughter:

I wasn't a boy, what she wanted me to be and what the whole family wanted . . . then beyond that, the second one to come after me was also a girl and she said that if you were any good, if you weren't a boy, you should bring a boy. (Yvonne, #32)

Predictably, the negativity pervades her youth. Her mother did not work:

. . . she didn't understand that [I would want to] . . . she prescribed [laughs]for me the three professions—like a nurse, a teacher, a social worker—that's it. If you don't do that then . . . please don't do anything. That's why, when I say I'm going to architecture, she goes 'Ugh!' She went ballistic because architecture to her means a guy wearing a hard hat and going to the construction site and she says, 'You're not going to go there with your high heels.' I say, 'I never thought that I was going there in my high heels, either.'

The clash of wills permeates the respondent's life. Her desire to attend university was opposed on the grounds that 'Women don't go to universities.' Although she ultimately succeeds in achieving a professional occupation, her career takes a downward spiral as she is laid off during the recession of the early 1990s and struggles with debilitating depression and increasingly marginalized employment in temp services. Now living on Ontario Disability payments, she sees that her generation 'broke from the past' and was 'in some sense sandwiched because we are not quite as advanced as . . . our kids.' As she speaks, she struggles with the meaning of this transformation. Her life is a 'bridge' between the traditional role of women in her culture and the new reality, but it is also a 'burdened generation' since they had to struggle to break from the past and also serve as role models for an upcoming generation. Looking back on her life—on her brief happiness as a successful building designer—she wistfully concludes, 'the thing is, I wanted [to be an architect] because I'm good at it. You should see the things I drew.'

Discourses on Working in a Changed Social Reality

Clearly, many women, especially those coming from a traditional family setting, cannot help but become aware through the course of their lives of an ongoing social transformation that directly impacts their paid as well as their unpaid work lives. 'I look at my daughter and . . . boy! Totally different. Totally!' (Carol, #55). The interviews often echo with comments about it being 'a lot different today' and living 'in a different world'. A 52-year-old married woman with three grown children and a job as a program co-ordinator in a non-profit organization sums up a positive view of this social revolution:

> Gloria Steinem was one of my heroes. They [feminists] made a lot of changes that people my daughter's age [18 years old] would just take for granted. As a child of the fifties and the *Leave It To Beaver* family that didn't work, I'm delighted that we don't have to think that's where we [women] have to be. (Nicole, #45)

A married woman who emigrated from the Barbados and who consciously decided not to have children similarly comments: 'I didn't have a difficult childhood, but my mother did. I was making sure [by remaining childless] my life wasn't like that. I saw her make so many sacrifices and put everybody first' (Shantell, #46). Not surprisingly, this transformed social reality is not seen as an unmitigated improvement. Later in the interview, Shantell (as cited earlier in Chapter 3) adds:

> I think that we lost something—what the women did. They are so confused and so afraid that they don't know if they're coming or going. We have gone out and helped men bring home the bacon, then we still prep it and cook it, too. We now have two jobs instead of one.

Of course, the impact of this new social reality is far from uniform since among our research participants there are women who have lived lives that mirrored their mothers'—working for a short period prior to marriage and then dedicating the remainder of their lives to their husbands and children. In other instances, a few women grew up with mothers or grandmothers who were the exceptions in that they were very socially active and/or professionally accomplished. One interviewee reports that she was aware of the possibilities available to women outside the home since her paternal grandmother played a foundational role as a woman scientist in Canada. Some grew up outside of Canada and were rooted in different social patterns. However, despite this diversity of experience, the clear majority speak of being so far removed from the realities and framework of their mothers' lives that it now seems like foreign terrain.

Discourses on Navigating Employment in a Changing Reality: Control, Drifting, and Luck

> I'm sorry that I'm not young now because . . . I would have the courage to go after the kinds of jobs that I perceive to be suitable to me [rather] than to my gender. (Becky, #54)

Since these women typically grew up in households where adult women's education and employment were not eulogized and where public values clearly questioned women's ability to combine family and paid employment, the attitudes towards education and career planning they encountered in their youth were, at best, ambivalent. Most women, in Nancy Mandell's term, were somewhat inclined to 'drift' when young. Most would marry; most would end up working for some portion of their adult life; but plans to target particular educational or career goals were decidedly uncommon. Over and over, women—even those whose work lives have been tremendously successful and accomplished—speak of a fortuitous conjunction of events or simply good luck rather than purpose and planning. For example, a woman who played a central role in the advancement of health care for women in the province of Ontario remarks:

> I didn't choose [the health care profession]. I always thought it chose me in a way . . . that I was kind of invited into it. And, I have always thought it strange to this day that people can say that I am going to be a [health-care professional]. (Rita, #1)

Another woman speaks of the good luck of being able to take advantage of, first, a maternity leave vacancy and, later, a vacancy created by retirement. Combined with her supportive women managers, these fortuitous opportunities allowed her to pursue her work aspirations: 'it was being in the right place at the right time . . . it was working with wonderful people (Lorna, #13).

Similarly, a woman who is executive director of a non-profit organization is ambivalent about the personal significance of her employment path. She doesn't want to 'make too much of it—it's a job'—but realizes that it could be understood as a 'career': 'I am not sure it is a vocation or career. It is a job' (Margaret, #4). And, again, her path to this 'work' was happenstance. She pursued a particular graduate program because it was the one that accepted her and upon graduation took a position even though she 'was not looking for work'.

Women's tendency to ambivalence and **drifting** are, of course, not necessarily restricted to heterosexuals and married women. In a period when women's education was not prioritized, it is not surprising that, regardless of personal circumstances and marital status, many women did not fix on an educational plan. A lesbian who has four children and currently holds a professional position also speaks of drifting:

Yeah, I had no idea what I wanted to do, I just thought I went to [university] for four years, got my BA ... as far as I knew that was what I was going to do forever and after six or seven years I just thought 'I can't', you know. 'I'm tired'. (Phyllis, #3)

Her new career direction is attributed to 'luck': 'I found another field by accident.'

The pattern is echoed in the experiences of a 50-year-old lesbian who is currently a housing manager and who had held a variety of non-traditional jobs. Although she speaks of 'freely choosing her path', she quickly acknowledges that the major turning points have been the result of luck rather than of planning. 'Sometimes I've sort of fallen into it; it's not been freely chosen or imposed. I've just stumbled on it. Like getting into the [plumbing] and [construction business]—that was not something I [looked for] (Pamela, #11).

A 57-year-old visible minority immigrant to Canada points out that one of the pivotal events in her life was taking a position at a Toronto hospital. However, interestingly, the source of this reorientation in her life was external, 'the major change was somebody pushing me to take the position' (Malina, #15).

It would seem that rather than self-conscious planning and perseverance, the turning points in employment experienced by many midlife women often are marked by good fortune and external forces. A 50-year-old woman who is currently employed as a university professor describes the decision to go to graduate school as 'the most very deliberate choice in my life' (Linda, #42). Yet, earlier in the interview, she explains this decision in terms of being encouraged as an undergraduate by a professor to pursue graduate studies. Again, it seems the luck of being at the right place with the right opportunities and support combine to make the difference.

On the one hand, midlife women do speak with pride of 'having grabbed' (made the decisions) or 'made the most of' opportunities when they appeared. However, they are quick to acknowledge that they did not self-consciously plan for or seek out those self-same opportunities.

This lack of intense purpose and planning, of course, allows women to be flexible and to make **compromises** as they navigate the intersections between their family life and their education and paid work life. It is important to note that many of our respondents indicate that, on occasion, they have given up on education or employment in order to accommodate the plans or aspirations of their partners. This pattern of accommodation is a particularly common event when women are young, upper-middle-class, and in heterosexual relationships. The gender script of the 1950s placed the responsibility for such concessions directly on women's shoulders:

My mother was a wonderful, wonderful woman but she let me know before I got married at 20 and told me it was totally up to the woman to make the marriage work—that she was to make her husband happy and that you never go to bed angry. (Carol, #55)

Not surprisingly, in this social context women often were willing to uproot them-selves and make sacrifices in response to their husbands' needs. Several interviewees report moving from community to community as they followed both their hus-band's educational career and then his paid employment. In some instances, this is now viewed with resentment. Carol, who is 56 and currently working as the man-ager for a non-profit resource centre, recalls her husband's having talked her into giving up her job and moving to another country, only to find that he had also trans-planted his girlfriend and was spending much of the week with her. Although now divorced and re-established in a job in a different city, she reflects back with anger at sacrificing so much control over her life:

> I'm not happy about it . . . one of the major things that I have felt coming back to Toronto was I didn't have any control over [pause] things just all happened so quickly and I didn't have control over what was happening. The only con-trol I had was to get the hell out, which I did . . . he had a car loan in my name and I had to pay off the car loan when I got back here . . . I got financially screwed. But, I had no control over any of that cause I let him look after all the finances (voice trails off) . . . I didn't take control. No, I had very low self-esteem and I didn't take control when I should have taken control.

Regrets about Education

Predictably, the tendency to drift early in life may leave a legacy of regret and unful-filled dreams. Repeatedly, the women interviewed indicate some measure of regret for their educational drifting—the absence of decisions either in the direction of their studies or their failure to complete or further their education:

> I wish I had a university education. (Nicole, #45)

> I sometimes wonder what would've happened if I had been able to go to uni-versity right after high school because I wanted to be a lawyer. That's what I wanted to do. It would've been interesting if I had been able to do that. . . . I graduated [high school] in June and got married in October. . . . By 23 I had two kids. (Catherine, #61)

In particular, lack of post-secondary education is seen by many as the root of contemporary restrictions on their working lives. A 57-year-old health-care worker who decided to attend university explains her regrets:

> What led up to that [decision to continue her education] . . . was . . . well, we [my husband and I] were always encouraging the children to go to university . . . constantly, and, uh, I thought how could I constantly encourage the chil-dren and harp all the time . . . I was actually harping, and not go myself. And,

plus . . . and I don't know how to explain it, but I thought . . . I had this feeling of something else I had to do. And, I don't know what it was but it had to do with going back to school. You just have this feeling. You know, you're content for a few years doing what you're doing . . . and I did all kinds of work, you know . . . with the union, all kinds of work, you know . . . with women . . . women and work. I've been looking at this throughout my whole life really and then . . . that to give a voice, you had to have an education for anyone to listen. (Gidget, #64)

A number of other women suggest if they had pursued some sort of professional accreditation (becoming a lawyer figures prominently) they would now be in a much better position to accomplish what they desire. A 56-year-old divorced woman with no children comments, 'I might have got more education, gone to university. I bite my tongue when I say that because I've learned so much. I just don't have a piece of paper that shows that' (Brenda, #51).

The following comments typify this strongly defined pattern of responses that focuses on educational paths not taken. A 54-year-old woman with two grown children who holds a satisfying professional position remarks, 'I think if I had it all to do differently and if I could have the same husband and children, I would be a lawyer' (Nancy, #2). Later in the interview, she speaks of the possibility of returning to school in the future so that she is ultimately able teach at a post-secondary institution.

A 50-year-old married woman with no children followed a typically circuitous path in pursuit of her education and career: 'I twice went back to school. I had started out as a registered nurse and decided I wouldn't want that for my whole career so I went back to school' (Margaret, #4). Later, she returned to graduate school to assure herself promotion as management. Although these efforts have resulted in considerable professional success, she speaks of paths not taken. '[If I had my life to live over] I might work in a different field, in a more creative field. I might work in something more related to writing or more creative endeavours . . . maybe in the arts.'

A 57-year-old visible minority immigrant to Canada who is currently a health-care worker speaks of regrets about both missed educational opportunities and the belated timing of her education:

[What would you have done differently in your work life?] I would have gone and started my education program long before I even immigrated to Canada . . . so most of my education was done after I got married, after I had my children, which was a very difficult thing to do. I would have really continued my education . . . there would have been an opportunity to go overseas and educate myself . . . I should have done that a long time ago. (Malina, #15)

Even the most accomplished women characterize their educational and employment decision-making as flawed. A 52-year-old (who jokingly refers to herself as a 'fesbian leminist') in a committed relationship with no children, who did obtain a professional degree and who has achieved considerable success in the public service, also describes her past in terms of drift:

> In hindsight, I might have probably got into the public-service sector sooner. I started off as a [profession] for five years. And, I might have thought of doing it in the federal government as opposed to the province, because I would prefer to live in Ottawa if I could. (Sharon, #5)

Although, unlike many of her contemporaries, she had the foresight to start with professional credentials, she looks at her past as less purposive and strategic than she might have wished.

These regrets about not pursuing education or training or particular employment opportunities while younger often blur into uncertain (or plentiful) possibilities for the future. A number of women—including those who have achieved considerable success in paid employment—discuss the possibility of 'going back to school' so that they can either further develop their credentials or move in a distinctly different direction as they approach their late fifties and sixties. In short, for many, it seems that the path that 'luck' and external forces have provided may be filled with a measure of success and economic rewards but, at this point in life, may lack the level of personal satisfaction and/or accomplishment they desire. Yet, they still have a sense of possibility and change, and further education is repeatedly envisioned as the key to these new employment directions.

Contributions and Satisfaction

Despite regrets about educational paths, concerns about compromises, and a pervasive lack of intentionality, the overwhelming majority of women speak in very positive terms about their employment experiences. Most speak with a measure of pride about the contribution they have made through the course of their paid work and most report they feel very positive about their current work position. Indeed, their work may be an important ingredient in their feelings of self-worth. 'Without paid employment, I would miss feeling valued. If I'm not working, part of my identity is gone. I don't want to be just a "mother of two daughters". I've been thinking about that' (Judy, #50).

From deli clerk to chief financial officer—the prevailing sentiment is that they feel that they have made a significant contribution through their work life and that their future in the public domain holds possibilities of further self-realization and fulfillment. What is absent here, by and large, is a sense of midlife as a crisis or as a moment for critical self-reflection and personal dissatisfaction. There is considerable self-reflection but it does not translate into a negative or critical assessment of their life courses. Even among women who are planning to move in another educational or occupational direction, most speak in strongly positive terms:

I do. I love my job. I am ready to move on and do something else related to that, but not because I don't like my job. I just think it is time for me to do that. . . . I feel very satisfied professionally. I have made an important contribution. I feel like I am making a contribution. (Nancy, #2)

Another woman, who over a number of years went from being a public school teacher to juggling several low-paying contract teaching positions at a university, indicates no sense of regret or dissatisfaction: 'I adore the jobs' (Ruth, #6).

A 53-year-old woman, who grew up in abusive foster homes and struggled for years to leave an abusive marriage, has worked her way up to a position as project superintendent in municipal government. Although not highly paid or particularly well-educated, she is emphatic about her work satisfaction:

There are good days and bad days. But, basically I'd rather be doing that than anything else. I believe in social housing and [if] you believe in something you can do something that might be nasty and you might not like that well— but if you believe in it, you will do it. (Mia, #10)

Gwen (#79), a 56-year-old part-time deli clerk who has held her job for 17 years, may not be as effusive about her sense of accomplishment but she does not express regrets about her employment situation:

Gwen: In some aspects, I hope I have made some contribution.
Interviewer: What would you do differently if you had your life to live over?
Gwen: Nothing. I have enjoyed the two jobs [previously worked as a hair-dresser] that I have worked. I wouldn't change a thing.

Given our sampling procedures (see Appendix), the women we interviewed are active in their communities. Many have been able to fuse their social activism with their employment, and it is not surprising that many of these women are particularly enthusiastic about their contributions through work and their enjoyment of the job.

Joyce (#59), who has integrated her paid employment with political work and community activism in the lesbian and gay community, can quickly sum up her viewpoint:

I love my work. It's great . . . I feel very excited about my life and I've learned from everything that's ever happened to me. . . . I think I'll be sitting in this chair counselling until my brain goes. . . . I don't have the kind of job where I'm looking forward to retiring at 65. I will do this work as long as I'm effective at this work. And, I see myself still doing consultation as I get older, in the lesbian/gay/trans community.

A 52-year-old mother of two, who has been employed for 21 years as a personal support worker in a seniors' residence, speaks in positive terms about her work contributions:

> And, I make a difference with the employees. Offer a lot of emotional support to the employees . . . a lot are single mothers . . . I really have a big role to play with negotiations and contract negotiations, especially, with shift-sharing and flexible scheduling. So, because we are predominantly female, that [flexible scheduling] sort of works for working mothers. There I think I've made good headway. (Gidget, #64)

Catherine (#61), a 59-year-old woman currently employed as community outreach co-ordinator for a major urban hospital's inner-city health program, talks enthusiastically about how 'very exciting', 'unique', and 'challenging' she finds her work to be. A 58-year-old Jamaican immigrant to Canada, who is currently employed as a program evaluator for a major metropolitan health centre, is consistently positive in her assessment of her contributions in paid employment and her enjoyment of her work: 'I don't do anything [at work] I don't like at this point . . . I've chosen to work in policy and displaced people and I think I've made a good impact' (Shana, #63).

The same enthusiasm and satisfaction are heard in the comments from a 54-year-old unmarried woman who is currently executive director of a major group providing education and policy support on HIV:

> I really like my job. It's extremely time-consuming and energy-consuming, demanding . . . . I've been doing jobs that I absolutely love and feel totally committed to and do like to come to work every day. But I have no job security beyond however long the next grant goes . . . from a financial perspective, I've had to do my own savings, because I have no pension plan. (Jennifer, #60)

It seems likely that at least some participants in our research indicate such positive responses to their paid employment because they have been able to combine social activism and income. As discussed in more detail below and in Chapter 8, it may be that many women in the boomer generation were fortunate in terms of living during a period where various social movements fused into powerful social forces—forces that resulted in public policy and institutional initiatives. However, as evident in the final comment above, commitment to community activism in the workplace may come with an immediate and/or long-term penalty in terms of income security and financial well-being.

Is Midlife Work a Crisis for Women?

Some other researchers have tended to draw attention to women's expression of dissatisfaction during their midlife years. Norella Putney (who published out of the

University of Southern California 'Study of Generations') found that boomer women in midlife are 'more depressed and have lower self-esteem' than their mothers' generation (as cited in Wright, 2005: 181). It is suggested that the generation of women born after World War II has faced considerably more stress since they are increasingly expected to navigate the uncertainties of both family and paid employment. In this vein analysts suggest that the midlife woman feels 'not in control of her life' and as a result ends up 'exhausted, used up, and overwhelmed' (ibid., 181–2). Sue Shellenbarger (2005) urges similar conclusions based on her review of the literature. She points out, for example, that 73 per cent of midlife women (40–54 years old) agree that life is much too complicated compared to 55 per cent only 15 years ago. Further, the title of Shellenbarger's mass-market book—*The Breaking Point*—underscores the popularity of this view of contemporary middle age as stressful and crisis-laden, especially for women.

Of course, we did interview women who report feeling trapped, unhappy, and dissatisfied. A 56-year-old woman, who followed a string of secretarial jobs into a position as a health-care worker, is blunt about her dislike for her job; her desire, if she could afford it, is to leave her job because she feels her work does not allow her to make an important difference or contribution (Vera, #8). Much of her life satisfaction is derived from her volunteer work over many years with the Canadian Girl Guides. Another 50-year-old woman, who is a visible minority and recent immigrant to Canada and who is currently unemployed, indicates that she loved her work prior to coming to Canada and felt she made an important contribution in that work. Currently, after unsuccessful efforts to use her education in Canada and having settled for low-wage, low-skill work as a mother's helper for a short period, she bitterly condemns the 'volunteer' work that she is encouraged to undertake by her employment counsellor as unfulfilling and demeaning: 'But, I believe the system in Canada . . . [it] says to people, "Okay, study well, be educated, buy your ticket, come to this country and work as a volunteer". . . . It's new slavery' (Amina, #9). A 59-year-old divorced woman with two children also paints a poignant picture.

> I don't feel good about my work life because I believe I was intended to something quite different . . . something more creative, like writing. I'm told that I show talent in writing. However, I don't like talking about that talent because of modesty and I may not have that talent. I'm not sure of myself in that area. I think I failed myself by not achieving anything in that area. (Becky, #54)

A 53-year-old married, unemployed woman with adult children, who has been extremely active in the Toronto community, weeps when she recalls her employment history:

> . . . someday I'll be able to talk about this without crying . . . well, because I think there have just been such limitations on what I have been able to do and I know that my potential was a lot greater, and although I'm in a real good place right now, as of this year doing about the level of work that I want to be

doing, maybe a little under still, there were years of doing almost nothing. (Susan, #16)

For years Susan struggled with depression; remaining secluded in her home left her with a sense of emptiness that was not lifted until her late forties when a happy confluence of medication, improvements in her physical health, religion, and involvement in feminism opened the doors to what, she now hopes, will become personally meaningful paid employment.

Certainly, we found evidence of women who had struggled with disappointing and unsatisfactory experiences in paid employment. However, responses that characterized paid employment experiences in essentially negative terms were uncommon. Overall, the majority of the women we interviewed indicated that they felt that they had indeed made an important contribution through their paid work and that they felt positive or very positive about their current work situation. While the women typically made it clear that their workplaces were not idyllic and that there were drawbacks, for the clear majority, the central message was consistently a positive one.

Making a Home at Work

By the early 1990s analysts were suggesting that the workplace was increasingly supplanting the family as the centrepiece of personal life (Hochschild, 1997). While the home, particularly with the pressures of children, family finances, and work/family compromises, was being experienced as a heavily conflicted social locale, the workplace, it was argued, was orderly, tranquil, and predictable. In this context, men and women could have their emotional needs for closeness, even intimacy, more easily satisfied. As a result, men and women were spending more time at 'work' rather than at home. Some argued that this was particularly applicable to women workers, since they were more concerned about the emotional elements in their personal lives and were highly skilled in interpersonal relationships. While this is an interesting perspective and certainly both men and women are spending more time in the paid labour force (Marshall, 2006), our interviews do not suggest that most midlife women generally find a sense of **community** and belonging in their work environment.

Some women do. A 52-year-old university professor in a same-sex relationship and with no children indicates that her work community is an important one, 'where I spend most of my time and energy' (Linda, #42). However, it does not seem to be the case that most middle-aged women are able to satisfy their needs for community and connection at work. In fact, the very diversity of work experiences that typifies so many women's life courses means that friendships and connections often are left behind in various locales:

I'd say that a sense of community has always been important to me. And, I'd say that my communities have changed as I go through different periods in my life. When my children were younger, it was the baseball, hockey, dancing communities . . . today, it's different communities. (Anita, #12)

Various friendships may remain important but the new workplace does not necessarily build on any sense of connection with others.

For many midlife women, there may be various other 'communities' that exert a stronger pull on their time and energies and that are not linked to their paid employment in any fashion. Pamela (#11), a lesbian in a long-term relationship and with two children at home and employed full-time as a public housing co-ordinator, has been very much involved not only in the gay community but also as a volunteer and board member in HIV/AIDS organizations. Malina (#15), a 57-year-old married immigrant from Africa, 'loves her work' but finds herself more engaged in her religious and cultural communities in Toronto. Gail (#14), 56 years old and married with two children and currently employed as a full-time community development officer, immediately identifies her religious community as the most important community for her. This is a group of friends who share a 'spiritual bond' and whose 'common faith connection' has lasted for years even though they do not necessarily attend the same church. This does not preclude an important sense of connection through her paid work. For more than a decade, she has connected with three other women who do essentially the same job but in different parts of the province—'we remained very close friends.' This original group has now grown to 12—men and women—who share and provide a network of work information and support with one another and whom she describes as 'good friends'. It would seem that these are 'virtual' friends since they rely on e-mail to keep in touch and share information. In short, it is not that there is no sense of community at work but that other communities—in this instance, the religious community—appear to take primacy.

In other instances, community at work may be not only secondary but also problematic and conflicted. Midlife women's very success at moving up the work hierarchy may militate against a sense of camaraderie and community. One woman explains that as a supervisor she feels conflicted about friendships with subordinates:

And, I'm the boss, which also makes another distance in terms of relationships. When I was younger, I've always been very adamant about that and I don't talk to people socially. But again, with my turning 50 what's also started to happen . . . there are women in the office who have asked me to go socialize with them, which has never happened to me before in my life. And, so I asked them, 'Well, don't you have a concern because I'm your boss that that will make you uncomfortable in some way?' And, they say, 'No, you're just a great lady.' I went, 'Oh.' So it was cool. (Anita, #12)

It would seem, then, that with increasing age and a greater sense of control at work and at home, this woman is able to be more flexible about her sense of connectedness with fellow workers. Yet, while her age may provide this opportunity, her life experience also makes her cautious about the significance of these connections.

However much she may enjoy socializing with her co-workers, she remains acutely aware of the limitations of any workplace sense of belonging:

> Otherwise, it's like you've just fallen off a cliff. Because I've watched when people leave here, for example, to go to another firm and it's like they don't exist any more. You're not in the same club. So, I'm assuming that will happen when I retire.

Institutional hierarchies can also place other obstacles in the path of community. Another woman, for example, talks of being caught between the needs of her poorly paid employees for an increase in salary and her board of directors, who insist on fiscal restraint. She becomes, on the one hand, the nag who is persistently raising the issue of inadequate pay to the board and, on the other, the bearer of bad news as she delivers the message to employees that no increases will be forthcoming. Clearly, in such a context, it is difficult to situate oneself as a member of a work community, and women's age, experience, and career advancements may each hinder the development of connection at work.

In workplaces where the women are on an equal footing with other workers and where a sense of community is buttressed by the role of organized labour, women may be much more enthusiastic about their sense of connection at work. Mia (#10), a 55-year-old single mother who is employed as a special projects co-ordinator, comments:

> My co-workers are among my best friends. We have a saying at the housing company that we are one family and we grieve together, we laugh together, we celebrate together, we play together, we lean on each other. My co-workers have become my best friends.

Interestingly, when asked about her prospects for retirement, she first identifies community as what she would miss about her paid work: 'I would miss the sense of community. I would miss the sense of accomplishment. I would miss the money (laughs).'

The majority of women we interviewed do not describe their sense of work community in such strong positive terms. Far from being a community, some workplaces—at least at some times—may seem more like war zones. Linda (#42), though her work community is important to her, comments, 'I have put up with very patronizing, very prejudicial, very antagonizing behaviour [from both men and women].'

Another woman talks about the drudgery of dealing with a very chauvinistic boss. Although a supportive and humorous male co-worker makes this situation tolerable and does provide a sense of connection at work, this workplace is not experienced by the interviewee as an important source of community. Not surprisingly, other women report the opposite experience, although they are quick to point out they know camaraderie at work is atypical:

I've always had these wonderful supportive males—which is very unusual. And, even now, I can say to my boss 'I'm having a PMS moment' and he'll laugh and say 'I'll leave you alone today.' And, that's unique. (Anita, #12)

To some degree the possibilities for friendship, support, and community are the luck of the draw. By midlife many women have managed to find their way into emotionally neutral or supportive contexts. This does not, as indicated above, suggest that they experience their workplace as a community or that it supplants their sense of connectedness in other areas of their lives.

Finally, some women describe their participation in the world of paid work as an obstacle to the creation of a sense of community. Margaret (#4), a 53-year-old married woman with no children and a busy career as a chief executive officer, remarks that the very intensity of her career combined with her family responsibilities have tended to make it more difficult for her to establish a community of female friends:

Margaret: [Careers] make you compromise—on the amount of time I have for friends and family, excluding my husband, . . . so what's fallen by the wayside have been some of those friendships.
Interviewer: If you hadn't compromised in order to maintain your career?
Margaret: I would have had maybe more broader or long-term friendships . . . I would say probably having deep friendships.

Clearly missing from almost all of these comments is any notion that the workplace is seen as a promising context for achieving a sense of personal connection and community.

Staying Home: Ambivalence and Agency

It is not the case that the midlife women expressing satisfaction about their family/work lives are all high-flying, executive success stories. A number of those who report midlife contentment followed the traditional track and devoted their entire adult lives to their families. Others compromised their paid working lives by taking part-time, dead-end employment so they could 'be there' for their families. Predictably, women who have been full-time homemakers for all or most of their adult lives are less likely to identify as feminists or to identify with the women's movement and are more likely to be involved in socially conservative community groups.

The more closely midlife women adhere to the full-time homemaker model, the more likely that they will be emphatic that their focus on the family was/is not the result of 'giving in' to societal pressure or to pressure from their husbands. Many explain that they wanted to stay home with their children and many explicitly state that they felt both in control and that they were making an important contribution. As Pamela notes, 'Yes, I don't regret the fact that I stayed home and looked after my kids. I have no regrets there whatsoever.'

The full picture of their experiences, however, is more complex and subject to interpretation. Financial 'common sense', cultural values, the lack of alternative child care, the absence of well-paid or interesting employment, and other factors may combine to produce the full-time homemaker 'choice'. The emphatic tone of their comments speak to these women's sense of pride and satisfaction in their choice of family life over paid employment and also to their defensiveness about making a decision that increasingly appears 'old-fashioned' and a poor fit with dominant norms. For example, a working-class woman who throughout her life was a full-time homemaker is quick to point out that although she was and is a full-time homemaker she holds important financial assets in her own name and that she is responsible for all the family finances. Her husband comes home and turns his pay-cheque over to her. She wants to make it clear that in no sense did she feel like the 'little woman' dependent on her husband's largesse.

Nonetheless, it is apparent that whether midlife women remained in the home or returned to paid employment, many felt torn, particularly by their child-rearing responsibilities. Nicole (#45), a 52-year-old married woman in full-time employment and with two children currently living at home, describes the combination of powerlessness and ambivalence contained in her negotiation between being at home and being at work:

I did the part-time when my son [first child] was four months old. It was obscene in those days that women had only four months of maternity. I don't think that was good for him, any more than for me, but that's what I had to do.

Yet, exiting the paid labour force exacts its penalty, as Nicole explains:

when I had my second child I stayed home. So I was out of the workforce for six years. It was very hard to come back. I worked for a volunteer centre for a year, but it was only part-time. I needed something more substantial. So, I got work at my children's school as an educational assistant. [I was] very overqualified, but an opening in that daycare happened [so I took it].

She feels that with both children she was forced (by financial pressures on the family income) to **compromise** between paid work and her young children. Yet, as she recalls the complex considerations, it is apparent that the debate still echoes, somewhat unresolved, in her mind:

Going back to work when my child was small was a major sacrifice. I would have preferred to stay home. I was glad I could do that with my daughter. . . . It was a risk and it was hard. . . . We sacrifice a lot for our kids. . . . I liked being home with my kids. It was a very fertile time in many ways but you do lose touch. Someone once told me that when you're out of the workforce, you can never again achieve the levels where you could have been had you never stayed out of it. Mind you, that was a trade-off. I wasn't in a career that I cared about much, anyway. I always wanted to be a mother—that was my biggest driving force.

Yet, with grown children and a job that she 'loves', she now mentions her regret several times at not getting more education, not going to university, since that would make her current work life more rewarding.

Finally, we interviewed several midlife women who, for various reasons, have exited the paid labour force and are not looking for work. Several of these women were able to resolve their dissatisfaction with their employment situations by opting for home responsibilities. A 59-year-old married woman, who emigrated from Spain to Canada as a child and who stayed home full-time when her children were young and then returned to paid work, now describes herself as a 'stay-at-home mom'. Five years ago, she lost her job (a job she found troublesome) when her company closed and since that time she has not had paid work. Although her children are now grown and essentially gone from the family home, it is clear that for her being 'in the home' and local community is an expression of control and connection:

> People work so hard and you wonder, 'Why are they doing it?' When you turn around . . . they might not be there; and you're not taking it with you. So, you know, in that sense . . . you ask me if I am going back to work? Well, . . . maybe. I am enjoying my life, you know—even talking to you right now and otherwise I would not have been able to do it. Or, you know, I have the phone and my people call me and I have time for them or someone needs something . . . I am available. So, maybe that's the luxury I have. Because I'm not going to work . . . but that's the choice I've made. So, I see life that way. (Lenora, #41)

Similarly, a 52-year-old married woman who was a stay-at-home mom with her three children—now all in their twenties—is back full-time in the home because she is on disability leave. It is clear throughout her interview that she dislikes her present work position—as a nurse's aide. Not only does she feel that she doesn't make a difference and that she must function as a subordinate, she feels ethically compromised since the people she provides care for are not getting the care they should be getting. The disability leave has allowed her to remove herself from a disheartening work situation and focus more time on her family and community activities. Although she recognizes that financial need means that if her disability leave ends she will have to find another job, she now feels empowered to take that control:

> I've come to the conclusion that even if I were able to go back to my job that I had, I think I would quit at this point and go on EI and then find something else. I would just forge ahead. I've reached a point where I really don't care for what I'm doing and I would really have the push, the momentum to change. (Vera, #8)

These comments suggest both the diversity of meanings and complexity of feelings attached by members of the baby-boom generation of women to being 'full-time in the home'. As discussed further in Chapter 8, there remains the traditional discourse about 'being there' for the children, but other explanations also speak to the desire for connection and community as well as to the use of 'homemaker' as an exit strategy from unsatisfying paid work. It is possible that contemporary young women, who experience dramatically foreshortened work careers or no 'times out' from paid labour, will be less likely to conceptualize full-time homemaking in the same manner.

A Fortunate Generation at a Fortunate Moment?

With the exceptions noted above, the clear majority of midlife women we interviewed arrived at a satisfactory paid work arrangement for themselves. Even those who disliked their paid work were able to negotiate 'time out'. This pattern clearly invites explanation, since the popular culture often conceptualizes midlife women, especially, in the area of paid employment as a benighted group. Past their physical prime in a culture (and workplace) that often prioritizes physical attractiveness, past the socially and culturally significant rites of passage of marriage and child-bearing, often facing insecurity in both the workplace and their family roles, and having been buffeted by a less-than-enthusiastic world of employment, this female boomer population is one from whom much more sombre appraisals of working life would be expected.

A number of explanations might be offered to explain this pervasive tendency in our interviewees to express satisfaction, happiness, and fulfillment. As psychologists remind us, the general tendency of persons in most populations is to adopt a positive stance when discussing their lives. However, since a significant minority of women spoke frankly and even emotionally about their dissatisfactions, it does seem clear that the interview situation allowed women the space in which to reflect critically as well as positively on their histories of paid work.

It does seem likely, as suggested above, that the women we selected to interview were more inclined to positive experiences in their paid work. In their diversity, they are primarily urban and not rural or suburban and, as noted in the discussion of our research methodology (see Appendix), they came to our attention through their social activism. Although their community involvement was extremely varied, this pattern may have been instrumental in providing access to social support mechanisms. Further, as socially involved women, they may have an advantage that also is demonstrated in their proclivity to be more proactive in their own lives.

Also, the midlife stage in the life course may entail benefits that are overlooked from traditional societal perspectives. As these women tell their stories it is clear that many of the issues and troubles of youth have been negotiated. Life is often conceptualized as a positive evolution towards greater empowerment. As Anita (#12), a 52-year-old married woman with three children at home who leads a very busy work life as a chief operating officer, comments, 'I think [in] every part of my life, I'm more in control. But that's because I was less in control.'

Simply by virtue of their life stage, most midlife women are no longer caught between the needs of very young children and the pressure of a young family's finances. Difficulties in relationships with partners and spouses have been in one way or another ironed out or transcended. Viewed from a midlife perspective, it is possible to be more philosophical about trials and tribulations: 'each step was a step—I wouldn't be here if I hadn't been there' (Linda, #42).

Most are no longer struggling to decide what 'to be' or fighting to get a 'foot in the door'—although they may now be thinking of starting a new chapter in their work lives. Many have a wealth of experience behind them and many have achieved a satisfying modicum of success and achievement. Most have bounced around at least a bit in terms of occupations and careers, but this is regarded as experience that led directly to their present situation. Talk about earlier struggles and dissatisfactions is couched in terms of a contemporary sense of greater control and fulfillment that they have now achieved. Among many of our interviewees is a sense of options at work, of not being locked in, and of having the chance to make significant changes. A 56-year-old woman speaks for a number of our interviewees: 'I feel that I could make a change and take a leave of absence and still come back to that job if I wanted to. So, there are some options' (Gail, #14).

Women who are primary wage earners for their families do not necessarily have that option since their income is the mainstay of the family economy. However, among our interviewees even these individuals often comment that they are anticipating greater work freedom later on in their lives; for example, as their partners complete education and assume a greater role in providing family income.

Further, it may be that the sheer range of activities included in so many of their lives means that they haven't a sense of having been devoted unreservedly to any one thing. For example, one woman recounts a personally and economically disastrous second marriage. Despite the enormous hurdles she encountered, particularly in terms of resolving her financial difficulties and locating new employment, she clearly feels triumphant at this point of her life. For this woman, as for her age cohort, the path to personal success and satisfaction was not simple, but it is not seen now as particularly troubled. So, for many women there are any number of paths forward. For example, women who stayed full-time in the home are able to locate their lives in respect to diverse relationships with extended family members, with grandchildren as well as children and spouses. Even if paid employment and family responsibilities offer little personal sustenance, community-based volunteer activity—often with traditional organizations such as the church and Girl Guides—also provides a sense of meaning and self-worth. Many of this generation of women were able to enjoy an unusual historical nexus in which new avenues were opening up and old restrictions were breaking down, while many old avenues also remained open.

Catching the Wave in a Period of Economic Prosperity, Cultural Transition, and Individuation

The socio-historical context in which midlife women came of age, that is, during the 1960s and 1970s, was a time of general economic well-being and expansion and was accompanied by expansion of the welfare state that provided individuals with considerable latitude in exploring alternatives (Gindin and Stanford, 2006). For example, the family wage still existed, high-wage industrial work for men was widely available, governments talked of full employment, and it was possible for women to launch initiatives to take part in highly paid men's work. In this regard the popularization of the women's movement was very important since it provided a cultural rationale for challenging the employment status quo. A variety of government reports and Royal Commissions, along with new provincial and federal agencies, provided growing evidence that the terms of women's participation in paid labour was unfair and should be questioned. Not surprisingly, many women—such as 'Women Back Into Stelco'—took the opportunity to challenge traditional male employment enclaves and to demand changes from organized labour.

Today's midlife women often found themselves launching their careers or work lives at an advantageous time and place. Until the mid-1970s the economy was booming and working-class wages were going up. 'Women's' jobs were growing by leaps and bounds; the public sector (in which women enjoyed greater opportunities) was expanding rapidly; and even traditionally male occupations were opening to women. This perspective is borne out by Louise Earl's examination of boomer women's labour participation rates, full-time employment rates, rates of unemployment, and earnings levels. As anticipated, she found that boomer women were more likely to work and more likely to work full-time than had the preceding generation of women. Since they were seeking employment, they also had higher unemployment rates than older women but lower ones than the following generation of women (Earl, 1999). They out-earned paid women workers of both the preceding and following generations of women.

Another indicator of this pattern of economic opportunity and prosperity is reflected today in the fact of the substantial wage gap between workers under age 35 and their older counterparts. In the last two decades, the percentage of men and women under 35 who are employed in low-paying jobs (earning less than $10 per hour) has grown, while the percentage of men and women age 35 and older who are employed in jobs paying $25 per hour or more has increased (Morissette and Johnson, 2005: 10). Part of this wage differential can be explained in terms of length of experience in the paid labour force; but the fact that the gap between older and younger workers' hourly wage is growing suggests other factors are at work—notably, the growth of precarious, non-standard employment, especially among young workers.

The dramatic movement of women, particularly wives and mothers, into paid employment also was supported by profound cultural changes, notably in family life and personal relationships. This was a period in which a relatively narrow range of traditional pathways to adulthood and paid employment was being replaced by a growing number of alternatives for both men and women (Moen and Han, 2001). In a process termed **individuation** the traditional narrow path from girl to woman and from marriage to motherhood was being supplanted by a dizzying range of individually constructed options (Jones et al., 1990). In this context, stigmas attached to alternative life choices were steadily eroded. The negative stereotype of 'the old maid' was replaced by the 'cosmo girl'; common-law marriage was no longer the shameful choice of the socially marginal. Family life increasingly transformed into a variety of shapes as blended families, stepfamilies, single-parent families, and gay and lesbian families became more visible and more socially legitimated ways to form intimate relationships and/or have children and as more people sequenced through a variety of these different family constellations (Gerson, 1985: 214). Even the timing of the family life course became more disparate as increasing numbers of university-educated and professional women postponed marriage and/or mother-hood until their late thirties and even early forties. At a time when working-class women are becoming grandmothers, these women are still caring for toddlers (Rubin, 2001).

In retrospect, many women who came of age in the 1970s and 1980s clearly were not penalized for their drifting because they were living and working in a period of relative state generosity and general economic prosperity. This situation is reflected in the increasing provision and generosity of maternity leave provisions. One of our interviewees, for example, was able to adopt two children as a single mother since she had access to reasonable maternity leave at her place of employment. By 2001, even Canada's Employment Insurance program had increased the length of paid maternity/parental leave from six months to one year. Although Canada still ranks rather poorly in comparison to the generosity of other Western countries, this pol-icy (along with the more generous leaves offered by some employers) has had a dra-matic impact on women's and men's lives. Within the first year of the improved leave provisions, there was a 24 per cent increase in the number of individuals taking this leave and an 80 per cent increase in the number of fathers taking time to be with their babies (up from 3 per cent in 2000 to 10 per cent in 2001) (Nelson, 2006: 346–8).

Of course, in more recent years this pattern of increased benefits for employed parents has been considerably offset by more conservative social policies emanating from governments that have refused to address the need for an adequate child-care system in Canada and that have reduced public spending on such social programs as welfare benefits. However, the neo-liberal agenda was not to be fully deployed until the 1990s. Unemployment Insurance benefits, for example (now called 'Employment Insurance'), were much more generously available into the 1980s and, as was the case with at least one of our interviewees, at this time one could claim UI even when one had chosen to leave a job. This alternative made it easier to switch careers and find new, more satisfying directions. In addition, since many women would achieve their greatest successes in the public sector, the generosity of public-sector spending often translated into increased opportunities for women to train or retrain and, thereby, redirect their working lives.

... someone encouraged me to apply for this one-year internship training job at the Cross Cultural Communications Centre that was a collective, non-profit, dealing with race relations and anti-discrimination and it was a training position. You could only qualify if you'd never worked in the field before ... they don't offer those internships any more. It was fantastic and that was funded through Ontario. Do you remember Ontario used to fund lots of non-profit groups? (Phyllis, #3)

In the present political-economic context, with dramatic restraints on state-provided benefits, including EI and reductions in funding for public agencies, such change is markedly more difficult. As Phyllis comments:

Frankly, if there hadn't been any increment I'd have probably quit except for the fact that you don't get EI now if you quit so I wouldn't have been able to because I was the only income of the family. So, that put a lot of pressure on me and I was pretty unhappy during that period.

Many midlife women are fortunate to find themselves where they want to be in terms of career, work, and family. They are no longer juggling the need for child care or facing the increased economic pressure on young families. If employed, their age (not old and not young) and work experience often translate into some autonomy and responsibility at work, a reasonable income, and some sense of job security.

In short, there is a reasonable basis for suggesting that the boomer generation of women were, in many respects, particularly fortunate. The institutional configuration of structural forces—notably, economic, familial, and educational—provided a wealth of opportunity and support. Further, the powerful social movements of the day—not only the general women's movement but also the dramatic growth of lesbian and gay culture, the successful struggle to legitimate abortion, social campaigns (as reflected in International Women's Day events and Women Back Into Stelco) to address racism, poverty, and social inequality—all provided a tremendous sense of personal possibilities. Women working in dirty, noisy steel plants were pioneers; women fighting for child support from dead-beat dads were social activists. For many, it seemed not only that another world was possible but that they were in the vanguard moving towards it.

Globalization and Economic Restructuring: The 'New' Economy

Although midlife women were lucky in terms of the timing of their entrance into paid employment, they are approaching retirement at a much more problematic moment. As widely discussed in the mass media, massive social and economic changes are producing a **'new' economy**. In particular, the employment revolution is rooted in information technology, global economic shifts, transformations in systems of production, the consolidation of corporate power, the growth of a global market and a global labour force, deepening inequalities between North and South, the weakening of national governments, and the increased power of supranational agencies (such as the WTO and World Bank) (Shalla, 2006). These elements weave together a profound transformation in work experiences and opportunities. The change is very evident in traditional manufacturing cities such as Hamilton and St Catharines (Lewchuck and Robertson, 2006). The growth in global competition—supported by the breaking down of trade barriers—in auto and steel manufacturing has produced a dramatic loss of traditionally male jobs. The last several decades have seen a virtual exodus of manufacturing plants to low-wage, non-unionized locations—in Korea, Taiwan, China, the southern United States, the maquiladoras of Mexico, and so on. This process has been exacerbated as computer-assisted technology (for example, robotics) has further reduced the manufacturing labour force in Canada and the US. This decline in manufacturing employment has also meant a dramatic reduction in the strength of traditional labour organizations. Despite massive protests, the CAW, United Steel Workers, and other traditional labour organizations have not been able to pressure governments to address the dramatic loss of well-paid, unionized employment.

The jobs that have been stimulated by information technology tend to be service-sector, low-wage, and non-unionized work. For example, the recent increases in call-centre work speak to this growth area in the new economy (Buchanan, 2006). Of course, call-centre work is eminently transferable to other areas and other countries. Efforts to unionize workers or to improve wages and benefits may result in the rapid exporting of work to India or the Caribbean. Further, this service-oriented work lends itself to a rethinking of the worker–employer contract. Since in service work the principal cost is in wages (as opposed to the physical manufacturing plant and equipment) and since the work is often characterized as low-skilled (women's) work, employers have introduced a variety of methods for reducing labour costs. For example, **service-sector employment**, which is the most rapidly expanding area of the Canadian economy, is much more likely than manufacturing work to be part-time, contract, and precarious (Fox and Sugiman, 2006). Employers sculpt their workforce to match the ebb and flow of demand and thus further maximize profitability. This objective is, of course, also achieved by keeping wages low and benefits low or non-existent.

Meanwhile, government intervention in these developments has been minimal. Global competition is reflected in pressures on governments to reduce deficits and establish balanced budgets. Failure to do so can result in a reduced credit rating from world financial institutions and, therefore, an increased cost for borrowing. This neo-liberal approach to governance is also rooted in the political conservatism of the Thatcher–Reagan–Mulroney era of the late 1970s and 1980s that laid the groundwork for popular acceptance of a belief in reduced public spending and trickle-down economics. **Neo-liberalism** is premised on a belief in competition and individualism as core social values. Individuals and corporations should succeed or fail based on their personal efforts and should not be interfered with. The poor and the **near-poor** are assumed to benefit as corporate growth trickles down to the common man and woman in terms of improved wages and so on. State-supported welfare recipients are said to jeopardize this 'natural' process by relying on state 'handouts'. The premise is that they must be made so uncomfortable by their inadequate support payments that they learn to take responsibility for themselves. When the state is 'too generous' or 'too large' or 'too involved in providing support for the less fortunate', it interferes with the natural economic competition that produces innovation and progress.

Predictably, this ideology became a rationale for dramatic reductions in state functions and state funding. The government-funded Employment Insurance program is a classic example of this transformation. The program has been so radically reduced—primarily by creating restrictions on eligibility for unemployment support payments—that the number of EI recipients is markedly down and employees' contributions actually are producing a massive surplus. As noted above, the direct result of these changes is that workers lack the flexibility and opportunities they previously enjoyed.

In an economic order in which corporations are consolidating their power, in which workers and their organizations are under attack, and in which governments appear unwilling or unable to balance the equation, it is not surprising to find analysts depicting the 'new' economy as the **'grim' economy** (Gindin and Stanford, 2006). This is the economic context in which midlife women will be approaching their 'retirement' years. Not surprisingly, they express considerable unease about the prospects for their 'golden years'.

Retiring from Employment in the 'Grim' Economy

Just as midlife women's lives were conditioned by the social and economic events of the 1960s and 1970s, today they face a present and future that must be located in the context of a leaner, meaner economic system with fewer and less generous state supports. Most Canadians today face a work world that is increasingly insecure, competitive, and challenging. As Susan McDaniel comments, the issues have become 'finding work, keeping work, whether work will continue, and whether it will provide an income on which people can live. These concerns are well justified in light of the massive economic restructuring that has taken and is taking place in Canada in the 1990s and now in the 2000s' (2003: 165). Certainly, these economic realities have impacted midlife women. Some have found themselves downsized out of a job and others have felt the pressure to update their technological skills so they remain competitive in the labour market. Many midlife women are indirectly impacted as adult children remain in the home while they struggle to advance their educational credentials or when they return home as a result of employment problems— boomerang kids (Matarazzo, 2006). Similarly, as the typical family's primary caregiver, midlife wives and mothers may be called upon to provide emotional as well as financial support if a spouse becomes a victim of economic restructuring. Even apparently benign transitions, such as early retirement or long-term layoff of spouses, may have considerable impact on midlife women's lives.

Since one of the outstanding features of the new economy is the loss of traditionally high-paid 'men's work' in manufacturing as well as in the public sector, midlife men may be particularly vulnerable to economic marginalization (ibid.). As midlife men struggle with the decline in traditionally male employment sectors, as well as the ageist tendencies of the labour market, and find themselves juggling part-time, contractual, and insecure work, they may discover quite unfamiliar terrain. This instability is reflected in the 25 per cent of dual-earner families in which women have become the *primary* wage earners (Sussman and Bonnell, 2006). Although seemingly a victory for feminists, it is likely that such shifts in traditional roles are accompanied by considerable stress and upheaval in families and, again, midlife women may carry an additional emotional burden (McDaniel, 2003).

This trend towards the loss of 'good jobs' is accompanied by state policies that seem largely intent on reducing support for families. Cost-cutting measures in the provision of health care to Canadians have meant not only that patients are sent home much earlier to be cared for, but also that patients often require considerable family assistance while in a health-care institution (Armstrong et al., 2001). If, as suggested by many, there is a shift towards user-paid health-care options, increased financial and caregiving pressures will directly impinge on families, most especially those not in a position to pay. This stress is particularly problematic given that increasing numbers of seniors are living well into old age. Midlife women are likely to find themselves with at least one older parent, parent-in-law, or extended family member who will live on as an aged senior and require family assistance or support. As the state continues to fail to provide adequate institutions and programs to provide care for aged seniors, it is likely that midlife women (and men) will find themselves increasingly called upon to make up the shortfall. Further, individual solutions, such as employing a personal support worker to assist the senior to live at home, are likely to intensify financial pressures at midlife and to be available only to those who are relatively well-off.

Staying in the Paid Labour Force

Analysts are anxiously speculating about the future viability of government pension provisions as well as health care. Recent newspaper headlines—'Are aging boomers going to bankrupt Canada?' 'The picture, if we don't do anything, is quite distressing' (*Toronto Star*, 20 July 2002)—speak to the grave concern that even with rapid increases in the numbers of younger immigrants, the Canadian economy cannot sustain so many senior and aged citizens. This apocalyptic vision suggests that so many baby boomers will survive into old age that they will place an insupportable burden on the pension system as well as on health care. As discussed in Chapter 1, the dependency ratio, that is, the number of retired people who are dependent on the productive activities of younger workers, will become so lopsided that pension plans will run out of funds and younger workers will find the systems depleted when it is their turn to retire (Longino, 2005; Morissette and Ostrovsky, 2004).

One of the solutions to the retirement of baby boomers is to encourage/expect more and more seniors to assume post-retirement employment and, thereby, defer dependency (Longino, 2005). This pattern is already emerging. In 2005 more men and women aged 55 to 64 were employed—spending an hour a day more in paid labour than they were in 1998. Over the past 20 years, women aged 55–64 are spending exactly the same time on unpaid work, have increased their paid work by one hour, and have decreased their active leisure by one hour (Marshall, 2006). Furthermore, employment after age 65 (the welfare state assumption of retirement age) has also increased. Between 1996 and 2001, while the total senior population grew by 11 per cent, the participation of seniors in paid employment increased by 19.6 per cent. Women 65 and older increased their share of the employed senior workforce to 32.1 per cent (Marshall, 2006).

Many of the women in our research population indicate that they will remain active in the labour force, part-time or full-time, well past their sixty-fifth birthdays. For many, this intention is simply a result of financial uncertainties or shortfalls. The exceptions here are the small numbers of women who have worked continuously in well-paid jobs, who have secure or even indexed public pensions, and who have few, if any, dependants to support. For these individuals, retirement, even early retirement, is 'in the cards' and their discussions centre on post-retirement choices and adventures. A 52-year-old senior government official anticipates a well-financed retirement commencing when she turns 60.

> It might be writing, it might be reading . . . reading stories to kids in school or doing some literacy stuff. Those are the kinds of stuff that hit me. . . . And, the other thing that I am starting to think about, and I am not sure if this would ever happen, is international work. Because, apparently, a lot of developing nations are looking for people with my skills set to help them set up a legal system or something like that. (Sharon, #5)

Such expansive dreams, however, are the exception. When asked if they have financial concerns as they approach retirement, the clear majority indicate that they do. Their reasons are myriad—they are self-employed and do not have a pension plan; they are paying off their children's educational expenses; their work has been low-paid and savings are insufficient; they are hobbled by the financial costs of a divorce; or, simply, they can't afford to retire. For many there is a remarkable murkiness about their retirement plans, if any, and their ability to afford retirement. Most women are talking of the need (and desire) to continue to work for pay, if only part-time. While many of these women express a desire for shorter and/or more flexible hours, they also reveal an undercurrent of uncertainty about future financial needs:

> I mean, I have colleagues who are unemployed (retired) and I say, 'What about your kids' education? Aren't you worried about it?' 'No. That has been paid for years ago.' I mean they have been able to put away enough money and we haven't. So we will see. I guess we can always sell the house. (Nancy, #2)

This pattern of insecurity is conditioned in part by the fact that many of these women are social activists and are, as a result, employed in NGOs (non-government [social support] organizations)—a sector of the economy that, in recent times, has been dramatically underfunded. Others, as mentioned above, have followed discontinuous career paths or worked in traditionally poorly paid women's occupations; and some, even though they have achieved considerable success at this point in their lives, face reduced financial returns on employment because of employment gaps or moves.

It's hard to know about [my financial situation after retirement]. One of the reasons why I'm staying [at my job] is that I like it, but that I'm accruing a pension. It won't be long; it won't be big. I will have only been working 13 years . . . so I will get some pension. (Catherine, #61)

Will Women Be Able to Manage the Costs of Retirement? Knocking on Wood

I have no retirement plan at this point. I have a small pension . . . my mother figures that, when she goes, that will take care of me. My husband's an artist so he's self-employed; he will work till he drops. For me . . . I've been thinking, if I could go in and get my BA and go to Teacher's College, I [could] even work as a supply teacher. (Vera, #8)

Midlife women's levels of paid employment and their economic status do not bode well for retirement and old age. The **occupational segregation** of employment by sex, with its resultant lower income for women employees, disadvantages them. The tendency of many women to juggle motherhood and paid employment by opting for part-time employment for some period of their working life, or to exit the paid labour force, may jeopardize those women's ability to save adequately for retirement (Statistics Canada, 2006). While continued employment might provide a partial solution to this economic shortfall, women over 55 may find that they are under increasing pressure to provide the care for a spouse or ailing older relations. Further, a healthy spouse may look forward eagerly to retirement and want his wife to join him in 'Freedom 55'—or 60. Here again, a woman's familial relationships may pull her out of the paid labour force and leave her with inadequate financial resources when she finds herself spending a decade or more as an elderly widow (Barnett, 2005). It is worth noting in this regard that, currently, in the US in long-term nursing-home care, women outnumber men by a ratio of roughly three to one (Hatch, 2005: 20).

Interviewer: What do you think you'd miss if you did retire?
Shana (#63): The money!
Interviewer: Will financial concerns figure prominently in your future decisions about paid work?

Shana: Yeah. Definitely. Because I have no money . . . I would like [my financial situation] to change for the better, but I'm not sure that it will [she knocks on wood].

Older women's economic situation may be particularly jeopardized by their family status. Women over age 65 who find themselves widowed or divorced or who have never married are particularly vulnerable. If women have devoted some portion of their adult lives to unpaid labour in the home, they may find that the loss of access to much of their spouses' pension income (in Canada, widows typically receive half of the amount of their husband's pension income) results in a sharp reduction in their quality of life.

At the beginning of the twenty-first century, unattached senior women have the lowest incomes and assets and the weakest social networks (Statistics Canada, 2006). While the movement of increased numbers of single women who have held professional careers can be expected to alter this pattern, it still is likely that widows and divorcees will find themselves financially disadvantaged in terms of pension incomes. Currently, fewer than half of women aged 55 to 64 are employed, in contrast to 62 per cent of comparable males. Among employed women, only 38 per cent have employer-sponsored pension plans, up only 1 per cent from 1980 and reflecting no growth since the late 1990s. Predictably, these patterns translate into greater dependence on inadequate government transfer programs (Old Age Security and Guaranteed Income Supplements). In 2003 over half the total income of women 65 and over came from these sources, in contrast to slightly more than 40 per cent of comparable men's income (Statistics Canada, 2007; Marshall, 2000).

I think I will have to be [employed until] at least 65. I can't even imagine retiring before then, financially. Not because I wouldn't want to. I don't have anybody else to support me. I'm totally relying on my own income to take care of my current and future financial needs. It's not like I have a husband with a pension plan or anything. So, I've got to do it myself. (Jennifer, #50)

Financial shortfalls in retirement are not rooted simply in gender inequalities and family role. Historical shifts in the economic order suggest that post-retirement financial security will become increasingly problematic. The new economy with its waves of layoffs, workforce reductions, and restructuring—along with its off-shoring of employment and strides towards non-standard employment—undermines traditional pension benefits. The women and men who have been laid off or downsized out of work may be unable to find new permanent employment with pension provisions. At the same time, they are not likely to be able to maintain a high level of RRSP investments. Similarly, the decline in unionized employment means that various work benefits, including generous pension provisions, have steadily eroded. As a result, pension coverage in Canada has fallen among males of all ages and among females under age 45 (Morissette and Johnson, 2005: 7). While midlife women may seem to be no worse off, since they are no less likely to be covered by a pension, these trends indicate they, too, will be less able to share in the pension income of their spouses. The overall picture is exacerbated by a general trend among employers to reduce and contain the costs of pension benefits.

More general economic trends towards intensified patterns of **social inequality** ensure that retirement and financial ease in old age will become an increasingly class-based phenomenon. Predictably, families in the top quartile of income earners have tended to increase their financial preparedness for retirement, while the rest of Canadians have not been able to do so. Also, as might be expected, individuals who not only have access to good employer-sponsored pension plans but who also can afford to contribute to RRSPs fall into the top quartile of privilege. Families, especially lone-parent families who already struggle with low income, have experienced either a deterioration or stagnation in their retirement preparedness since 1986 (Morissette and Ostrovsky, 2005). Women who are poor single parents and members of low-income-earning families at midlife are more likely to find themselves ill prepared for the financial as well as the non-financial realities of retirement (Schellenberg et al., 2005a). Not surprisingly, those whose financial situation remains the same or improves post-retirement and those who are able to take early retirement and those who plan for retirement while still employed (by developing leisure activities or hobbies, by becoming involved in volunteer work, or simply by gathering information about retirement) are more likely to enjoy life during retirement (Schellenberg et al., 2005b).

Unfortunately, relatively little evidence from our respondents suggests they have a strong financial foundation for retirement or prospects for early retirement. Most of them are quite aware that this is an important issue but, for most, a clear path out is not apparent. For many, continuing to be employed, even into their seventies, is seen as a partial solution, as is a shift to part-time work or consultancy work. Whether this will be feasible in light of health factors, family caregiving responsibilities, and employment realities remains to be seen. However, aging and staying in their job may become increasingly problematic:

> . . . if you [as an employer] can get someone who's like I was when I was 34 or 35 and pay them a whole lot less, why wouldn't you? And, I think many of the social service agencies will be looking at that, because all the funding is being cut back. So, why would you want to hire me and pay me what I've been making—and I'm not going to work for less—if you can get somebody else who, in fact, has got another 20 years to be able to give back to you. (Elise, #62)

As midlife women move into the ranks of seniors, they may increasingly confront the harsher consequences of their vanguard position.

Key Concepts

Community A term used in a wide variety of ways to refer to those non-familial individuals with whom one experiences a significant sense of personal connection. Historically, a community often referred to those individuals who shared (or had shared) a defined geographic location. In recent years, the term is frequently also applied to those individuals who share interests, social causes, and/or specific experiences, and connections may be entirely virtual (on-line) while retaining their personal and societal significance.

Compromise The effort by women to balance their family and paid employment aspirations/felt obligations through such mechanisms as part-time employment, self-employment, home-based employment, employment of nannies, time-out from paid employment, reliance on extended family for child care, and so on.

Drifting A term popularized by Nancy Mandell that refers to the tendency of many young Canadian women to not fully commit to any particular life course. In the presence of unclear and/or conflicting gender role expectations, many young women keep open as many options as possible.

Generation A term clarified in the recent work of Susan McDaniel (2004) that refers to the likelihood that individuals who are born into a common socio-historical moment are likely to face similar issues, concerns, social and economic forces, and social movements. Given this shared temporality, these age cohorts are likely to evince discernible life course patterns.

'Grim' economy A term popularized by Sam Gindin, Jim Stafford, and others that refers to the fact that the emergence of the so-called 'new' economy since the 1980s has had a profoundly negative impact on the lives of many Canadian workers, including those engaged in labour movement activities, those employed in manufacturing and industrial production, and those confronting the prospects of 'precarious' employment in the burgeoning service sector of the economy.

Individuation A term popularized by Lorna Marsden, Charles Jones, and Lorne Tepperman (1990) that refers to the historical emergence through the course of the twentieth century of a wide diversity of potential life course paths, family forms, and so on.

Near-poor Those individuals who are not below the unofficial poverty line designated by Statistics Canada's low-income cut-offs, yet who often live in very straitened personal circumstances. Poverty activists urge more consideration of their plight.

Neo-liberalism The emergence and popularization since the 1980s of a body of ideas that reflect classical liberalism, such as the emphasis on free markets and trade and a view of society as atomized individuals rather than a collectivity. These ideas are reflected in social policies that encourage dramatic reductions in state funding and urge greater self-reliance. Neo-liberalism is reflected, for example, in reductions in employment insurance benefits and welfare payments and increased demand for alternatives such as workfare.

'New' economy The economic order that emerged out of the micro-electronic revolution. Advances in computer technology have permitted the robotization of much manufacturing and resource extraction work and the dramatic expansion of service-sector employment. Most analysts view economic globalization (including the off-shoring of employment and increased use of migrant workers) as a key facet in the new economy.

Occupational segregation The continuing tendency of women to be employed in traditionally 'female' jobs and men in traditionally 'male' work. For example, women work as nurses while men work in construction. This pattern has tended to keep women in low-wage, service-based, and insecure sectors of employment.

Patriarchal culture The prevailing beliefs, values, attitudes, and norms in social systems through which men in general dominate over women.

Service-sector employment Those jobs, other than resource extraction and industrial manufacturing, that characterize modern economies. This loose group of economic activities includes financial/business services, personal/health-care professions, education, retail/wholesale sales, distribution activities, and so on. Work in this sector of the economy tends to be labour-intensive and is often characterized by 'bad' job traits such as precarious employment, low wages, and lack of opportunity for advancement. Service-sector employment has expanded dramatically in recent years and women play a central role in this type of work.

Social inequality The wide array of ways in which 'power' is differentially distributed in societies. In contemporary Canadian society, gender, age, sexual orientation, social class, disability, visible minority/race status, and recent immigrant status figure prominently in patterns of differential access to power.

Questions for Critical Discussion

1. Describe the ways in which the 1950s model of women's role in the family continues to resonate in the lives of contemporary midlife women. What strategies do women use to resolve the conflict created by 'the grip of the past'?
2. If the modern generation of young women were to be subject to an equivalent amount of social and personal change, what kind of future society would they inhabit?
3. Taking several of the quotes in this chapter, distinguish between the roles of 'luck' and 'agency' in the interviewees' lives.
4. How might the work lives of immigrant women of colour and lesbians differ from those of midlife women who have followed a more traditional life course?
5. Consider the level of work satisfaction described by these diverse women and explain the social and historical roots for their reactions.
6. Why would the notion of midlife as crisis appeal to normative views of aging and women?
7. Some analysts argue that the boomer generation of women has been unusually fortunate—particularly in their experiences in the labour force. Critically evaluate this argument.

Chapter 7

Health and Well-Being

In this chapter, we explore the contradictory themes of loss and decline, agency and control. We begin by examining physical decline and social loss as inevitable consequences of physiological 'slowing down'. We look at the ways midlife women incorporate changing physical abilities into their day-to-day lives. We then examine a key area in which midlife women experience ambivalence: beauty and appearance. Discourses on thinness and attractiveness overwhelm some midlife women who have internalized a cultural association of 'youthfulness' with 'moral responsibility'. We then turn our attention to concerns about menopause, sexuality, depression, chronic illness, and fears of breast cancer. Finally, we focus on questions of spirituality and meaning by examining how midlife women seek, and eventually find, balance and meaning in their lives.

Aging necessarily brings concerns about **health and well-being**. Midlife women are aware that getting older may mean a loss of physical ability and the eventual worry of losing their independence or of becoming a burden to their families. As Sharon (#5) said: 'I don't want to be put in a home [if I lose my mind]. At that point, you've lost all control.' But midlife women also experience aging as spiritual maturation, as a time of renewed hope and deepening meaning in their lives. In short, health, like intimacy and paid employment, represents ambivalent experiences for midlife women.

Themes of vulnerability and decline do permeate many midlife women's health narratives. In the introductory chapter we talked about how the literature on aging associates midlife as the beginning of decline and loss. Changes in reproductive capacity and presumed diminishment of sexual inclination accompanying menopause are culturally positioned primarily as losses. Physical losses occur and midlife women know they must ready themselves for changes in their health status. According to Ruth (#6): 'The older one gets, the more one is concerned about one's health and well-being from the perspective that you are getting older, and you're not the same as you once were.'

At the same time, themes of agency and connection are evident. Physical alterations do not determine social experiences of aging. For many women, midlife signals the beginning of journeys of self-discovery. Midlife is a time of freedom, independence, and autonomy, all of which bring our women considerable pleasure and opportunities for deeper connections to activities and people they enjoy.

Just the evolving nature of life is wonderful, and the older we get the more wonderful we are—again, health problems aside. I know fabulous women in their seventies, just fabulous, and so I think that gives me a lot of hope about the second half of life. I think that in midlife you can look forward with all kinds of glee. (Susan, #16)

Discourses of Loss and Decline: Slowing Down

Discourses of loss and decline dominate conversations about aging in the West, whether in the academic literature or in conversations at the mall. Young and old alike operate within this discourse. Personal experiences with aging parents and grandparents become woven into images in the popular media. Aging in Canadian society, once any delightful interludes of 'Freedom 55' and 'sexy sixties' are passed, is understood as marked by ill health, decline, marginalization, and isolation. The elderly are not only not valued, they often are seen as a burden and an unpleasant reminder of mortality. Ageism in this social context is not only about how older people are treated, it also is about how older people self-label and the ways in which they internalize ageist beliefs. A central task for midlife women is coming to terms with what Gullette (1997: 8) has called 'declineoldageanddeath'.

At midlife women are beginning to acknowledge changes in physical capacity. They no longer feel as strong or as flexible as they did when younger. Some, like Rita (#1), who is a married mother of five employed in health care, talked about not being able to play the sports she once loved. She has asthma and worries that her stressful life could cause health problems in the future. She regrets the lack of balance in her life and the loss of her youthful energy. There is a nostalgic tone as she remembers the physical freedom she enjoyed as a child.

I remember that when I was a kid, there were times when I ran, and I would move into that place that I would feel that I could run forever and it was so liberating that I couldn't believe it. I would love to be able to feel that again, to get back to that place.

Malina (#15), a 55-year-old immigrant, says about the closing down of the athletic side of her life: 'I'm still hoping that maybe, maybe I will be able to do more in terms of exercise.' She talks wistfully about her desire to walk with her husband on the Way of St James[1]:

Wouldn't it be remarkable to go on that? But I can't even think about something like that now, because I certainly don't have the strength for that. So that aspect has closed down.

Margaret (#4), who is married but childless and in her fifties, also talks about being less able to be involved in active sports and worries about the impact on her health of this lower level of activity. She has loved sports and physical activity all her life, but finds that it takes more and more of a push to become involved in physical activity. She also has fewer and fewer women friends who engage in sports, so finds it harder to find people to go biking or skiing with. Fortunately, she and her husband like doing these things together.

Those in good health seem to be invigorated by activities and opportunities open to them at this stage of their lives. One focus group participant continues to ride a motorcycle. She is determined not to give it up 'until she is in a wheelchair'. But even active midlife women are ambivalent about the future. They want to remain active but realize that they may not be able to control their physical well-being and are anxious about what lies ahead. Although Martha (#49) has a job she enjoys and finds fulfilling, next to her family, athletics are the most important thing in her life. Understandably, she worries about being able to continue her athletic involvements as she ages. Having supported her mother through a painful and debilitating illness, she doesn't want to be in pain, and she doesn't want to be physically incapacitated. She wants very much to 'live an active elder life':

> I recognized that I probably won't aspire to climb Mount Everest—somebody has asked me to go sky-diving, and I said, 'You know what, No'; whereas two years ago . . . [pause] . . . I don't need to do it; I don't have to do it; and, in some ways, I don't want to do it. I don't find it a compromise. I hope that I maintain my health.

Slowing down and moving away from physical activity are relative. Ironically, women who are most athletic may also be most aware of their physical decline. Anita (#12) has three children and a very demanding job. Despite being very active, she sees herself as needing to accommodate her changing body:

> My body's falling apart; it's really doing me in. I love working out, and I . . . I do all sorts of things, and my working out has sort of changed. When I was younger it used to hurt a little, my knees; I would do very aggressive exercising and cycling. I cycle; I rollerblade; I do yoga. I used to go to the gym, but now it's too much work. And I now find that I do yoga at home, and garden, which I read in the paper on the weekend: when you turn 50 you garden. I'm out there with my shovel and I'm throwing dirt! I have lots of injuries. But overall I'm very, very healthy; but I'm very physically fit and overall quite strong. But I had to change what I do to accommodate my body, which has decided it's going to do different things. And the biggest pain in the butt, and it is only a pain in the butt, is my feet. I have arthritis now in both my feet.

So, while many midlife women feel healthy and physically active, they are aware of loss of capacity and energy levels. This dominant response varies since some accept and others regret the changes. As Margaret (#4) said: 'The fifties is a time when you are more vulnerable. You have to adapt.' The element of control is a key. Neither the gradual slowing down—or, as one woman described it, the 'deterioration'—nor the sudden changes in health status are within their control. Cancer, specifically breast cancer, is the perceived greatest threat for the women in this study—and some, like Mia (#10), feel that death has become an unpredictable factor: 'You never know when death is going to occur.'

Threatened Health: Things You Cannot Control

Most midlife women realize they can no longer take their health for granted. They are starting to feel the aches, pains, and losses associated with aging. Losses of energy, of hearing or eyesight, and of memory foreshadow the incapacities they associate with aging. Tara (#75), a health-care worker from Niagara, described the natural progression of aging:

> You do feel different, your body's different. You take for granted every day when you're in your twenties and your thirties; you don't really think about aches and pains. And when you do get into your forties and fifties you're starting to feel pains that you probably didn't even know were there before and all of a sudden it's you can't even, you can't ignore them; it's very real.

Nicole (#45) probably would agree:

> I know bodies wear down. I'm having aches and pains that began when I turned 40. I notice some things about my body and my hands, and my memory, so I do perceive a slowing down.

For these women the appropriate analogy is a gradual 'wearing down' until the aches and pains can no longer be ignored.

While these midlife women feel healthy now, they worry about how this situation could suddenly change. Clearly, the popular perception is that aging can quickly translate into a profoundly unpleasant physical reality. Susan (#16) said that she 'dreaded the deterioration that comes with old age. I intend to be as healthy as possible . . . to stay as active physically as possible . . . but it's a nightmare to think of deteriorating health because you can't do anything about it.'

Several women talk about the spectre of a rapid change in health. As Barbara (#78) says: 'That's really uncertain because you can be perfectly fine, then all of a sudden, you know, you just don't know.' Sharon (#5), too, talks about how a health crisis can make life 'turn in a second':

> I worry, I can tell now that I don't heal as quickly as I did—I don't get over colds and those kinds of things as quickly. And I think [about what would happen] if I was to have some kind of accident or illness or something like that. I am also of an age where I have friends who have cancer and of course, most of those guys are dead, sadly. But many are living with HIV now. When you think about things like that, you realize that your life could turn in a sec-

ond. And this cough that won't go away and all of a sudden, bang, something else. So I think about those things more than I used to, certainly.

There is no illusion in most of these women that decline can be forestalled forever.

I don't take my health for granted but, thankfully, I feel healthy. My body shape has changed, but that's a middle-aged thing—I'm . . . I had a kidney stone three months ago and that alarmed me, like, 'Oh, is this the beginning of something?' and then they found something on my liver, and I had a test on Monday. I don't get the results for another two weeks . . . when I'm thinking about this, I think, 'Oh, great; this is the beginning of the end of my good health.' (Phyllis, #3)

It is important to realize that even healthy midlife women live with a nagging subtext: their well-being can be shaken at any moment. This inevitability conditions their thinking, feelings, choices, and plans. Women who have struggled with health issues and crises are even more concerned. For Elizabeth (#81), a stroke was a wake-up call:

It took away part of my sight, which was very life altering. And, of course, I'm a smoker and I thought, 'Okay, you idiot.' But everything's fine. That's what they [the doctors] told me, 'You had a stroke.' I figured [it was caused by] clogged arteries, but they told me, 'Everything's fine. These things happen.' $125,000 and you went to school for how long? And this is the answer, 'These things happen'?

Living with the legacy of an existing health concern not only frustrates any sense a person might have of control, it can contribute to a profound reorientation in the perception of self and others.

Healthism and Weightism

Middle-aged women typically internalize messages of health promotion regarding diet, exercise, and smoking. **Healthism and weightism** refer to the ideas that individuals can control their health and their weight—indeed, that they have a moral obligation to do so. This individual attribution is reflected in public health messages that focus on individual responsibility. The intentions of the women we interviewed to stop smoking, start exercising, or lose weight are tinged with guilt and their comments full of stated and implied 'shoulds'. They are anxious to be slim, healthy, and fit and feel guilty if they gain weight or slow down. Many women refer to exercise as an important part of their lives, either being generally physically able, or wanting still to engage in physical activities. Their comments reflect a contradictory combination of carpe diem, realism, and self-acceptance—a little regret and a little worry.

We are not surprised to find that smokers want to quit, and many women explicitly state that they want to lose weight and exercise. Ten women mentioned smoking and four of those indicate they 'have to quit'. Others want to quit or feel guilty for not quitting. References to smoking ranged from regret about having smoked to defiance about the habit. Kendra (#77) was regretful: 'If I had to do it all over again I wouldn't smoke.' Although she was taking better care of herself, and had started an exercise program, she 'still can't give up smoking!' Becky (#54), too, was regretful:

> I've been a smoker all my life so I'm concerned about all the smoker's diseases. I'm not worried enough about them to quit smoking yet, but soon!

Janet and Sophia are typical of those who respond to the open-ended health question with a certain amount of defiance about their smoking.

> I must say I'm still a smoker. Now, I know; I don't have to be given a lecture. I know about smoking, but I still do it and it is a very hard thing to give up, and it is definitely affecting my health at this stage of the game. (Janet, #72)

> My drawback is that I smoke; and right about now I don't give a shit. I don't. I don't care. I've tried to quit. I give up. (Sophia, #74)

Mia (#10) feels guilty and immobilized by the pressure to make healthy life choices and she worries about having a second heart attack. She had a minor heart attack 18 months ago and recognizes that she 'should' begin to exercise and 'should' lose weight. She takes full responsibility for her heart problems, but is unable to initiate the changes she feels she must.

> So I have to take control but so far I have been blindly going ahead smoking, not taking care of myself, and I know I have to, I just don't know when I'm ever going to get myself in control. . . . If I lost weight, and if I quit smoking, and if I got more exercise, I would probably be able to go off of most of the medication that I'm on, and my heart would be a lot healthier for it. I will never have a 100 per cent heart, I've never had one since I was born; but in the last 30 years I've brought this on myself. If I had not started smoking and if I had started to exercise and if I had started to watch my weight 30 years ago, I wouldn't be in this health position that I'm in now.

Women's feelings about their responsibility for their poor health practices are often complex and contradictory. In accepting the prevailing individualistic discourse on health, many women do blame themselves, with the attendant feelings of shame or guilt. They castigate themselves for their failures to diet, exercise, eat properly, lose weight, quit smoking, and so on. However, midlife women may also recognize the sheer impossibility of incorporating better health practices into their day-to-day lives. In these instances and at these moments, they may erupt in an angry, wilful refusal, which amounts to a demand for a sense of agency captured by the phrase 'to hell with it'. What is missing in these discourses is an appreciation for the structural roots of poor health practices—the stresses of the double day, the general loss of leisure in Canadian society, the health impacts of environmental degradation, the multiple stresses of impoverishment, and so on. Anger is addressed to all the 'should-sayers' (notably, the media) rather than to the societal context that creates and sustains unhealthy lifestyles. This theme of self-blame is evident in many midlife narratives of resolve, such as that of Terry (#66):

> I think I am in lousy physical health. I think I should be toned up and I am grabbing a little piece of flab right here. I looked at myself; I am getting a little jolly as I reach for a glass of wine and so on. I think I definitely need to get a grip. So, in terms of physical health, I am a little ashamed of it. I don't like it. It doesn't fit in with my younger image of myself. I have been a little self-indulgent and I think I need to . . . the big 'D' word . . . to become, you know, disciplined and do it. I promised myself that once this contract is over, I am getting back into walking an hour a day and getting back into swimming and just make it a focus. So, I am in a little . . . 'observing myself' mode here and I don't like that part of it.

Midlife women internalize health promotion messages to the extent that they feel guilty if they do not present as slim and fit. Amy (#20), a 58-year-old widow and mother of two sons, describes her dilemmas with diet and exercise:

> I went on these exercise kicks. I would join the health club and work out for six or nine months, or I would, you know . . . I went to Weight Watchers and I tried to control my dieting and become, you know, because everybody's supposed to be pencil-thin. And, you know, that whole silly advertising thing that they've dumped on women. And I would say to you that I eat pretty basic, pretty stable food. I think that I try to eat by the Canada Food Guide. I try to eat in smaller portions. So I'm trying to eat better and I'm trying to take my vitamins and I'm trying to do all the things that you're supposed to.

The idea that diet and exercise are fundamental strategies to looking and feeling young would not surprise anyone who scans the covers of women's magazines. It is difficult to find an issue among them without at least one article focused on losing weight through diet or exercise. The implication that body size and shape are within an individual's control fuels the sense that overweight is a personal failure. Body dissatisfaction is big business in terms of cosmetics, exercise, aging (Wolf, 1997). In fact, the exercise movement has been co-opted by the media to make women feel guilty and dissatisfied about their shape and size.

Negotiating Societal Pressures to Appear Slim and Youthful

How do midlife women interpret cultural proscriptions to remain youthful? And how do they balance cultural demands with obvious signs of aging? McLaren and Kuh (2004: 49) find evidence of what they refer to as the 'turning-50 effect'. In other words, women feel more dissatisfied with their bodies in their fifties than they remember feeling when they were younger. These feelings of dissatisfaction appear in midlife and apparently continue until old age. Clarke interviewed 22 Canadian women aged 61 to 92 about physical changes associated with aging, particularly those related to weight. Most of these women are unhappy about their own weight and 'lament the loss of their youthful figures' (Clarke, 2002a: 433). Several say they have been 'fat' all their lives and are still unhappy with what they feel are their over-weight bodies. In Clarke's study, even women in their eighties want to lose weight. An 86-year-old woman thought her legs were fat and unattractive. The only women in Clarke's group who want to gain weight are two women in their nineties! It seems women are never old enough to relax about their weight.

In a society preoccupied by weight, it is not surprising that weight is a source of discontent for midlife women. A recent study of a large cohort of 54-year-old women in Britain found that nearly 60 per cent were dissatisfied with their bodies and nearly 80 per cent wanted to lose weight (McLaren and Kuh, 2004). Interestingly, even those who weren't dissatisfied with their bodies wanted to lose weight and almost half of those in the study were actively trying to lose weight. Clearly, body dissatisfaction cuts across all body sizes, although heavier women expressed more dissatisfaction. Women with better health were less likely to feel dissatisfied with their bodies and were less likely to wish to lose weight. Predictably, women who felt dissatisfied with their bodies tended to avoid such situations as wearing bathing suits, physical activity, and physical intimacy (ibid., 51). Body dissatisfaction is associated with feelings of depression, diminished sexual feeling, and marital dissatisfaction (McLaren and Wardle, 2002: 180). There is some evidence that decline in physical activity among menopausal women is tied to their resistance about wearing revealing athletic clothing. Body dissatisfaction in middle-aged women is also tied to smoking, unhealthy weight-loss tactics, and disordered eating (ibid., 181) as they struggle to control their weight.

Women in our culture face a societal expectation that they appear healthy, young, slim, and 'beautiful'. Changes in body shape, wrinkles, and stiffness all signal both aging and threatened health status. Clarke (2002a) found that women internalize cultural standards of beauty in that they think of overweight people as unattractive and as 'having let themselves go'. The majority think of wrinkles negatively, although some describe 'earning' their wrinkles. A few women resist the negative connotations of wrinkles, but not of weight. Although they say they value inner beauty over outward appearance, the majority think they were more attractive when younger.

Economic and social pressures to appear youthful are strong, even for those aware of the oppressiveness of these messages. In Chapter 1, we saw some of the comments of women who feel marginalized because of their age. They talk about their experiences of feeling old and devalued because of the way others react to them. They feel judged—and found wanting—because of their maturing bodies. It is not unusual for middle-aged women to say they are surprised when they look in the mirror and realize how old they look (Gubrium and Holstein, 2003: 212). As Amy (#20) tells us: 'I see the aging in my parents and I see the aging in myself. If I look in the mirror I think, "Well, you're not 21 any more, kid."'

Having internalized cultural messages about aging, midlife women are ambivalent about whether to accept or work to forestall aging. Participants in Banister's (1999) interview study involving a small sample of Canadian midlife women (aged 40–55) talk of internalizing 'derogatory messages' and carrying on a sort of inner dialogue between the cultural standards valuing youthfulness (which they reject) and falling into the trap of worrying about their appearance (ibid., 527). Women also feel ambiguity about their typical weight gain. While they feel strong and capable, they regret that they are not as thin or beautiful as they would like.

In Banister's study, women have a heightened awareness of less time to live, which is exacerbated by a loss of their youthful appearance, youthful energy, and loss of fertility (Banister, 1999: 529). Physical changes challenge their sense of identity and self-esteem (ibid., 530) and leave them feeling vulnerable. Their inner sense of youthfulness feels at odds with the face and body they see in the mirror and this discrepancy may create a sense of self-alienation (ibid.). They are unhappy with outward signs of aging even though they don't necessarily want to hide their wrinkles or grey hair (ibid., 531).

At work, middle-aged women feel particularly conscious of weight and other visible signs of aging. While women of all ages may experience sexism in the workplace, midlife women begin to experience the 'double whammy' of sexism and ageism (Sontag, 1972) at this stage in their working lives. As Trethewey (2001) argues, this perception leaves women to navigate a path between reproducing and resisting the discourse of decline. Participants in Trethewey's study describe struggling against grey hair, an aging face, weight, and fatigue. They also make an effort to exercise and to wear stylish clothes and hairstyles so that they can pass as younger than their age. Granted, these are women of privilege. As white, middle-class professional women they are able to afford trainers, expensive clothes, and so on. They also talk about a positive side to their experience of growing older in the workplace. They are more likely to be listened to because of their experience and they feel a certain freedom that goes along with self-acceptance and a shift in priorities. Freedom from sexual innuendo or unwanted sexual advances is also an advantage of age, although the down side of this sense of freedom is that of feeling invisible.

Although we see that some women carry the desire to be thin into old age, generally, older women are less likely to report body dissatisfaction, which may reflect a change in attitude or it may simply be that when these midlife women were adolescents and young women, the cult of thinness was less prominent than it is now, so they were less likely to be socialized into weight preoccupation (McLaren and Wardle, 2002: 179–80).

The struggle between accepting and resisting the discourse of decline is evident in Tamika's (#58) comment:

Well, I can't be working that long, for one thing [laughs]. I hope to retire. If my health is good, I'd like to keep working. When do women retire? It depends, if I—I hate to look ancient on the job. If I look really old at work, you see, . . . if I start to look, I don't dye my hair, you see, and I hope not to, but I will try to make it look . . . well-groomed.

Many of our midlife women express this sense of ambivalence as they talk about their aging bodies. They both reject and internalize societal negations of aging. There is also considerable diversity among women in terms of whether rejection or internalization dominates. Some women are more comfortable in their skin than others. Although they are aware of the changes in their bodies they are not preoccupied with weight and appearance. For example, Phyllis (#3), a 47-year-old lesbian mother of two, appears to accept completely her changing shape and weight: 'My body shape has changed but that's a middle-age thing. . . . It's just wider. I'm not alarmed or concerned and I have no idea how much I weigh and never have.'

Others, like Jennifer (#60), a 50-year-old, never-married woman, remain as preoccupied with weight in middle age as they were in their twenties and thirties:

I feel totally self-conscious about my body image and my weight, particularly my weight. It's constant . . . I work out faithfully . . . but it's still a constant thing about my life. From a health perspective . . . I don't feel as horribly overweight as I did before, but I still feel self-conscious about it.

In some instances, arriving at a point of acceptance about one's body is a long journey. Nicole (#45), a 52-year-old mother of two and married to her second husband, described the roller-coaster of living with an eating disorder. As she explains, she was finally able to be free of her dieting cycle when she recognized the pattern and could see how destructive it was. She was quite heavy in her twenties and lost about 30 pounds with a great deal of effort. In her thirties she was exceptionally thin—too thin. In retrospect, she describes her slimming experience as an eating disorder. While she attributes her weight gain to an unhappy marriage, she connects her weight loss to increased self-confidence that enabled her eventually to leave the marriage. As she explains: 'When I lost the weight, I gained so much self-esteem that I decided I probably didn't need to stay in this marriage.'

But the weight loss was a double-edged sword. Although never diagnosed, she felt she was 'borderline anorexic'. Now, at midlife, with a settled family life, she seems far more accepting of her appearance and weight. Although she likes to look well, she has stopped worrying about her weight. 'I'm not nearly as neurotic about it as I used to be. I don't worry about my weight as I used to. I'm not worried about the grey hair. Those things don't bother me like they used to.'

The twin discourses of loss/decline and thinness/beauty exert an ideological and practical control over midlife women's lives. Ambivalence about aging is structured into the institutions and culture so pervasively that midlife women understand and experience the message as 'aging bodies ought to disappear'. However, most midlife women also understand that being thin and beautiful is attached to discourses of youth where these attributes are demanded if women are to successfully leap the hurdles of 'finding a relationship' and 'making a living'. At midlife, those great tests of self-worth are now generally perceived as in the past; for good or ill, most middle-aged women are past concerns about finding 'the love of their life' and making their way economically in the world. They have already muddled through, and aging not only brings a sense of loss and decline, it also means freedom from these earlier demanding agendas. Freed from the harsher proscriptions about appearance, they often find they are at liberty to experience more independence and self-expression.

Discourses on Sexuality: Time to Retire?

It may be a misnomer to refer to a **discourse on aging sexuality**, for it is unusual to consider older people as sexual. The image of a silver fox—an older man who has retained some youthful vitality—may be an exception. It is harder to imagine a parallel image reflecting a sexually attractive older woman. At a certain stage, old is simply not thought of as sexually attractive. Middle-aged women are deemed sexy only if they are able to mimic the appearance of younger women. Middle-aged men seem not to have to struggle as much to be thought of as sexually attractive. In Western culture, aging men can be sexy, aging women cannot. Media commentators appear constantly to be amazed that Demi Moore would have snagged her much younger husband, Ashton Kutcher. Yet, there is no comment on the series of '20-something' girlfriends enjoyed by her ex-husband and age-contemporary, Bruce Willis. Endless other celebrity examples could be cited.

For women, menopause signals the end of procreation and, as the media would have it, the loss of sexual attractiveness. Certainly, midlife women internalize the idea that menopause means a dwindling interest in sexual intimacy. Koster and Garde (1993) argue that expecting interest in sexuality to gradually decline may be a self-fulfilling prophecy. Indeed, menopause could have the opposite effect, signalling a period of sexual interest, free from worries about pregnancy and focused on one's own sexual needs (Gott and Hinchcliff, 2003). Australian researchers found that women aged 60 to 92 expect their sex lives to improve as they get older, as the meaning of sex shifts from reproduction to their own pleasure. Women who grew up with limited contraception welcome the freedom from worries about birth control that accompany menopause. They also are influenced by increased attention paid to female sexuality in the media—although they aren't necessarily able to discuss their thoughts with their male partners, who they feel are more traditional (ibid.).

The gendered inequities surrounding sexuality certainly do not disappear as women age. A midlife heterosexual woman's sexual experiences typically hinge on her partner's availability and willingness; a midlife heterosexual man's sexual experiences depend more on his physical ability—an obstacle Viagra and other 'erectile dysfunction' drugs have removed for many men. Women in the Australian study 'sexually retire' when their partner dies or is unable to experience sex. Men retire sexually when they encounter health problems or erectile dysfunction—whether or not they have an interested partner. Widowed men are more apt to seek another partner if they are still sexually active, whereas widows do not (ibid.).

We did not ask about changes in sexuality. Sexuality was not raised as a midlife concern by participants in the community-based focus groups, and these informed the development of our interview guide. Perhaps sexuality is not a topic that will arise in the context of a focus group unless specifically addressed. Very few women mentioned sexuality in our interviews. Judy (#50), who identified herself as a feminist, said that she wishes it were possible to have open discussions of sexuality among women. Only three participants mentioned sexuality. One isn't interested in sex any more (Ameya, #97), while two others mention declining interest—one with seeming acceptance and one with ambivalence. 'People usually say better sex will give you a better relationship. Well, it's somehow true. But now, maybe I am getting older mentally . . . comfort is even more important than physical needs' (Lucia, #96). And Jane (#18) comments, 'The only change has been in my libido which . . . I will probably start working on that. That happened at menopause where I don't have the same type of libido I had before—lower sex drive, so I don't know . . . I still care about it once or twice a week, but it's not the same kind of feeling.'

We *could* interpret the fact that sexuality was so infrequently raised by our participants as a reflection of its relative unimportance to these women, but it could also reflect a cultural proscription against middle-aged women introducing sex or sexuality into an interview. Academics, in general, assume that sex is neither important nor relevant to older people and have ignored sexuality and aging—whether in studies of aging or studies of sexuality (ibid., 64). According to our interviewer's notes, one respondent did make the point that in her opinion it had been an oversight not to ask about sexuality. We are left to wonder whether failing to raise the topic in our interviews reflects our own ageism. Have we so internalized the discourse of the asexual older adult that it didn't occur to us to ask about sexuality?

Discourses on Menopause: Raging Bodies

Menopause, the end of menstruation, has become synonymous with female midlife. It is a major focus in the literature in women's health and has received far more attention than any other health concern. Menopause is the biological marker of middle age, defined by a long list of symptoms and a presumption of declining sexual interest and attractiveness. Menopausal *symptoms* (note the medical language) include hot flashes, night sweats, insomnia, memory changes, palpitations, psychological symptoms, vaginal dryness, decreased sex drive, blood pressure changes, depression, forgetfulness, and a quick temper. Symptoms of menopause have given rise to a class of jokes; is there anyone who hasn't heard the one about the menopausal woman . . . ? Such stereotyping contributes to the social definition of middle-aged women as incompetent, erratic, unpleasant, and unreliable.

Because these symptoms are presumed to be caused by an estrogen deficiency, menopause is treated as a medical condition. Menopausal women become 'patients' whether they are healthy or not. The dominance of the biomedical model sees menopause as a biological event and ignores the influence of cultural and psychosocial factors (Huffman and Myers, 1999). When menopause is anticipated as a condition to be treated allopathically, alternative approaches that focus on nutrition and exercise are ignored. The menopause literature, situated within allopathic medicine, describes menopause using terms such as pelvic atrophy, ovarian dysfunction, and estrogen deprivation (Rostosky and Travis, 2000: 193). More recent holistic health literature finds that menopause is not particularly problematic for many women (ibid., 196). Margaret Mead, the noted anthropologist, reported evidence of what she referred to as menopausal zest (see Lock, 1995: xiv).

Because menopause has been defined as a lack of estrogen, the obvious *treatment* has been hormone replacement. Hormone replacement therapy (HRT) became widely used in the 1960s. New York gynecologist Robert Wilson was an influential advocate of HRT, and an article focusing on his treatment was published in *Newsweek* in 1964. Wilson's work was later detailed in *Feminine Forever*, which promoted estrogen replacement therapy to prevent the unnecessary 'tragedy' of menopause. When first introduced, HRT was thought to be a short-term treatment to relieve hot flashes, night sweats, vaginal dryness, and other related symptoms. In theory, HRT would provide both physical and psychological relief. Research also suggested that HRT had the additional benefit of preventing bone density loss associated with osteoporosis, so it became used long-term to prevent osteoporosis and heart disease. For four decades the use of HRT was heavily promoted by physicians and the pharmaceutical industry. Increasingly, women became concerned about negative side effects, such as depression and mood swings, weight gain, fluid retention, and high blood pressure in addition to concerns about increased risk of breast and ovarian cancer and stroke.

Like many women, Catherine (#61) felt ambivalent about taking HRT because she worries about a link to cancer.

Well, I worry about the menopause stuff and what the effects of HRT are, but I feel like I have no choice because of the quality of life I have now, I have no quality of life if I'm not taking it. So that concerns me, am I setting myself up for cancer?

In 2002 a major US research project was stopped midway when the evidence became clear that HRT produced increased rates of cancer and heart disease in women (see Worcester, 2004). Now, the standard advice appears to be to use HRT only if needed for unmanageable hot flashes and to use it only for a short time. For some women, HRT is a godsend for dealing with severe menopausal symptoms, but the notion of HRT as a solution to aging has been abandoned.

These recent events speak not only to the continued medicalization of women's bodies but also to women's justifiable fears about such medicalization. Since the advent of the modern women's movement, mainstream medicine has been exposed as having played a very problematic part in aspects of the medical management of women's lives in such practices as unnecessary Caesarean sections and hysterectomies, dangerous breast implants and contraceptive devices, the prescribing of mood modifiers without recourse to counselling, and the symptomatic 'treatment' of aging women's bodies through cosmetic surgery.

In this context it is not surprising that menopause is associated with deterioration, inevitable weight gain, and reduced elasticity—in other words, more wrinkles and more sagging. Rostosky and Travis (1996: 284) note that 'Popular images and stereotypes of women in the menopausal age range are overwhelmingly negative.' The study of menopause has been dominated by the medical model—so menopause is both understood and treated as a disease rather than a normal stage of life. 'Medical discourse strongly influences women's self-definitions and experiences of their bodies' (Banister, 1999: 527–8) and once again produces a self-fulfilling prophecy.

Although the stereotype of menopause is of an extended period of discomfort and incompetence, women's experience of menopause actually is varied and complex. For Judy (#50), menopause triggered an awareness of her own mortality and awakened a desire to take better care of herself:

Menopause was significant. I thought of it as a phase, a challenge not to think of it as a medical problem. I took it as a challenge. It was inconvenient and uncomfortable at times, but that too would pass. In some ways it was important because I became more aware of looking after myself. I wasn't doing that in the past. I became more in tune with how I feel physically when I normally wouldn't have paid attention to myself. I never cared for myself. I became more aware of my mortality, too. There were lots of people dying and who died around my age. I had lots of symptoms, which were pretty horrible when working with lots of kids. I just told myself I needed to look after myself. It lasted three years. So, then I thought that this was going to be great, getting rid of this nuisance! Although, I really didn't think about it lasting three years.

Middle-aged professional women worry about their 'leaking bodies' (Trethewey, 2001) and in the workplace are self-conscious about visible evidence of hot flashes and excessive sweating. Trethewey (ibid., 202) describes this feeling as another way that professional women feel 'othered'. They struggled, first, as professional women in male-dominated fields, then as mothers in the demanding and unpaid work of raising the next generation, and, in midlife, as menopausal women. Anita (#12) is married and the mother of three children. She has a responsible job and describes herself as generally well grounded. However, menopause was distressing because of the physical symptoms and because she experienced panic attacks for the first time in her life. She could manage the hot flashes and learned to wear layers at work and have a fan:

But I was like freaking with all these panic attacks. And then I had to go to speak at this conference. I start driving, I get to the bridge and I can't go over. And my heart was pounding, I pulled over to the side of the road, and I realized . . . I'm a driver, I drive in snow, rain, hail, fast, crazy, comfortable, no problem. All of a sudden I can't get over the bridge!

A common complaint for women who found menopause difficult was hot flashes. Joyce (#59), a 49-year-old lesbian, had stopped having daytime hot flashes, but still had to deal with night sweats:

I've had night sweats now, for probably about four years, so I'm kind of used to it. And we put central air in this year, thank Christ, or I wouldn't even be sleeping this summer.

But hot flashes are not the whole story. Deirdre (#52), who experienced what she called 'volcano flashes' for years, found menopause a relief. She was happy to stop menstruating (and to stop buying tampons and dealing with 'messy things') and she found she had more energy. Women who had 'no problem' with menopause feel lucky because they know they had an easier time than many of their friends.

Women sometimes likened the changes of menopause to the changes of adolescence—and felt similarly unprepared. Women in Banister's (1999) study talked about having unanswered questions about menopause. For them, for the most part, useful information comes from other women, not health-care professionals. As is the case for one of our respondents, women may not always agree with their doctors about whether or not they are experiencing menopause. Anita (#12) illuminates this difficulty:

Last year I went to see a doctor. I love doctors. He said, 'Do you have your period?' and I said, 'Yes'. He said, 'Well then you're not in menopause.' I said, 'No. I'm in menopause. I'm telling you.'

Discourses on Depression: Wretched/Gloomy/Miserable Bodies

Women may anticipate that they will be depressed as they approach menopause in the same way they anticipate that they will lose interest in sexual experience or become unattractive. Surveys show that women and their doctors expect women to become depressed and irritable with menopause (Avis, 2003: 91). However, as Avis points out (ibid., 92), research that supports the association of menopause with depression is based on clinic or patient samples—on women whose experience of menopause led them to seek treatment. These are unlikely to be representative samples. As Avis argues, depression experienced by midlife women may be caused by a number of other factors, including stress, poor health, other health problems, some of which are not diagnosed, and prior depression. The Ohio midlife study found that stress was a better predictor of depression than menopause. The best predictor of stress and depression is loss of resources (Glazer et al., 2002). As these findings regarding depression predict, women whose mood was generally positive before menopause experience generally positive moods during menopause (Dennerstein et al., 2001).

While popular discourse associates menopause and midlife crisis with depression, aggregate data suggest that depression affects midlife women less frequently than it affects young women. The Canadian National Population Health survey found that depression is more common among younger than older women and more common among women than men. However, women's depression rates begin to fall at age 45 and the trends for older men and women are very similar. Not surprisingly, depression in women is related to previous depression, feeling overwhelmed, out of control, and lacking in emotional and social support (Beaudet, 2000).

Few of the women in our research study talked about depression as a significant health problem in midlife. Catherine was an exception. She had what she referred to as a horrible menopause that included mood swings and depression. Not all women sense that they are experiencing mood swings. Malina wasn't aware of her changing moods, until her family posted a 'barometer' in the kitchen, with a movable dial to indicate her escalating moods. Then she began to wonder if she was depressed because of her mother's death, or because her husband had been away for a lengthy time, or was it simply menopause? Joanne (#53), a single mother with a heart problem, experienced emotional ups and downs during menopause.

> Emotional health, I seem to be falling apart more than I used to, and maybe it's because now I don't have the kids living there, so I don't have to hold it all in, so that they don't see it. And maybe just going through this menopause thing, I seem to be more emotional than I ever had been in my life. I've always been an emotional person, but I didn't cry as easy or get upset as easy as I do now.

Anita, whose panic attacks began with menopause, worries because her mother had suffered a debilitating depression at menopause.

> My mother went to bed for two years when she went into menopause. And my biggest fear is that I go over the side and am unable to function going into menopause. And I had this real hang-up about it because that's what my mother did. She had a breakdown. She basically fell apart when she went into menopause. . . . And I became at 16 the main caregiver in my home. (Anita, #12)

While few women talked about depression associated with menopause, several talked about other periods of depression. Sharon (#5) attributed the depression in her thirties to financial problems coupled with an unhappy relationship.

> I went through some really rough times in my early thirties where I can recall being depressed to the point of at least having some suicidal thoughts. I didn't

go on a subway for about six months because I didn't think I should do that kind of stuff. So, I am a long way from that. (Sharon, #5)

Susan (#16) talked extensively about weight gains and losses that she now thinks of as an eating disorder. Her account is full of references to low self-worth connected to feelings of lack of control. She has suffered from depression since she was a young teenager and had a particularly low period in her forties. She went on to describe the source of her angst:

> I guess one of the most telling things . . . is . . . [very quietly] I didn't identify that for 20 years . . . is that I've never had goals [crying] or dreams . . . it's just so sad. I just realized over the last 10 years or so . . . I've never felt that I had any significant amount of control over my life to be able to say this is what I aim for in a few years. Not at all . . . and I had just realized in the last while how very sad that is that I never felt like I had enough control. And it started then, because as a teenager I had lots . . . lots.

Chronic Health Concerns

The health of Canadians has improved dramatically over the lifespan of the midlife women in our study. Improved health is a consequence of better treatment of disease, better health habits, and improved standards of living as well as of health promotion efforts focused on quitting smoking, controlling weight, and maintaining activity levels. Midlife women live longer than in previous generations and can expect continued good health in old age. They have benefited from a rising standard of living, universal health care, medical discoveries such as insulin and penicillin, and, of course, the availability of birth control. When penicillin became available in the 1940s it had a dramatic impact on diseases such as tuberculosis, septicemia, pneumonia, and typhoid. By the 1970s, vaccines had become available to treat measles, whooping cough, and scarlet fever (Crompton, 2000: 12–13).

In Chapter 1 we talked about the longevity revolution. Life expectancy has increased over the past century and, typically, women live longer than men. However, as noted in Chapter 5, in Canada this longevity gap appears to be closing. Dropping rates of infant and maternal mortality also contribute to longevity. In 1921, 10 per cent of children died before their first birthday (ibid., 13). Now, that mortality rate is less than 1 per cent.

Both mortality and morbidity vary significantly among subgroups. For example, poor and racialized women are more likely to suffer from chronic disease and disability and die at an earlier age than white women with economic security. Life expectancy for women declines west to east, measuring within provinces from British Columbia to Newfoundland; and mortality rates are higher among rural and northern women. Immigrant women have lower mortality rates, presumably a result of the 'healthy immigrant effect' whereby selection and screening of immigrants favours those in excellent health. This advantage declines over time.

It is commonly thought that women have greater morbidity than men—in other words, that they are more frequently ill. Women are more likely than men to suffer from long-term activity limitations and chronic conditions, such as osteoporosis, arthritis, and migraine headaches. But to suggest that women have higher illness rates than men is an oversimplification—gender differences in health also are socially produced. Perhaps it is more socially acceptable for women to admit illness and to seek medical intervention. Perhaps doctors are more apt to label women's health concerns and distinguish them in terms of morbidity than as 'normal exceptions'. Women report illness, anxiety, and depression and single symptoms such as fatigue and headache more frequently. They also are more frequent users of health care (see Popay and Groves, 2000). However, it is not appropriate from these differences to conclude that women are not as healthy as men.

Women in our study experience a host of chronic conditions from cancer to diabetes; from cardiovascular disease to osteoporosis; from arthritis to fibromyalgia; from stroke to depression. Chronic health problems are a great source of stress for many of the women in the focus groups because they do not have the sort of medical benefits attached to full-time stable employment. For this reason, too, they cannot afford the drugs that would keep their chronic conditions under control (Lynn, 2001: 6).

Some women learn to live with chronic ill health. Becky (#54) is a divorced mother who does contract work and who also has had a series of health issues over the last two decades, most of which have been resolved with surgery. As she said facetiously, 'every time I want to lose weight I've had an organ removed.' The surgeries were not as life-changing, she says, as learning to live with osteoarthritis:

> Most of my leisure activities left my life because of the disease. Everything is a labour, even going up the stairs. I used to think that I just had to strengthen the muscles and I'd be fine, but I don't think that's true any more.

Brenda (#51) talks about two major health transitions. The first was having a large cyst removed. The second was being diagnosed with fibromyalgia. The second diagnosis came as a relief to her because she had been feeling poorly for a long time and was very worried about having a life-threatening illness. Her doctor attributed her health concerns to the standard package—age, weight gain, stress, and depression because of her marriage breakup. A new young doctor in a health clinic identified fibromyalgia:

> It was amazing, I started to cry. I was fearful of having the cancer my mother had, the depression my sister had, I couldn't figure out what to do with these pains, and I was previously told it was all in my head. I spend most of my days in pain, and there's help groups, but I'm alive!

Shantell (#46) moved to Canada from the Caribbean in her twenties. She is diabetic on injected insulin, and has lived with the pain of endometriosis for two decades.

She, like other midlife women we talked to, accepted living with a chronic illness with equanimity. As she says:

> I just take it one day at a time. You can't worry about the things that aren't happening yet. I am aware that my future, because of my history with diabetes, may not be as rosy as somebody else's, but there's no guarantee. I'll just do the best I can. . . . Whatever happens to my body because of the diabetes, I can't control. I can control how I take care of my body.

While many women feel they are taking steps to care for themselves and to be proactive about their health, others worry deeply about the future loss of function—of health matters being taken out of their hands. In some cases their concern stems from their first-hand experience working with the health-care system. Elizabeth (#81) worries that the arthritis she has will be crippling. Primarily, she worries about becoming a burden to her family. She has taken care of people in this situation at work and she doesn't 'want to end up like that'. She is clear that she would rather be dead than have her kids worry about 'what they are going to do with Mom'. Tara (#75) is worried about her future health because in addition to being, as she describes it, severely overweight she has a bad back from 25 years of front-line nursing. She has been told her health is at risk and 'it's finally sunk in that it's time to do something.'

For some, health concerns they encounter signal the beginning of old age. Pamela (#11) is a 47-year-old mother of two in a same-sex relationship. She recently recovered from an operation for bladder control, which for her was a turning point, as it is a procedure she associates with aging. She also worries about genetic predisposition to osteoporosis and breast cancer and wonders what she can do to prevent either of these. Deirdre (#52) worries about arthritis and cancer—arthritis because her mother had it and cancer because she has had it and because she smokes.

Echoing throughout our interviewees' reports are constant worries about illnesses associated with aging, genetic predispositions, and self-pressure to attempt proactively to prevent future health problems. Signs of deteriorating health surround middle-aged women. Many have experienced changes in their own health. Others have observed the deteriorating health of their parents, friends, or partners, and predict that they will have similar experiences. Gail (#14) talks about how difficult it is to see people she loves in pain: 'I have a friend now who is going through great pain. It can be a challenge. She's bedridden. She can't work. She's on disability. She has pain all the time.'

Becoming more aware of and in tune with oneself leads to a greater sense of control regardless of one's health situation. Margaret (#4) talks about having less control of her health in terms of 'anything can happen' and yet becoming more skilled at exercising personal control and becoming more resourceful as she ages. That sense of control seems to increase feelings of optimism. Indeed, despite the experience of physical loss and decline and the onset of chronic health issues, midlife women basically are optimistic about the immediate future.

The Spectre of Cancer

Illness can be a significant turning point for midlife women. In a sense, illness is an equalizer. As a focus group participant said: 'Everything is affected by your health. Whether you are rich or poor, an illness changes everything.'

Although heart disease and cancer account for the greatest numbers of deaths for women, cancer causes the greatest worry.[2] As Lorna (#13) said: 'Well, I guess no one likes that big 'C' word, right? Especially breast cancer.' Fear of breast cancer, in particular, is fuelled by public awareness campaigns such as Breast Cancer Awareness Month (October), Run for the Cure, and the Weekend To End Breast Cancer. Concern is exacerbated because the public health messages have focused on personal responsibility for breast self-examination, rather than on public responsibility regarding environmental causes of the disease.

Women in Robertson's Toronto study were far more worried about breast cancer risk than cardiovascular disease or stroke, even with a family history of the latter. One woman in Robertson's study said she felt 'invincible' as far as the other diseases were concerned, but not regarding breast cancer (Robertson, 2000: 224). Women with relatives with breast cancer talk about their breasts as a time bomb (ibid., 225). Robertson and others argue that the fear of breast cancer is disproportionate to the risk. On the other hand, the incidence is rising and so is the number of deaths.

Many women in our study talked about their deep fear of cancer, particularly of breast cancer:

> All you have to do is read the paper. Cancer is the number-one killer of women . . . statistically you've got to have a miracle not to have cancer in your lifetime . . . so sure, I don't want to have cancer. (Phyllis, #3)

Jennifer (#60) says: 'I'm terrified, just like all women are, of breast cancer.' Over and over, this preoccupation with genetic risk enters women's discussion of health concerns. Not surprisingly, the fear of cancer was exacerbated for women with relatives with the disease. They seem to have a very strong belief that biology may be destiny in this regard:

> . . . my mother died in her fifties from cancer; her mother had it, and her grandmother had it, so for sure that has an impact. (Margaret, #4)

> I am at the same age my mother was, when she was dying of cancer. (Rita, #1)

> I fear cancer because it's prevalent in my family. My mother had breast cancer and then it went to the bone. All but one of her sisters died that way. My older sister died of breast cancer. (Brenda, #51)

This fear of cancer is reinforced as midlife women await results of regular mammograms or a biopsy. Nancy (#2), a 54-year-old married mother of two children, describes her experience:

I just had a mammogram and that was scary, my first mammogram. I did the mammogram and they kept asking me to come back for more tests and finally they didn't find anything, they were getting a benchmark. But it took a very long time.

When viewed from a life course perspective, a turning point 'is a disruption in the trajectory, a deflection in the path' (Wheaton and Gotlib, 1997: 1). Cancer is such a turning point for too many Canadians. Indeed, the extent of the change occasioned by cancer has been referred to as an existential crisis. The fear that surrounds diagnosis and treatment encourages a search for meaning. As Arthur Frank (1991: 3) has said so eloquently: 'Being ill is just another way of living, but by the time we have lived through illness we are living differently.'

Eleven women in our study have been diagnosed with cancer. Lesley (#19) was 51, married, a mother of three daughters and a grandmother of two. In the interview she describes her initial reaction and her subsequent decision to frame her life differently:

The diagnosis was confirmed on December 1st, although I knew it by the middle of November. And then at Christmas, I received in the mail—there were all these subscription renewals and membership renewals and I put them all in the garbage can, because what am I going to need my magazines or my memberships for? I threw them in the garbage. We were at the cottage for Christmas and in that three days I made the decision to not be a victim of cancer. And I fished them out of the garbage and I renewed them for as long as I could, which was three years.

She describes the transformative effect of her cancer diagnosis:

Cancer gave me an out. . . . I was a fringe person in all groups all my life. But I never was truly connected to anybody, because I wasn't getting involved in any of them, I was just a visitor. And I think I was that way with all my relationships—my husband, my family. I've been that way, I can see, all my life, for various reasons. Then the diagnosis of cancer, and I immediately went, 'Oh, I don't have to be this way, I can change.'

As Lesley began to reach out to others, her relationships and her feelings of self-worth began to shift: 'I thought I was the only one that was in pain. Once you open up and say "I'm in pain" others say "I'm in pain, too." And you really need to support each other.'

A Midlife Search for Meaning

As we said at the beginning of this book, a study of middle-aged men gave birth to the notion of a male midlife crisis. A key issue facing men in Eliot Jacques's (1965) study is their confrontation with death. A number of women in our study talk about confronting death when a friend or family member dies or when they or someone they love is diagnosed with a life-threatening disease. Not surprisingly, by this age many women have experienced the death of one or both parents. The death of a parent, especially the second parent, is a major turning point for most people—a time to confront their own mortality (Aldwin and Levenson, 2001: 195).

A few women in our study are widows and another handful had experienced the death of a child or close friend. Some of the women we interviewed confront death as part of their work as palliative care workers or nurses, or have been acquainted with death and dying in their connections with HIV/AIDS care in the gay community. Confronting directly or indirectly one's own or another's mortality can be both a crisis and an opportunity for reflection. Stressful events can become meaningful turning points (Wethington et al., 1997). Pamela (#11) talks about experiencing the death of people who were close to her:

> I mean it's recreating; you think about recreating how you want to live the rest of your life, what things are important. You have to go through an evaluation. . . . It's like almost being 20 again and all that new stuff. It's happening right now to many of us. I don't know whether it's menopause, or whether it's coming to a place where you know more.

For some, the search for meaning is a spiritual search. Ruth (#6) has experienced the death of both parents, and had been close to two women friends who died of cancer. These deaths created a desire

> . . . to understand what one can never understand, regarding mortality, regarding what is beyond death, regarding the importance of life . . . or, indeed, if there is something outside of oneself—the Divine.

This longing for spiritual connection and meaning is also evident in the following remarks:

> It's not like we're not religious, but you wouldn't call us the practising religious. But yes, there is a time of sickness and a time of death it makes you wonder if there is something more out there than day-to-day life. (Lenora, #41)

Considerable evidence points to the connection between religion, **spirituality**, and health. The epidemiology of religion (Levin, 2001) refers to an impressive body of research investigating the relationships between religion and morbidity and mortality. Systematic reviews conclude that religious involvement has a statistically significant protective effect on health. The relationship persists when controls for health behaviour and socio-demographic variables are introduced (ibid.). Religion, as Levin (ibid., 201) describes it, is 'epidemiologically protective'. In other words, research suggests that those who consider themselves 'religious', whether they are rich or poor, male or female, reap a health benefit from their faith.

Our interviews support this link since these midlife women do tend to frame their experience of crises such as illness as spiritual journeys. In a focus group participant's words, 'the threat of death brought life, awakening, and freedom.' Similarly, midlife women in Howell and Beth's (2002) study talk extensively about spirituality. Many discover spirituality through 12-step programs related to recovery from periods of alcohol or drug abuse. Some return to religious practices they had long abandoned. Others actively seek out religious community. Some women in our study talk about how religion provides community and others refer to empowerment.

Most references to religion or spirituality are made in the context of finding meaning in illness or in the death of a friend or family member, or of confronting another significant issue in life, such as abuse. As Amy (#20) tries to explain, 'I think the spirituality is part of what's inside of you, and once you heal yourself you can deal with other people differently.' Thus, Esther's (#7) sense of spirituality developed out of her experience of abuse. As she described it, there was a point at which she said: 'there has to be more.' She made a decision: 'I have to live or die, and if I live it's going to be on my terms.' With that decision she left the abusive relationship, and eventually was drawn to Judaism for help in finding meaning in her experiences.

Carla (#26), who had lost both parents and a child, described her knowledge of death as a spiritual experience:

My base has been religious, and I would say that people who I've loved and been close to have died, their deaths are profound spiritual experiences for me. . . . Funerals give me great hope . . . I don't think words can describe it. Funerals increase the depth of my faith.

The larger social context for this religiosity and spirituality is contradictory. It is not clear whether religion and spirituality are becoming more or less important to Canadians. Worldwide, the rise of religious fundamentalism is perceived by many as threatening. The rise of fundamentalism in North America, especially in the United States, is regarded cautiously by many. Canada, on the other hand, appears to be an increasingly secular society. Attendance at religious services has declined in the post-war years. Less than one-third of Canadians attend religious services at least monthly, although 'over one-half (54 percent) engage in religious activities [prayer, meditation] on their own at least monthly' (Clark and Schellenberg, 2006: 3). Religious attendance at places of worship increases with age, as does the tendency to pray or meditate. Immigrants are more apt to engage in both public and private religious behaviour than Canadian-born citizens, although levels of religiosity vary among immigrants according to region of origin. As Clark and Schellenberg conclude, declining attendance may not reflect an increase in secularity.

Generally, religion becomes more important with age, and women, more than men, are more apt to say that religion is important to them and to have a high sense of religiosity (ibid., 6–7). The majority of our respondents were (or had once been) Christian or Jewish, so their comments often include images of a deity. On the whole, however, the existential search described by the women in this study was less about institutional religion than about a deeply personal spirituality. As Shana (#63) said:

> The whole religious part for me has never been a smooth process. But my spirituality, I'm comfortable, I'm secure. But the whole religion thing is confusing.

Judy (#50) said:

> I feel spiritual, I feel connectedness to life, a life force. I feel I have an old soul, that I've been around more than once, probably . . . .

For some women spirituality and feminism are linked. As Nicole (#45) explains:

> There is still something about Christianity that has never held me. It's so arid and dry and the beliefs are patriarchal, and like a lot of women in my generation we discovered the Goddess [a female deity] and all those other wonderful writers. I was drawn to all the stuff about the inner tribe. My life has been enriched by that. That's why I can't identify myself in any particular religious world.

An increased sense of spirituality is an important aspect of midlife development (Jung, 1960; Brewi and Brenna, 1999). Baby boomers are increasingly drawn to spirituality (Roof, 1999). 'As baby boomers age and grapple with their own mortality and the death of loved ones, there is a growing impetus to explore the meaning of life and the mystery of a spiritual afterlife' (Walsh and Pryce, 2003: 338). Babyboomer women separate the spiritual and the religious in a way that is likely unique to their generation. 'The baby boomer woman's spiritual journey is to find a connection between life and meaning and about finding a way to express it' (Payne-Stancil, 1997: 235).

It could be that age is important in the search for meaning—or, alternately, that midlife women are more apt to experience the kinds of life crises that precipitate a search for meaning. Indeed, as Crowther et al. (2002) argue, aging involves interdependent, biological, psychological, social, and *spiritual* processes. These authors make a strong case that positive spirituality be added to the model for successful aging proposed by Rowe and Kahn (1997). The meaning system provided by religion and spirituality 'provides the ageing person with resources to optimize the process of change and eventually to accept irreversible decline and its consequences' (Marcoen, 2005: 364). Certainly, for many women in this study, health, well-being, and spirituality are closely connected.

Shana (#63) describes how a connection to nature helped her endure the crisis of immigration. She grew up close to the ocean and feels that her sense of spirituality developed from her childhood connection to water. She describes how she used to:

... go to the ocean and meditate, and I started thinking the universe is bigger than me. You know, there's a reason for this and there's a reason why these things happen to you . . . like I'm close to God if I'm close to the ocean.

Susan (#16) experienced a loss of faith during a period of depression.

I had a major, major, horrible, horrendous depression around 40, and I don't think it had to do with the age . . . it was my circumstances at the time, and that was the time I lost all faith in God, which meant for me losing my whole way of looking at life and thinking about myself and everything, so it was awful. A year ago, I had a turning point in the opposite direction, and had a significant spiritual experience, and read a wonderful book on health in general, and for some reason the combination of whatever was going on jump-started me into a healthier way of living . . . started eating less and walking lots . . . and so have lost a lot of weight in the last year.

Some combination of spirituality and religion fosters a sense of equanimity for many midlife women. For Nicole (#45), her faith allows her to face death without fear:

I have an implicit faith in something, but it's sort of nameless. It's a balance and a harmonizing. I don't fear death. I like the idea of reincarnation, but I also want to wait and see what happens. . . . when I immersed myself in studying different religions in my thirties, I went to different kinds of churches and I tested a few things out, [so] I'm not afraid of death but I'm not in any rush.

Conclusion

For the women in our study, decisions to live more consciously are often triggered by an illness or a brush with death. Both experiences become more common at middle age. The experience of loss, whether of expectations for self or of physical or emotional kinds, prompts at least a transition, at most a transformation. Living more consciously leads to a greater sense of control regardless of one's health situation. Margaret (#4) talked simultaneously about having less control of her health in terms of 'anything can happen' yet becoming more skilled at exercising personal control and becoming more resourceful as she aged. That sense of control seems to increase feelings of optimism. Despite the experience of physical loss and decline and the onset of chronic health issues, midlife women seem basically optimistic about the future. For example, Gail (#14) simply takes time at this stage of her life to walk and enjoy being out of doors: 'I feel optimistic that I think my health is better than it was a year ago. I will take whatever comes and do the best that I can.'

Midlife women experience health concerns—from the minor (some loss of eyesight or hearing) to the major (cancer, diabetes, stroke, or heart disease). In response to worries about health and decline, women claim to think and act differently about their health in midlife. Regardless of class or ability, women make jokes about their ailments and share coping strategies. They talk about some of the ways they try to maintain their health as they age. These include the obvious ones of losing weight, quitting smoking, becoming 'clean and sober', beginning to exercise, or making an effort to live a healthy lifestyle by focusing on fitness, nutrition, and vitamins. They also describe a shift in their sense of self and talk about living more consciously as they age.

Women at this life stage face setback and health crises, and some face death, either through a life-threatening illness or as friends die. Nevertheless, they have developed a repertoire of strategies and have accumulated psychological resources that enable them to manage the exigencies they confront. Esther (#7) describes her situation as follows:

> I don't know, it's like, here I am, and I'm this woman, and I've been through all these things, and people might stop and say, 'oh, what an awful life', but that's the way it was, and there's no turning back, and there's no getting someone else's life. . . . I try to take away something positive from that, and say 'I won't treat people that way.' . . . At this age I feel like I have more control of my life, or I'm able to take more control and steer the boat where I want to be, and the rest of my life's up to me.

Perhaps, as Deirdre (#52) argues, the greatest health strategy is self-acceptance:

> When I think of other women, being self-critical is very important because then you know what your strengths and weaknesses are. I think the most important thing is to be comfortable with your body. I think you become more comfortable through self-acceptance: self-acceptance of your strengths, limits, whatever. I guess the values that really enrich one's life are the things we've been talking about throughout this interview. People are looking for meaning in life. I think it's in the ordinary things around us, appreciating what's around us. I can't really pin it down. I think I said it in the interview. Also, I don't think we're an island. Accept yourself, age gracefully, enjoy it. Be intellectually alive, curious, physically engaged, involved in community, family, friends. I don't believe in being some mythical physical being that culture says you should be. Have balance, interdependence, understanding of others, be more tolerant. We need to waste less time about ourselves.

Key Concepts

Discourse on aging sexuality Dominant social conversation that assumes aging men can be sexy while aging women cannot.

Discourses of loss and decline Two dominant social conversations about aging in which aging is associated with social losses and physical decline.

Health and well-being According to the World Health Organization, a state of complete physical, mental, and social well-being, not merely the absence of disease and infirmity.

Healthism and weightism The idea that individuals can control their health and weight, and, indeed, have a moral obligation to do so.

Spirituality A search for meaning that may or may not be associated with religious practice or the presence of a higher power.

Questions for Critical Discussion

1. How would you describe your current health and well-being? To what extent is your description tied to your age?

2. In Western cultures, aging is associated with loss and decline. Do you see any signs that the longevity revolution has begun to foster another, more positive discourse about aging?

3. The women in this study expressed feelings of guilt that they had gained weight and weren't exercising enough. Do men and women feel equally guilty about weight gain and lack of exercise? Does this vary for adolescents, young adults, midlifers, and older adults?

4. Why are older women not considered sexy while younger women are seen as the epitome of sexiness? When do women become unsexy? Are there examples from contemporary films that address this phenomenon?

5. Many women in this study talked about experiences of spiritual connection at midlife. In what social, cultural, or personal circumstances might spiritual meaning develop at earlier life stages?

6. Aging women's bodies are described as 'raging'. What adjective would you use to describe young women's bodies?

Chapter 8

Ambivalence and an Ambiguous Future

Midlife Women: The Demographic Tsunami

As midlife Canadian women living in the beginning years of the twenty-first century, we do not often locate our lives in terms of history or social forces. Encouraged by our culture to experience our biographies in individualistic terms—luck, chance, ability, beauty—and to be caught up in the day-to-day, month-to-month momentum of life, it is easy to go along without thinking of the ways our existence is framed by social and historical factors that most often are hidden from us (Hunt, 2002). In the preceding chapters we have sought to draw attention to the ways in which an entire generation of women were born into a historical and social moment of intense change and how that change now offers prospects for freedom and containment, progress and retrenchment.

According to the 2006 census, the baby boomers continue on track as a massive shift in the age profile. Baby boomers (born between 1946 and 1965) are now between 42 and 61 years of age and comprise the largest segment of the population—nearly one in three Canadians. Since women outnumber men in the general population, baby-boomer women constitute the largest gendered cohort in the population. As middle-aged women move into the elderly category in 2011, the proportion of seniors in the Canadian population is expected to nearly double and seniors will outnumber children. Government analysts anticipate that this huge demographic wave will 'have a major impact on the labour force, on public pension and health insurance plans and, in general, on the Canadian economy and society' (Statistics Canada, 2007: 7).

The midlife women interviewed here are part of this looming generation of senior women. Their sheer numbers suggest they are positioned to have a dramatic impact on the evolution of Canadian society. When the size of this age cohort is combined with its distinctive historical position—notably, its roots in the profound changes in the family, women's roles, economic restructuring, the partial dismantling of the welfare state, and so on—it seems poised to make a significant contribution to the discourses on both gender and aging. The nature of that contribution will depend on a wide variety of factors, but particularly on baby-boomer women's self-awareness as historical agents and their commitment to social change and agency.

Patterns within Individuation: Traditionalists, Radicals, and In-Betweens

At first glance, the impact of the great social changes that occurred in the second half of the last century may appear to have created an enormous variety of individual responses, contingent on the vagaries of luck, opportunity, ability, and so on. Certainly, research suggests that the lives of Canadians are characterized by increasing variability in the life course as traditional norms and institutions of social control (notably, religion and the family) decline in their influence. Old patterns of home-leaving, first union, first marriage, and first and last birth have disappeared as unattached adults, boomerang children, abortion, divorce, extramarital and premarital relations, and single parenthood have become more commonplace. While women's ages at family life transitions still are more homogeneous than men's, even the prevailing pattern—marriage in late twenties and children during thirties—may fade as biological constraints are reduced by reproductive technologies as well as by increased frequency of childlessness (Ravanera et al., 2004). Given these trends, it is not surprising that in our research we heard from women who were living very traditional lives—lives that mirrored those of their mothers' generation—and also from midlifers who were creating entirely new family forms—for example, as they established long-term relationships and marriages as lesbians with children. The diversity is so wide that it is often difficult to discern the commonalities, and some theorists (as discussed in Chapter 6) have, in fact, used this trend towards individuation to characterize life in the postmodern world (Jones et al., 1990).

However, within this trend towards life course diversification, it is possible to infer patterns and commonalities. For example, based on their interviews with middle-aged women, Howell and Beth (2002) argue for a developmental understanding of midlife aging. Specifically, they propose a three-stage developmental pattern. At first, their respondents struggle with the negative stereotypes of middle-aged women, exhibiting anger, confusion, and rebelliousness. During the second stage, they are reflective as they work out the changes in their lives, particularly in terms of their bodies, finances, and significant relationships. In the third and final stage, once they achieve clarity about their personal values and life circumstances (sometimes through 12-step programs or religion), they adjust to their midlife status with a modicum of emotional comfort. However, as Howell and Beth stress, these processes are not linear. Rather, women experience various changes at different times, some going through stages more than once and with markedly different levels of emotional distress.

While Howell and Beth offer an interesting effort to address the contradictory and complex patterns of midlife aging, as discussed in Chapter 1, we are more concerned here with women's roles as historical actors and in the framing of their lives by structural factors. Teasing out the patterns within the contradictions and diversity of middle-aged women's lives is a difficult and, at best, tentative undertaking. As discussed in the preceding chapters, boomer women have lived through many momentous changes—historical and social events that have produced an expansion of personal options and alternatives as well as profound shifts in institutional structures. As a result, their stories are a complex and sometimes contradictory weaving of triumphs and crises, joys and sorrows, and accomplishments and failures. However, we suggest that certain patterns—clusters of beliefs, values, and experiences—point to the confluence of historical and social pressures with individual biographies.

First, there appears to be a significant, though minority, contingent of midlife women whose lives are characterized by considerable continuity and traditionalism. They have maintained a more traditional life course and tend to embrace more traditional beliefs and values (Luxton, 1983). Despite the growing **urbanization** of Canadian society, there are numerous smaller towns, rural areas, and urban enclaves that both encourage and allow women to focus the bulk of their energies on marriage, motherhood, and family. These women are not necessarily excluded from the paid labour force, but their participation is likely to be pre-marriage and post-child-rearing and is frequently on a part-time, episodic, and/or marginal basis. More importantly, this participation in paid employment is subordinated to responsibilities in the home. Traditional values tend to emphasize women's roles as wives and mothers and the primacy of the family over personal concerns. Paid employment is accepted as a necessity while also often being experienced as a stressful distraction from familial responsibilities. This traditional life course is often buttressed by community-based, socially conservative institutions, such as the church, synagogue, or mosque. In immigrant communities even second- and third-generation women may be pressured and/or supported to embrace a traditional role in the family. Given the large (and growing) number of immigrant families in Canada and given that research is now documenting the impact of ethnic and cultural diversity on women's experiences of midlife, it is important to recognize the pressures towards traditionalism experienced by many midlife Canadian women in the Chinese, Muslim, Orthodox Jewish, Hindu, and other minority and immigrant communities (Wray, 2007; Ho et al., 2003; Zhan, 2005).

Here, it is crucial to emphasize that simple demographic or employment characteristics do not clearly identify the more traditional midlife women. In particular, contrary to some recent analyses, full-time homemakers and full-time paid workers do not provide categories neatly dividing the traditional from the non-traditional (Hirshman 2006). Several of our personal acquaintances[1] are full-time homemakers who still embrace a postmodern gender role. Claire, for example, was the daughter of a working-class mother who had been employed throughout her life. Claire did not marry until her late thirties and only upon discovering she was pregnant. She now has two children, aged 12 and 14, and in every superficial respect appears to be a stereotypical stay-at-home soccer mom. Although she is in her fifties and her children are relatively independent, she has no intention of taking paid employment (despite encouragement from her husband to do so). She irons her husband's shirts and is active in the local schools; but her husband does most of the cooking, home decorating, and household cleaning. She anticipates that her daughters will go to college or university and pursue some kind of professional employment throughout much of their lives, just like Claire's older sister, who is a married, childless lawyer. Claire's life as a full-time wife/mother is the result of a complex mixture of factors, including her lack of educational qualifications, her ability, with careful money management, to afford to stay home, and, prominently, her belief in the value of her role in the home and her enjoyment of her complex role in child-rearing and home-making.

Rachel is, in essence, a midlife stay-at-home mother because her husband's income means her paid employment is superfluous to their economic needs and because she prefers to be very involved in and supportive of her children's lives and to have time simultaneously to indulge her own creativity and to enrich her family's life; for example, by preparing homemade, culturally traditional meals for her family. She also spends considerable time providing care for her elderly parents. However, Rachel also is far from simply traditional. On her own, she immigrated to Canada from the Philippines to pursue her education. She has actively pursued and strongly emphasized the highest academic standards for her daughters, one of whom is already in graduate school, and she fully expects them both to pursue professional careers. While the lives of Claire, Rachel, and many others are framed around child-rearing and homemaking, what is not evidenced in their stories is a sense of having sacrificed self for family or children, a belief in the unequivocal primacy of women's roles as wives and mothers, and an acceptance of male superiority.

Conversely, there are certainly midlife women who are paid employees and inclined to embrace more patriarchal beliefs and values. They characterize their employment as a necessity (typically economic) and struggle to maintain traditional standards in the home despite their paid work obligations (see Luxton, 1983). Their comments suggest they believe that the best life course for women in general is marriage, child-rearing, and then grandmothering; they discuss their personal value in terms of their contributions as wives and mothers. Careers for women, along with feminism in general, are characterized as a threat or a mistake, particularly as evidenced in abortion and lesbian rights. From this perspective, women who do not devote themselves to their husbands and children are seen as missing out on the best life has to offer or as 'unnatural' or as, simply, bad wives and mothers. In short, it is the meanings that women attach to their lives and to the lives of other women that reflect their relative traditionalism rather than their status as stay-at-home mothers or full-time employees.

Most contemporary research suggests that relatively few midlife women are living out a completely traditional life.[2] Of course, this category and others are fluid and, indeed, change over the life course. A midlife woman may self-describe as traditional at 20, radical at 30, and ambivalent at 50. With this caveat, even midlife women who, for example, describe themselves as emphatically 'not feminists' are affected by the dramatic changes encouraged by the women's movement, the gay/lesbian rights movement, the sexual revolution, the movement of wives/mothers into paid employment, and the general secularization of Canadian society. Indeed, it often seems that their comments are referenced to the unspoken criticism that they should have had careers or that they are allowing themselves to be downtrodden in their marriages. However, while they may acknowledge the paths not taken, most steadfastly assert the moral and logical rightness of their lives. They were, for example, 'there' for their children and their husbands.

At the other end of the continuum are women who, for various reasons, seem to have more completely shed the 1950s discourse on gender. Among this more radical contingent, some had mothers or, even, grandmothers who were part of the feminist vanguard. Private and public equality for women along with accomplishments in the public domain were part of their earliest socialization and they never doubted the necessity of finding a path of their own. Some embraced a lesbian lifestyle in which they are the primary breadwinner; others are single parents who have long accepted the duality of their responsibilities to provide for their children both economically and emotionally; still others are intentionally childless and have thereby dodged the pressures of the motherhood script. Some grew into non-traditionalism as successes in education, at work, and/or in a career contributed to a rethinking of their self-worth as well as their life goals. These women sometimes express 'selfishness' and 'ambition' without a great deal of anguish or personal recrimination. They acknowledge coming home late, disappointing their children, and/or letting their partners (or adult children) shoulder the lion's share of the household work. Some become at ease with this more radical stance later in life as a result of divorce, a health crisis, or engagement with feminist organizations and issues. In each instance, their lives are such dramatic departures from the norms of the 1950s that there is relatively little spoken evidence of an ongoing inner or outer dialogue with the more traditional paradigm of the good wife and mother.

Finally, there are the clear majority of interviewees whose lives have been transformed by the social changes emanating from the 1960s and 1970s but who remain in some sense grounded in many of the beliefs, values, and social practices of the 1950s. In this context, it is important to emphasize how profound and pervasive the social changes have been. The basic forms of day-to-day life have been altered, including beliefs, values, normative standards, and social expectations. Like Alice in *Alice Through the Looking Glass*, midlife women have lived through a revolution in public and private behaviour. It would be inconceivable, for example, to the average midlife woman in the 1950s that gays and lesbians would be the main characters in television series; that there would be female celebrities who were openly lesbian; that extensive profanity would enter the lexicon of typical middle-class children; that there would be a public discussion of a US President's sexual antics; that gay and lesbian marriages would be legitimized by the state; that women's right to publicly display their breasts would be enshrined in law; that among students studying to become medical doctors, women would outnumber men; that a husband could be successfully prosecuted for raping his wife; that young women would play football and hockey on men's teams. Midlife women have experienced all this upheaval and much more, depending on their own personal and community roots. Yet, they have not been provided with nor have they produced themselves the structural changes—

state-provided child care, shared domestic labour, state funding of women's domestic work, 50–50 marriages, and so on—that would allow for an unimpeded move into a completely non-traditional reality. As a result, this third and largest segment of midlife women tends to be caught in the structured ambivalence discussed in Chapter 1.

Control and Compromise: The Ambivalent Generation

Given the profundity of the social changes experienced by baby-boomer women, it is not surprising that most of the midlife women in our research indicate that they are aware of living through a dynamic and important period. After all, for their mothers' generation, dodging the stultifying drudgery of household work and creating some agency in life was couched in terms of 'marrying a millionaire' or 'making a good catch'.[3] In contrast, midlife women know that some members of their generation opened up new possibilities for women in the labour force, rejected traditional heterosexual codes, and challenged many of the worst aspects of patriarchy. They are aware of being in various ways 'liberated' from the more punitive restrictions on women's lives—the shaming and ostracizing of unwed mothers, the stigmatizing of sexually active single women, the social constrictions imposed by the demand for 'ladylike' behaviour, and the generalized exclusion of most women, especially wives and mothers, from the public domain. The women's movement and the sexual revolution meant that as young women they were freer to control and explore their sexuality, including premarital sex, that they were aware of alternative sexual orientations such as lesbianism and bisexuality, and that they could consider voluntary childlessness along with other alternatives.

Although much of the role rigidity associated with being a woman has been eroded, much remains untouched. In various key respects, many midlife women's lives share a marked continuity with those of their mothers. For example, despite the feminist critiques of the ideology of romantic love and its role in dictating women's choices (Greer, 1970), midlife women typically embraced the belief that they would and should find a sexual/life partner and 'live happily ever after'. As evidenced right through to the present, wedding rituals with brides in white gowns being given away by their fathers are still popularly marketed as a pinnacle event in a woman's life. While the marriage may happen later in life and be preceded by a period of common-law marriage, the fundamental message remains the same. Similarly, the **motherhood mystique**,[4] despite feminist challenges and the voluntary childlessness movement (Nelson, 2006: 340–1), was taken for granted by most of our interviewees as a prerequisite to a fulfilled female existence. In these ways, many midlife women's lives can be seen to be framed by the traditional discourses—the primacy of interpersonal relationships over alternative life projects (such as adventures, explorations, artistic achievements, and so forth) along with the desirability of self-sacrifice, even self-abnegation, in support of those relationships. In this regard, often, the double day simply is to be managed or survived until a more reasonable life arrangement can be reached. Similarly, the failure of women to prioritize their own health and well-being also speaks to the continued acceptance of self-denial—a pattern that presumably explains the persistent tendency for women, regardless of age, to have lower self-esteem than men and for older women to report some of the lowest levels of self-esteem (McMullin and Cairney 2004).[5]

Further, gendered appearance norms still reverberate powerfully through many midlife women's lives—the enormous market for cosmetics, clothing (for women and their children), furnishings, and so on testify to women's perhaps uneasy acceptance of the need to satisfy certain image requirements. Even though this theme did not emerge as a significant dimension in our research and despite the fact many interviewees say that they are comfortable with their aging appearance, the sheer number of cosmetic products and procedures being offered to middle-aged women suggests that, culturally, there is some deep-seated ambivalence about wrinkles, age spots, grey hair, and so on. Certainly, the research that exists on the topic suggests that older women are much more likely than their male counterparts to use cosmetic and other techniques to reduce or mask the signs of aging (Hatch, 2005). Further, to the degree to which midlife women accept the requirement that they, as women, must live up to certain standards of appearance (weight, hair colour, youthfulness),[6] women also commit to a considerable unpaid employment in the service of consumption.

In short, various traditional assumptions about women's roles and responsibilities reverberate into the present, since the traditional structures supporting the family and paid work remain remarkably unchanged. In this context, it is understandable that midlife women would both embrace and distance themselves from feminism: 'I'm not a feminist but . . .' They accept that paid employment is part of the modern relationship bargain, but they are not provided with mechanisms for negotiating the conflicting demands of paid work and family. Daycare, for example, was and is to be individually negotiated and managed—employers and the state by and large have opted out of any responsibility for making this manageable (McDaniel, 2004). Frequently stressed and resentful of the double burden of earning an income and caregiving, women are encouraged to seek strategies to ease the burden rather than to challenge the overall arrangement. After all, they typically are employed in institutions and organizations where men occupy most of the key power positions and in which men, as a rule, continue to earn more money than women, especially wives and mothers (Frenette and Coulombe, 2007). As a result, it is not surprising that many employed midlife women seem to feel profoundly ambivalent about the compromises they have made (not being there for the kids) and their achievements (not getting the education they should have). Their lives, after all, are structured by contradictory demands and framed by inadequate social supports.

The bulk of midlife women in our research appear to be caught between agency and compromise, between clarity and ambivalence. Their lives are characterized both by conformity—most married and most had children—and by control—they divorce, they reject abusive relationships, they demand a financial say or assert economic independence, they pursue meaningful employment (or insist on time at home), they lobby for breast cancer research and support, they expect significant equality in their marriages, and their social world extends well beyond the family. The two tendencies—compliance and agency—often coexist in an uneasy and dynamic standoff.[7]

As these women now surge in a generational tidal wave towards their senior years they are likely to confront profound challenges. Whether they draw on their prior experiences with agency, their sense of themselves as 'pioneers', and their experiences with both community and social activism remains to be seen. Unlike many preceding and subsequent generations of women, this cohort has both the numbers and the historical experience to make its mark. Finally, current developments at the intersections between baby boomers and health, employment, and family suggest that, as women and as seniors, they will likely have little choice but to respond to emergent changes in the structuring of their lives.

Emerging Points of Resistance: Work, Family, and Health

In earlier chapters we discussed the conflict that midlife women have experienced as paid employees juggling their caregiving responsibilities and health-care concerns. In the near future, this struggle is likely to intensify dramatically. For example, there will be growing social (and likely economic) pressure on seniors, especially women (since they outnumber their male counterparts), to continue to participate in the paid labour force. Government officials are expressing alarm at the shortfall in the available labour force that will appear as the baby-boom generation passes age 65. Already, in Canada and globally, the need is being recognized for policy changes that will encourage workers to stay employed past retirement and fill this gap in the labour market created by reduced fertility and population aging. While immigration has been touted as a partial solution to the shrinking number of younger workers, this strategy cannot satisfy the needs of employers. From the governmental perspective, one preferred solution is to 'encourage' workers 65 and older to remain working (Townsend, 2006). While this approach is sorely lacking in specifics, the media have picked up on the theme and are lauding the benefits of continuing to be socially and intellectually engaged in the workforce past the retirement age of 65. After all, according to this rhetoric, 65 is the new 45 and workers can reasonably anticipate living into their early eighties. Of course, popular discourse about 'Freedom 55' and the glowing prospects for adventure and leisure for 'early' retirees would presumably disappear in this version of the future.

The emergent scenario holds both promise and threat for current midlife women. Many, as discussed in the employment chapter, have not accumulated the pension benefits of a lifetime of full employment. Working-class women, single mothers, divorced women, disabled women, and visible minority and recent immigrant women all are particularly likely to lack the material resources that would translate into a leisurely retirement (Arber, 2004). Postponing retirement would allow them to improve their economic situations as well as permit them to further develop jobs and careers that may have had a late start due to family responsibilities. In this respect, the recent elimination of mandatory retirement may be seen as a boon for women.

However, at present most women do not work past age 65 and many withdraw from the labour market before reaching that age.[8] Many analysts explain this early withdrawal in terms of two major reasons. First, women often face considerable caregiving responsibilities. Typically, women marry older men and as a result they may become caregivers as their husbands' health declines with age. Similarly, as discussed earlier, they are likely to shoulder the lion's share of care for aging parents and in-laws. In addition, there have been sharp increases in the numbers of boomerang children (adult children who return—or do not leave—the parental home) living at home while they seek to get an economic or employment toehold. This means that women's responsibilities as mothers (however reduced) may persist well beyond those of earlier generations. Finally, as indicated by several of our more traditional respondents, there may be the expectation that as grandmothers they will provide their adult children with the kinds of child-care services that are otherwise unavailable to working mothers. In addition, a small but growing number of grandparents (again, primarily grandmothers) are taking on full-time responsibility for their grandchildren because of their adult children's physical, emotional, or drug-related problems, or run-ins with the criminal justice system (coupled with the inadequacies of the social welfare system). All these caregiving responsibilities may mean that paid employment is simply too stressful or unmanageable for many midlife and older women.

Second, given that women have been encouraged to prioritize their family responsibilities regardless of their paid employment status, many midlife women find themselves in dead-end, uninteresting, poorly compensated, and non-prestigious jobs. Given the current trends in the 'new' economy—the growth of low-paid service-sector employment, the expansion in various forms of peripheral employment, the decline in the well-paid public sector, and the loss of well-paid, secure unionized work—it will likely be difficult for most women, especially 'older' women, to secure a 'good' job. Of course, even if their jobs are challenging or the workplace provides important social connections, the lack of economic rewards may make employment seem not worth the effort—particularly when there are other pressing and personal demands on women's time and energy.

Health is a crucial component to these shifts in family caregiving and paid employment. Clearly, catastrophic and life-threatening illnesses are going to undermine involvement in both areas. However, the so-called minor aches and pains of aging also are likely to impede involvement in family life, caregiving, and paid work and to be aggravated by burdensome responsibilities in the home or labour force. Aging often involves becoming familiar with a whole range of 'minor' health complaints. Pain develops in the soles of the feet (plantar fasciitis); teeth and gums deteriorate and need treatment; back pain from arthritis and disk deterioration is common; eyes not only become near-sighted but almost routinely develop cataracts and other ailments; even among young seniors arthritic joints impede mobility and patients join the long lines for hip and knee replacements. Psycho-emotional ailments, in particular depression, often accompany aging (Miech and Shanahan, 2000). A recent National Population Health Survey that followed a group of middle-aged (45–64) Canadians from 1994–5 to 2002–3 reports that 56 per cent of healthy, middle-aged adults died or lost their 'good health' over the course of this eight-year period (Martel et al., 2005). While paid employment and caregiving may be sources of enormous personal satisfaction and social connection, it is important to acknowledge that the typical **aging body** may have a limited capacity to continue to shoulder these responsibilities (Marshall, 2001).

On the one hand, policy analysts plan to call on older women (and men) to stay employed as the baby boomers turn 65. On the other hand, there continues to be a lack of concrete social support for women's paid and unpaid work and for the realities of health decline that routinely accompany aging (Twigg, 2004). Further, the growing inadequacies of the health-care system in responding to illness and disability in an aging population are accompanied by numerous reductions in a whole spectrum of social services that previously assisted women as single parents, mothers of disabled children, and so on, all of which suggests that there are going to be more and more pressures on women of all ages, including senior women, to fill in for the shortfall in caregiving in our society (McDaniel, 2004). The intensification that women have experienced in their responsibilities as wives and mothers—now that they routinely are expected to take paid employment to contribute some economic support to their families—will extend to older women in the form of 'encouragement' to continue their paid employment into their senior years.

Just as the women's movement of the 1960s and 1970s was able to catalyze the anger, frustration, and dissatisfaction of women who were treated as second-class citizens or rendered invisible because they were 'just women; just housewives', the growing pressures on midlife and older women may trigger a social reaction. These women, who were part of a generation that rejected the use of violence, abuse, belittlement, and stereotypes against women, may feel pushed to the limit by the prospect of an old age in which the only part of 'retired' they will be allowed to embrace is 'tired'.

Red Hats and Raging Grannies: Up Against Popular Consumer Culture

Midlife women occupy a key position from which to challenge the role of **popular consumer culture** and the market economy in women's lives (Katz and Marshall, 2003). Again, the sheer dimensions of this generational wave mean that it will have a marked impact on consumption practices and patterns. The fact that the popular culture has been deeply embroiled in presenting and marketing an often demeaning and negative image of middle-aged women places it on a collision course with the aging midlifers (Biggs, 2004). When almost every contact with the popular media—films, television, magazines, and so forth—embodies the direct or indirect message that age spots, wrinkles, grey hair, increased weight, achy joints, and poor vision are undesirable, the confrontation between the consumer market's models of attractive women and the realities of women's lives seems inevitable. When these social facts are combined with midlife women's generational experiences of agency, social movements, and community participation, the stage is set for an interesting engagement.

There are already some slight indications of collision between the discourse on beauty and aging women. Marcel Danesi (2003), in critiquing the ageist tendencies in our culture, argues that the current population of seniors is acquiescing to the popular culture and mass market message that aging simply implies decline and deterioration and, therefore, is to be avoided at all costs. The solution being grasped by the midlifers and the elderly is to endorse the ideals of youthfulness. From his viewpoint, seniors are seeking to look, talk, and 'groove' like teenagers and he urges them to face the fact that 'aging is OK' (ibid., 126). Significantly, the cover of his book presents the photo of an older woman in a tie-dyed T-shirt and flowery bell-bottom pants, standing on an idyllic beach and playing with a hula hoop. The solution to this frivolity, according to Danesi, is for aging Canadians to reject the mass marketing of youthfulness, to accept aging, and to recognize the wisdom that comes with experience. In short, he is urging both the rejection of a predominant 'teenager' culture and the re-establishment of traditional respect for seniors.

A well-established feminist tradition challenges the popular culture's commitment to ageism, especially as it applies to women. As discussed in Chapter 1 a number of second-wave feminists—Germaine Greer, Betty Friedan, June Callwood—were more than willing to tackle aging as a social issue. Much less likely to 'hide' or lie about their age, they also demanded a new set of attitudes. The American feminist Gloria Steinem, in a famous television encounter, commented, 'This is what 50 looks like!' If the current tidal wave of midlife women were to demand a less ageist perspective in the mass media and popular culture, they have a feminist canon to draw upon.

Further, there is an interesting link between aging and sexuality in the popular culture—particularly, given the advent of Viagra and like products targeting senior men. The second wave of the women's movement was intertwined with the sexual revolution and the sexual liberation of women. In the 1960s, women's movement advocates pressed for an expanded, 'liberated' understanding of women's sexuality—one not simply objectified and passive. Even the largely apocryphal representation of 'bra-burning' feminists speaks to the demand for a more natural relationship to one's sexuality in terms of body shape, in opposition to corsets and torpedo bras. In this context, it is revealing that recent books are arguing for an appreciation of older women as sexualized (Sheehy, 2006; Marshall and Katz, 2006).

Certainly, there is some indication that, at the grassroots level, older women may be rejecting the view that they are deteriorating or asexual. Heather Dillaway's (2005) interviews with 45 middle-class, heterosexual, menopausal women mirror our research results—the overwhelming majority of these women do not feel 'old' and do not interpret menopause as a sign of growing old. Unlike their mothers' generation, they had controlled their own fertility (with birth control, tubal ligation, and so on) long before the onset of menopause. As a consequence, the biological change did not mark a major loss in their lives. They do not tend to evaluate their worth or sexuality in terms of their ability to have a baby. Most of Dillaway's respondents, in fact, indicate they desire and enjoy sex and do not link menopause with a decrease in sexual desire or desirability.

In addition, some reflection of women as 'sexy' in their fifties, sixties, and seventies is already being marketed in the mass media. Despite the overarching double standard in much of the media, older women more frequently play leading roles as sexual and attractive characters—including, for example, Holly Hunter (49), Glenn Close (60), Susan Sarandon (55), Jane Alexander (67), Goldie Hawn (60s), and Diane Keaton (60s) (Holloway, 2007: R4). Unlike their media predecessors of past generations, these 'mature' women are uniformly presented as physically desirable and actively sexual—rather than as evil, frigid, or ridiculous. Admittedly, the messages in recent films are decidedly 'mixed'. Gender and age asymmetry remains the norm—in the 100 domestic top-grossing films of 2002 major male characters outnumbered females almost three to one, and the majority of female characters were in their twenties and thirties, while men were in their thirties and forties. Research also indicates that while both men and women in their sixties and older are 'dramatically' under-represented, male characters in their forties, fifties, and sixties are more likely to play roles as leaders and as those who wield occupational power, while older women are likely to be portrayed as goalless. Also, films that include middle-aged female major characters are often ultimately supportive of the motherhood mystique, present a decidedly young-looking old, and assume that a narrowly framed heterosexual nuclear family remains normative (Lauzen and Dozier, 2005; Tally, 2006). Nonetheless, within these significant limitations, new media representations do open the door to representations of older women as worthy of emulation and may ultimately provide the foundation for a model of mature womanhood that women actually look forward to attaining.

Imagining Midlife Women's Future

Midlife women appear poised between opportunity and retrenchment or, as Marshall suggests, between danger and opportunity (2006: ix). It is possible—no more and no less—that the combination of historical trends towards the increased subordination or exploitation of women, coupled with the boomer generation's experience with personal and societal agency, may encourage acts of resistance. After all, these women have managed to get through the major life hurdles. Finding a mate, deciding on motherhood, having (a) child/ren, finding a job, earning a livelihood, getting a divorce, facing the death of loved ones, and/or experiencing personal health crises have already happened and they, for better or worse, have survived. The major gendered 'risks' have been faced, and, increasingly, the big risk simply is 'running out of time'. As a cohort, they are not likely to meekly comply with a loss of freedoms or continued age prejudice (Longino, 2005).

A joke going the rounds on the Internet captures this midlife female feistiness. A middle-aged husband says to his wife, 'Honey, when we got married 25 years ago, you were a hot 25-year-old blonde and we lived in a one-room apartment, slept on the couch, and ate hamburger. Today, we live in a million-dollar three-bedroom condominium, have a custom king-size bed, and eat steak and lobster whenever we like. But, I'm married to a 50-year-old woman who's starting to show her age. It seems to me that you're not keeping up your end of the bargain.' His wife laughs and says, 'That's okay. You can go find yourself a 25-year-old blonde and I'll make sure you're back living in a bachelor apartment, sleeping on the couch, and eating hamburger before you know it.' If she speaks for her generation, this anecdotal middle-aged woman is not going quietly into that good night.

Clearly, the powerful ageist prejudices in the culture may still work to marginalize middle-aged women and their voices. Recent events such as the federal government's withdrawal of funding for Status of Women Canada speak to an increasingly hostile climate for gender equality advocacy. In general, the rise of political conservatism in North America and Western Europe and the successes of religious fundamentalists in Canada, the United States, and Europe necessarily raise concerns about setbacks in the historical struggle to liberate and empower women. However, despite this resistant social climate, feminism is far from dead, particularly in universities[9] and in major urban centres. Women's bookstores, shelters for battered women, addiction support organizations for women, sexual assault education and support groups, and university-based centres for feminist/women's studies, as well as numerous journals, books, and conferences, exemplify the continuing vitality of the women's movement.

Admittedly, as discussed in Chapter 1, the contemporary women's movement has been slow to focus on problems of ageism and the complex intersections among age, gender and class, ethnicity, sexual orientation, and ability. However, in this respect, the issue of age serves not only as a challenge to feminism but as an important stimulus to push forward with analyses that address the oppressions of women, across age, class, ethnicity, sexuality, and ability (Cruikshank, 2003; Wekker, 2004; Calasanti et al., 2006). From this perspective, midlife women may have a particularly significant role to play, not in terms of 'passing on' a feminist spirit to the coming generations of women, but in demanding a rethinking of feminist understandings of the complex interplay of culture, work, family, and oppression (Adkins, 2004; Barnett, 2006; Norris, 2006).

Perhaps Danesi is right; perhaps we are witnessing the **teenagering** of older women. But this may not be a bad thing for the women, for feminism, or for our society. The menopausal women who report that they 'feel like a teenager again'; the midlifers who join the **Red Hat Society** or become **Raging Grannies**; the middle-aged women who laugh and cry as they quilt, bead, knit, or fundraise; the women we talked with who 'loved, loved, loved' growing older—all offer a much-needed vitality. After all, in the 1960s, the feminist phrase—'I don't want a revolution I can't dance to'—spoke to the need for joy and self-indulgence in the pursuit of social justice. The looming generation of boomer women may offer a savouring of life and a rebelliousness of spirit—a blend of fun and wisdom—which is just what is necessary for confronting the historic hostility of conservatism and the selfish negativism of neo-conservatism.

Key Concepts

Aging body The biological realities of aging—menopause, increased rates of illness and disease, greater likelihoods of disability, and so on that are framed by societal realities determining the public perception and personal consequences of these patterns.

Motherhood mystique A term coined in the 1970s to refer to the powerful social ideology that becoming a biological mother was core to women's self-fulfillment and personal satisfaction. Related to this ideology are the beliefs that women who are unable to have children by defect are to be pitied and that those who choose not to have children are to be pathologized.

Popular consumer culture A newly identified area in sociology, consumerism refers to the tendency for many modern Western societies to be organized around the consumption of goods and services rather than their production.

Raging Grannies A worldwide protest movement that started in Victoria, British Columbia, in 1987. Dressing in the stereotypical 'granny' garb of bonnets and shawls, they sing hilarious and politically loaded songs in support of peace rallies, union gatherings, and various social protests. It would appear that they are very intent on having a good time as well as having their say (Acker and Brightwell, 2004).

Red Hat Societies A North American, profit-based organization of apolitical groups (chapters) of older women that are created (by one or several enthusiasts in a community) as an opportunity to meet, have fun, and challenge some stodgy images of senior women; inspired by a poem by Jenny Joseph containing the line, 'when I am old, I will wear a red hat'. Chapter guidelines, assorted merchandise including red hats and related novelties, such as pins and T-shirts, are marketed to midlife women through a website (www.redhatsociety).

Teenagering A term used by Danesi (2003) to refer to the social pressures that encourage older men and women to act, talk, dress, and present themselves in a manner previously considered appropriate only to youth.

Urbanization The ongoing process in Canadian society in which increasing numbers of Canadians live in or closely adjacent to heavily populated city areas and less and less frequently in rural areas or small towns.

Questions for Critical Discussion

1. The media pay a great deal of attention to the impact of population aging on the economy and on the society as a whole. What kinds of societal shifts are reasonable to expect as an increasing proportion of the Canadian population is elderly and aged?

2. The authors describe the continuum (from traditional through innovative to iconoclastic) along which midlife women may be seen to have lived their lives. What contemporary forces are affecting young women's paths along this same continuum today?
3. The authors distinguish between demographic traits of women and the personal meanings women attach to their roles in the family and the economy. Explain this distinction and consider how it might play out in other areas of our society.
4. Thinking of the midlife women you have met, what strategies have they employed to navigate between their more traditional roots and the demands of contemporary society?
5. What are the messages in the popular culture about middle-aged women and how are these messages communicated? Consider your personal response if you were middle-aged and female.
6. The growing popularity of gender-conservative religious fundamentalism, in Canada and globally, may be a potentially important determinant in the lives of middle-aged women. What other social factors are likely to play a key role in the life course of Canadian women over the next 20 years?

Study Design and Sample Characteristics

The Study Design

This study focuses on a group of women born at mid-twentieth century who were interviewed when they were in their fifties. This group of women is of particular interest to us in that they came of age in the midst of dramatic social changes triggered, in part, by the popularization of the women's movement. Because they were implicated in this significant cultural shift—whether or not they were actively engaged—we expect them to experience midlife in a way that differentiates them from cohorts that preceded or followed them. Further, they are part of a massive demographic shift—the baby boom—which is changing the age patterns of Canadian society.

We designed the study to interview women about their family, work and health, the meaning and timing of significant life events, regrets, and hopes. The first step in the research involved a pilot study conducted by Mandell in Toronto and Ottawa in 2000. Nine focus groups included 64 focus participants—midlife women from a diverse range of class and ethnic backgrounds. These women identified three key areas of concern in their lives: changing family arrangements, ongoing concerns about money, and worries about changes in their health status (Lynn, 2001). These focus group findings were used to design an interview protocol directed to exploring midlife women's experience of family, career, and health transitions. Pilot interviews were conducted early in 2002. The authors then developed and tested the interview guide, finalizing the questions after an initial analysis of five pilot interviews. Most of the interviews were conducted by a doctoral student who was herself a midlife woman. The interviews explored women's views on intimacy, love, and friendships; paid, unpaid, and volunteer work; and how they felt about their health. We wanted to explore similarities and differences in how women of differing class, ethnicity, race, ability, and sexual orientation experience these dimensions and how this experience has changed over the course of their lives. The interviews were open-ended and allowed women to describe their experiences in as much detail as they wished. The interviews lasted from one to three hours.

The study design is based on feminist qualitative research principles, with the primary tool being a personal, open-ended interview (see, e.g., Naples, 2003; Giele and Elder, 1998). The project's goal is not only to learn more about the lives of midlife women but to place individual experiences in historical context. We wanted to give voice to the thoughts and experiences of this cohort as they pass through middle age.

The population of midlife women to be interviewed was developed through contacts with diverse social agencies, community groups, or comparable organizations in the Greater Toronto Area and southern Ontario. These organizations, all of which are directed specifically to women's issues, were asked to post or distribute a flyer outlining the purpose of the study and providing contact information. The same flyer was sent out with all e-mail contacts. We made a conscious effort to maximize diversity in terms of social class, ethnicity, immigration status, sexual orientation, and ability by selecting organizations attached to diverse populations. For example, immigrant women's associations, lesbian groups, and church-based women's groups were contacted in the research process. We also solicited participants through representations at meetings, posters, and word of mouth. A secondary strategy was to employ a snowball technique whereby one participant refers another to the project through word of mouth. The results were further amplified by an interview project conducted by students in an undergraduate Women's Studies course who undertook interviews with midlife women they contacted.

Sample Characteristics

The results presented here represent the experiences of 110 midlife women. This figure includes 63 interviewed by the midlife doctoral student, 29 conducted by the undergraduate Women's Studies class, and 18 conducted by the researchers and several research assistants.

Forty-seven (approximately 43 per cent) of the 110 women were married and three respondents were currently cohabiting. Only two said they had never been married. Eight women were widowed, and 20 per cent were separated or divorced. Several once-married respondents indicated that they were single rather than separated or divorced when asked their marital status, but in discussing relationships they referred to a previous partner or spouse. Some women objected to categorizations of 'single' or 'married' or 'with a partner' and declined to answer. Ninety participants described themselves as heterosexual, nine said they were lesbian, and one respondent described herself as bisexual. Eighteen per cent of respondents were childless, and another 18 per cent were grandparents.

Seventy-five per cent spoke English as a first language. (The rest spoke one of: Italian, Spanish, German, Cantonese, Portuguese, Farsi, Yoruba, Arabic, Croatian, French, Persian, Sindhi, and Patois). Fifty-five per cent were born in Canada. Immigrants came to Canada from Italy (7 per cent), Jamaica (6 per cent), United States (4 per cent), Germany (4 per cent), United Kingdom (3 per cent), Guyana (3 per cent), Hong Kong (2 per cent), Iran (2 per cent), Portugal, Belize, Spain, India, Barbados,

Nigeria, Macedonia, Iraq, Croatia, Switzerland, Tanzania, and St Lucia (each at 1 per cent). For those not born in Canada, immigration years ranged from 1946 to 1999, and half of the respondents immigrated in the late 1960s and mid-1970s, the peak immigration years in the twentieth century.

Most of the women interviewed described themselves as white when asked about race; however, this descriptor was often coupled with others (for example, 'white Muslim Canadian', 'white Jewish Canadian', and so on). Some respondents declined identifying race or ethnicity, so the following is suggestive rather than conclusive; 73 per cent were white, 11 per cent were black, and the rest said that they were First Nations, Middle Eastern, Asian, East Indian, and Indian.

Most of the sample had some post-secondary education: 20 per cent had completed a BA, 20 per cent had completed community college or technical school, and 12 per cent had completed a master's degree. Of the rest, 17 per cent had completed high school, and 11 per cent had a bachelor's degree 'in progress'. Respondents were asked to indicate total family income and to describe their feelings of financial well-being. Yearly income for 30 per cent of the sample was above $80,000 and the household income for 16 women was less than $20,000; for 21 women, income ranged from $60,000 to $80,000 a year. Regardless of income, most felt they were 'financially okay' (30 per cent) or 'financially comfortable' (23 percent). One-fifth (18 per cent) said they were 'struggling financially'. Interestingly, there was no relationship between income and feelings of financial well-being. Some women in the upper-income range (more than $80,000) felt they were struggling, some felt okay, some were comfortable. Clearly, feelings of financial well-being are influenced by factors other than income.

Interviews done as part of the class project did not include questions about the women's movement. Of the 81 women who were asked their feelings about feminism and the women's movement, over one-third described themselves as feminists, and 21 would not call themselves a feminist; five women said 'maybe' and two said that 'sometimes' they would consider themselves feminist. Some of these women rejected the idea of labels entirely. Some midlife participants thought that women were better off before the women's movement and spoke with nostalgia about 'the way things used to be'.

Most women in the sample described themselves as 'able-bodied' (48 per cent). The most common health problems mentioned were depression (9 per cent), cancer (7 per cent), arthritis (4 per cent), smoker (4 per cent), alcoholism (3 per cent), and mental illness (3 per cent).

Given the sampling process—locating women through women's groups and organizations—the research population is made up of women engaged in some form of social involvement at this point in their lives. However, it is important to note that many of these women-based groups and organizations were not specifically feminist in nature; some of the religious-based organizations might be considered explicitly anti-feminist.

In the quotations cited in the text, pseudonyms have been used and any potentially identifying characteristics have been altered so as to maintain interview confidentiality.

Notes

Chapter 1

1. Once individual choices became detached from particular ages, the discourse of crisis could be assigned to any age with any event depending on the societal context. For example, Robbins and Wilner (2001) have written about the 'quarterlife crisis' for young adults in their mid-twenties.

Chapter 4

1. Discourses constitute an interrelationship of themes, statements, forms of knowledge, and positions held by individuals in relation to these ideas. They consist of ideas and practices that share a common view and reflect a specific world view. Discourses suggest procedures and practices that constrain what we can feel, think, and do, and through their effect on behaviour they shape our experiences. Finally, discourses evolve through collective conversations people have about their lives.
2. This finding makes us wonder if the accepted postmodernist life course notion of the self-project is based primarily on the needs and lives of men rather than of women. While we agree that actual experiences, not simply past socialization processes, become forces for self-discovery and self-construction, we also understand that for midlife women, there is no self-actualization in the absence of others. Midlife women use intimate relations as vehicles to achieve self-actualization. Both men and women experience many transitions over their lifetimes, but these are no longer predictable or linear. A male view of fashioning one's life course as being a primarily solitary, autonomous, and largely independent series of actions ignores moral and emotional concerns that connect women to the actions of intimate others. Women's transitions are unpredictable but still tied to the fate of others. For example, many of our midlife women talk about returning to work after age 50 or about taking up new employment careers or entering university or graduate school in order to retrain for a new career. These are not activities their parents' generation would have undertaken because the age of 50 meant time to plan for retirement; but for contemporary midlife women, age 50 means a time of diminished responsibilities to others and hence more time for oneself.

Chapter 7

1. The Way of St James, or El Camino de Santiago, is a footpath taken by Christian pilgrims that begins in France and crosses Spain, ending in the city of Santiago de Compostela. There are several routes, all several hundred kilometres in length.
2. Half of Canadian women die of heart disease and cancer, but half of all deaths of women in their fifties and sixties and almost half for women in their forties are due to cancer (Statistics Canada, 2005: 58–9).

Chapter 8

1. Both of these 'informants' were not interviewees but rather middle-aged women who, as friends of the authors, were invited to comment on the research project and its implications for understanding their own lives.
2. This group may be considered a minority insofar as the majority of Canadian women are now evidencing life course patterns that are inconsistent with the traditional one—common-law marriage, single motherhood, full-time employment during all or most of adult life, childlessness, and so on. These categories are fluid and change over the life course. While discussing her life, a midlife woman may indicate that she was traditional at 20, radical at 30, and ambivalent in middle age. Here the reference is to the predominant orientation in a woman's life course as perceived at midlife, and the 'groups' are understood as loose categories intended to be suggestive rather than definitive.
3. This version of feminine agency, of course, is perpetuated in the popular media in films such as *Pretty Woman*.
4. The mainstreaming of the motherhood mystique is very much still with us. Celebrities are often evaluated on their perceived abilities as a mother. Ironically, even members of the 'feminist' generation have joined the chorus. In a recent interview, the anti-Vietnam War crusader and actor Jane Fonda indicates that 'her biggest regret is: "I wasn't a better mother"' (*National Enquirer*, 2007).
5. This impact on 'self' is also suggested by research that indicates women, regardless of age, have lower self-esteem than men. Predictably, older women and lower-class women experience the lowest levels of self-esteem (McMullin and Cairney, 2004).
6. Not all midlife women will focus on appearance norms. Depending on individual and group contexts, women may be much more occupied with addressing racial or economic inequalities, health challenges, disability concerns, or something else. See, for example, Dillaway (2005).
7. It is important to emphasize the ongoing and dramatic shifts that may occur in women's position regarding gender traditionalism. Pivotal personal events—diagnosis of breast cancer, denial of promotion, divorce—may prompt a profound rethinking of one's self-perception. Similarly, historical events—the Montreal massacre, the war on terrorism, the election of a female Prime Minister—may resonate in terms of shifting self-definitions.
8. As they age, women are less likely to be employed than their male counterparts.
9. The situating of so much of contemporary feminism in the university has long been contentious (Egeland, 2004). Perhaps the boomer generation of women may help liberate the women's movement from the university.

References

Acker, A., and B. Brightwell. 2004. *Off Our Rockers and Into Trouble: The Raging Grannies*. Victoria, BC: Touchwood.

Adamson, N., L. Briskin, and M. McPhail. 1988. *Feminists Organizing for Change*. Toronto: Oxford University Press.

Adkins, L. 2004. 'Passing on feminism: From consciousness to reflexivity?', *European Journal of Women's Studies* 11, 4: 427–44.

Agnew, V. 1993. 'Canadian feminism and women of colour', *Women's Studies International Forum* 16, 3: 217–27.

Aldwin, C.M., and M.R. Levenson. 2001. 'Stress, coping and health at midlife: A developmental perspective', in M.E. Lachman, ed., *Handbook of Midlife Development*. New York: John Wiley and Sons, 188–214.

Arber, S. 2004. 'Gender, marital status, and ageing: Linking material, health, and social resources', *Journal of Aging Studies* 18, 1: 91–108.

———— and C. Attias-Donfut, eds. 2000. *The Myth of Generational Conflict: The Family and the State in Aging Societies*. London: Routledge.

————, K. Davidson, and J. Ginn. 2003. *Gender and Ageing: Changing Roles and Relationships*. Maidenhead, UK: Open University Press.

———— and J. Ginn, eds. 1991. *Gender and Later Life: A Sociological Analysis of Resources and Constraints*. Newbury Park, Calif.: Sage.

Armstrong, P., H. Armstrong, and D. Coburn. 2001. 'From medicare to home care: Globalization, state retrenchment and profitization of Canada's health care system', in Armstrong, Armstrong, and Coburn, eds, *Unhealthy Times: Political Economy Perspectives on Health and Care*. Toronto: Oxford University Press, 1–6.

Arnold, L.B. 2000. '"What is a feminist?": Students' descriptions', *Women and Language* 23, 2: 8–18.

Avis, N.E. 2003. 'Depression during the menopausal transition', *Psychology of Women Quarterly* 27: 91–100.

Baines, C., P.M. Evans, and S. Neysmith, eds. 1998. *Women's Caring: Feminist Perspectives on Social Welfare*, 2nd edn. Toronto: Oxford University Press.

Banister, E.M. 1999. 'Women's midlife experience of their changing bodies', *Qualitative Health Research* 9, 4: 520–37.

Barnett, B. 2006. 'Focusing on the next picture: Feminist scholarship as a foundation for teaching about ageism in the academy', *NWSA Journal* 18, 1: 85–98.

Barnett, R.C. 2005. 'Ageism and sexism in the workplace', *Generations* 29, 3: 25–30.

Beaudet, M. 2000. 'Psychological health—depression in how healthy are Canadians?', *Health Reports* 11, 3: 66–73. Ottawa: Statistics Canada Catalogue no. 82-003-XPB.

Beaupre, P., M. Turcotte, and A. Milan. 2003. 'Junior comes back home: Trends and predictors of returning to the parental home', *Canadian Social Trends*: 28–34.

Beauvoir, S. de. 1989 [1949]. *The Second Sex*. New York: Alfred A. Knopf.

————. 1986 [1977]. *Old Age*. Middlesex, UK: Penguin.

Beck-Gernsheim, E. 1998. 'On the way to a post-familial family: From a community of need to elective affinities', *Theory, Culture & Society* 15, 3: 53–70.

———. 2002. *Reinventing the Family: In Search of New Lifestyles*. Cambridge: Polity.

Bernard, J. 1972. *The Future of Marriage*. New York: Bantam Books.

Biggs, S. 1997. 'Choosing not to be old? Masks, bodies and identity management in later life', *Ageing & Society* 17, 5: 553–70.

———. 2004. 'Age, gender, narratives, and masquerades', *Journal of Aging Studies* 18, 1: 45–58.

Brabeck, M. 1989. *Who Cares? Theory, Research and the Educational Implications of the Ethic of Care*. New York: Praeger.

Brewi, J., and A. Brennan. 1999. *Mid-life Spirituality and Jungian Archetypes*. York Beach, Maine: Nicolas Hayes.

Brody, E. 2004. *Women in the Middle: Their Parent-Care Years*, 2nd edn. New York: Springer.

Browne, C. 1998. *Women, Feminism, and Aging*. New York: Springer.

Buchanan, R. 2006. '1-800-New Brunswick: Economic development strategies, firm restructuring, and the local production of "global" services', in Shalla (2006: 177–200).

Buschman, J.K., and S. Lenart. 1996. '"I am not a feminist, but": College women, feminism, and negative experiences', *Political Psychology* 17, 1: 59–75.

Butler, R.N. 1975. *Why Survive? Being Old in America*. New York: Harper & Row.

Calasanti, T.M. 2006. 'Gender and old age: Lessons from spousal care work', in Calasanti and Slevin (2006: 269–94).

——— and K.F. Slevin. 2001. *Gender, Social Inequalities, and Aging*. Walnut Creek, Calif.: AltaMira Press.

——— and ———, eds. 2006. *Age Matters: Realigning Feminist Thinking*. New York: Routledge.

———, ———, and N. King. 2006. 'Ageism and feminism: From "et cetera" to center', *NWSA Journal* 18, 1: 13–30.

Campbell, L.D., and M.P. Carroll. 2007. 'The incomplete revolution: Theorizing gender when studying men who provide care to aging parents', *Men and Masculinities* 9, 4: 491–508.

Castells, M. 2004. *The Power of Identity*, 2nd edn. Malden, Mass.: Blackwell.

Chow, I.G.Y. 1993. 'An assessment of factors influencing Chinese Canadian and Caucasian women's identification with feminism', unpublished manuscript.

Clark, Warren, and Grant Schellenberg. 2006. 'Who's religious?', *Canadian Social Trends* no. 81 (Summer): 2–9.

Clarke, L.H. 2001. 'Older women's bodies and the self: The construction of identity in later life', *Canadian Review of Sociology and Anthropology* 38, 4: 441–64.

———. 2002a. 'Beauty in later life: Older women's perceptions of physical attractiveness', *Canadian Journal on Aging/La Revue Canadienne du Vieillissement* 21, 3: 429–42.

———. 2002b. 'Older women's perceptions of ideal body weights: The tensions between health and appearance motivations for weight loss', *Ageing & Society* 22: 751–73.

Cohen, L. 1984. *Small Expectations: Society's Betrayal of Older Women*. Toronto: McClelland & Stewart.

Connidis, I.A. 2002. 'The impact of demographic and social trends on informal support for older persons', in D. Cheal, ed., *Aging and Demographic Change in Canadian Context*. Toronto: University of Toronto Press, 105–32.

——— and J.A. McMullin. 2002a. 'Sociological ambivalence and family ties: A critical perspective', *Journal of Marriage and Family* 64, 3: 558–67.

——— and ———. 2002b. 'Ambivalence, family ties, and doing sociology', *Journal of Marriage and the Family* 64, 3: 594–601.

Copper, B. 1997. 'The view from over the hill', in M. Pearsall, ed., *The Other within Us: Feminist Explorations of Women and Aging*. Boulder, Colo.: Westview Press, 121–33.

Cousins, S.O., and K. Edwards. 2002. 'Alice in menopauseland: The jabberwocky of a medicalized middle age', *Health Care for Women International* 23, 4: 325–43.

Covey, H.C. 1988. 'Historical terminology used to represent older people', *Gerontologist* 28: 291–7.

Craig, M.L. 2004. *Ain't I a Beauty Queen? Black Women, Beauty and the Politics of Race*. Oxford: Oxford University Press.

Crompton, S. 2000. '100 years of health', *Canadian Social Trends* 59 (Winter): 12–17.

Crowther, M.R., M.W. Parker, W.A. Achenbaum, P.A. Parker, W.L. Larimore, and H.G. Koenig. 2002. 'Rowe and Kahn's model of successful aging revisited: Positive spirituality—the forgotten factor', *The Gerontologist* 42, 5: 613–20.

Cruikshank, M. 2003. *Learning To Be Old: Gender, Culture, and Aging*. Lanham, Md: Rowman & Littlefield.

Curran, S.R. 2002. 'Agency, accountability, and embedded relations: "What's love got to do with it?"', *Journal of Marriage and Family* 64, 3: 577–84.

Danesi, M. 2003. *Forever Young: The Teen-aging of Modern Culture*. Toronto: University of Toronto Press.

Dennerstein, L., E. Dudley, and J. Guthrie. 2002. 'Empty nest or revolving door? A prospective study of women's quality of life in midlife during the phase of children leaving and re-entering the home', *Psychological Medicine* 32, 3: 545–50.

———, P. Lehert, E. Dudley, and J. Guthrie. 2001. 'Factors contributing to positive mood during the menopausal transition', *Journal of Nervous and Mental Disease* 189, 2: 84–9.

de Vries, B. 1996. 'The understanding of friendship: An adult life course perspective', in C. Magai and S. McFadden, eds, *Handbook of Emotion, Adult Development, and Aging*. New York: Academic Press, 249–68.

——— and C. Johnson. 2002. 'The death of friends in later life', *Advances in Life Course Research* 7, 299–324.

Dillaway, H.E. 2005. '(Un)changing menopausal bodies: How women think and act in the face of a reproductive transition and gendered beauty ideals', *Sex Roles: A Journal of Research* 53, 1/2: 1–17.

Doherty, R.W., E. Hatfield, K. Thompson, and P. Choo. 1994. 'Cultural and ethnic differences on love and attachment', *Personal Relationships* 1, 4: 391–4.

Duffy, A., and N. Pupo. 1992. *Part-time Paradox: Connecting Gender, Work, and Family*. Toronto: McClelland & Stewart.

Dufour, L.R. 2000. 'Sifting through tradition: The creation of Jewish feminist identities', *Journal of the Scientific Study of Religion* 39, 1: 90–106.

Duxbury, L., and C. Higgins. 2001. *Work–Life Balance in the New Millennium: Where Are We? Where Do We Need To Go?* Research Report No. 7314. Ottawa: Canadian Policy Research Networks. At: <www.cprn.org/en/doc.cfm?doc=52>.

Earl, L. 1999. 'Baby boom women—then and now', *Perspectives on Labour and Income* (Winter): 14–19.

Egeland, C. 2004. 'What's feminist in feminist theory?', *European Journal of Women's Studies* 11, 2: 117–88.

Elder, G.H., ed. 1985. *Life Course Dynamics: Trajectories and Transitions, 1968–1980*. Ithaca, NY: Cornell University Press.

Ephron, N. 2006. *I Feel Bad about My Neck and Other Thoughts on Being a Woman*. New York: Random House.

Evans, M. 1998. '"Falling in love with love is falling for make believe": Ideologies of romance in post-enlightenment', *Theory, Culture & Society* 15, 3/4: 265–75.

Fairclough, N. 1989. *Discourse Analysis*. Cambridge: Polity Press.

Fast, J. 2005. 'Caregiving: A fact of life', *Transition* 35, 2: 4–9.

Featherstone, M., and M. Hepworth. 1991. 'The mask of ageing and the postmodern life course', in M. Featherstone, M. Hepworth, and B.S. Turner, eds, *The Body: Social Processes and Cultural Theory*. Thousand Oaks, Calif.: Sage, 371–89.

Ferudi, F. 2003. *Therapy Culture: Cultivating Vulnerability in an Uncertain Age*. London: Routledge.

Fox, B., and P. Sugiman. 2006. 'Flexible work, flexible workers: The restructuring of clerical work in a large telecommunications company', in Shalla (2006: 74–95).

Frank, A.W. 1991. *At the Will of the Body: Reflections on Illness*. Boston: Houghton Mifflin.

Frenette, M.S., and S. Couloumbe. 2007. *Has Higher Education among Young Women Substantially Reduced the Gender Gap in Employment Earnings?* Ottawa: Minister of Industry, Statistics Canada Catalogue no 11F0019MIE-No. 301.

Friedan, B. 1984 [1963]. *The Feminine Mystique*. New York: Dell.

———. 1993. *The Fountain of Age*. New York: Simon & Schuster.

Gannon, L. 1999. *Women and Aging: Transcending the Myths*. London: Routledge.

Garner, J.D. 1999. 'Feminism and feminist gerontology', *Journal of Women & Aging* 11, 2/3: 3–12.

Gee, E.M., and G.M. Gutman. 2000. *The Overselling of Population Aging: Apocalyptic Demography, Intergenerational Challenges, and Social Policy*. Toronto: Oxford University Press.

Gergen, K. 1991. *The Saturated Self: Dilemmas of Identity in Contemporary Life*. New York: Basic Books.

Gerson, K. 1985. *Hard Choices: How Women Decide about Work, Career, and Motherhood*. Berkeley: University of California Press.

Giddens, A. 1992. *The Transformation of Intimacy: Sexuality, Love and Eroticism in Modern Societies*. Stanford, Calif.: Stanford University Press.

Giele, J.Z., and G.H. Elder Jr, eds. 1998. *Methods of Life Course Research: Qualitative and Quantitative Approaches*. Thousand Oaks, Calif.: Sage.

Gilleard, C., and P. Higgs. 2000. *Cultures of Aging: Self, Citizen and the Body*. London: Prentice-Hall.

Gilligan, C. 1982. *In a Different Voice: Psychological Theory and Women's Development*. Cambridge, Mass.: Harvard University Press.

Gindin, S., and S. Stanford. 2006. 'Canadian labour and the political economy of transformation', in Shalla (2006: 379–94).

Glazer, G., R. Zeller, L. Delumba, C. Kalinyak, S. Hobfoll, J. Winchell, et al. 2002. 'The Ohio midlife women's study', *Health Care for Women International* 23, 6/7: 612–30.

Globe and Mail. 2007. 'Need an at-home aphrodisiac? Try a mop', 9 Aug., L4.

Gotleib, A. 1994. 'Saying goodbye to *Healthsharing*', in E. Dua, ed., *On Women Healthsharing*. Toronto: Women's Press.

Gott, M., and S. Hinchcliff. 2003. 'Sex and aging: A gendered issue', in S. Arber, K. Davidson, and J. Ginn, eds, *Gender and Aging: Changing Roles and Relationships*. Philadelphia: Open University Press, 63–78.

Greer, G. 1970. *The Female Eunuch*. London: Paladin.

———. 1991. *The Change: Women, Aging and the Menopause*. Toronto: Alfred A. Knopf Canada.

Gubrium, J. F., and J.A. Holstein. 2003. 'The everyday visibility of the aging body', in Gubrium and Holstein, eds, *Aging Bodies*. Walnut Creek, Calif.: AltaMira, 205–27.

Gullette, M.M. 1997. *Declining to Decline*. Charlottesville: University Press of Virginia.

Harding, S. 2006. *Science and Social Inequality: Feminist and Postcolonial Issues*. Urbana: University of Illinois Press.

Hatch, L.R. 2000. *Beyond Gender Differences: Adaptation to Aging in Life Course Perspective*. Amityville, NY: Baywood.

———. 2005. 'Gender and ageism', *Generations* 29, 3: 19–24.

Hernandez, Greg. 2007. 'ABC lauded for most gay characters', *Globe and Mail*, 8 Aug., R4.

Hirshman, L. 2006. *Get to Work: A Manifesto for Women of the World*. New York: Viking.

Hislop, J., and S. Arber. 2003. 'Sleepers awake! The gendered nature of sleep disruption among mid-life women', *Sociology* 37, 4: 695–711.

Ho, B., et al. 2003. 'Caregiving for relatives with Alzheimer's disease: Feelings of Chinese-Canadian women', *Journal of Aging Studies* 17: 301–21.

Hochschild, A.R. 1989. *The Second Shift: Working Parents and the Revolution at Home*. New York: Viking.

———. 1997. *The Time Bind: When Work Becomes Home and Home Becomes Work*. New York: Metropolitan Books.

Hockey, J., and A. James. 2004. 'How do we know that we are aging? Embodiment, agency and later life', in E. Tulle, ed., *Old Age and Agency*. New York: Nova Science, 157–72.

Holdsworth, C. 2007. 'Intergenerational inter-dependencies: Mothers and daughters in comparative perspective', *Women's Studies International Forum* 30: 59–69.

Holloway, D. 2007. 'Age is nothing but a number', *Globe and Mail*, 1 Aug., R4.

Holstein, J.A., and J.F. Gubrium. 2003. *Ways of Aging*. Malden, Mass.: Blackwell.

hooks, b. 2000. *Feminism Is for Everybody: Passionate Politics*. Cambridge, Mass.: South End Press.

Hooyman, N.R. 1999. 'Research on older women: Where is feminism?', *Gerontologist* 39, 1: 115–18.

——— and J.G. Gonyea. 1999. 'A feminist model of family care: Practice and policy directions', *Journal of Women & Aging* 11, 2/3: 149–69.

Howell, L.C., and A. Beth. 2002. 'Midlife myths and realities: Women reflect on their experiences', *Journal of Women & Aging* 14, 3/4: 189–204.

Huffman, S.B., and J.E. Myers. 1999. 'Counseling women in midlife: An integrative approach to menopause', *Journal of Counseling and Development* 77, 3: 258–66.

Hulbert, K.D., and D.T. Schuster, eds. 1993. *Women's Lives through Time: Educated American Women of the Twentieth Century*. San Francisco: Jossey-Bass.

Hunt, K. 2002. 'A generation apart? Gender-related experiences and health in women in early and late mid-life', *Social Science and Medicine* 54: 663–76.

Hurd, T.L., and M. Brabeck. 1997. 'Presentation of women and Gilligan's ethic of care in college textbooks, 1970–1990: An examination of bias', *Teaching of Psychology* 24, 3: 159–66.

Jacques, E. 1965. 'Death and the mid-life crisis', *International Journal of Psychoanalysis* 46: 502–14.

Jones, C.L., L. Tepperman, and L.R. Marsden. 1990. *Lives of Their Own: The Individualization of Women's Lives*. Toronto: Oxford University Press.

Jung, C. 1960. *The Stages of Life: Collected Works*. Princeton, NJ: Princeton University Press.

Katz, S., and B. Marshall. 2003. 'New sex for old: Lifestyle, consumerism, and the ethics of aging well', *Journal of Aging Studies* 17, 1: 3–16.

Kaufert, P.A. 1997. 'Women's resistance and the breast cancer movement', in M. Lock and P.A. Kaufert, eds, *Pragmatic Women and Body Politics*. Cambridge: Cambridge University Press, 287–309.

Kemp, C.L. 2004. '"Grand" expectations: The experiences of grandparents and adult grand-children', *Canadian Journal of Sociology* 29, 4: 499–525.

Kershaw, P. 2005. *Carefair: Rethinking the Responsibilities and Rights of Citizenship*. Vancouver: University of British Columbia Press.

Kesterton, M. 2006. 'Social studies: A new coinage?', *Globe and Mail*, 13 Nov., A20.

Koster, A., and K. Garde. 1993. 'Sexual desire and menopausal development: A prospective study of Danish women born in 1936', *Maturitas* 16, 1: 49–60.

Kranz, K.C., and B.C. Long. 2002. 'Messages about stress in two North American women's magazines: Helpful? We think not!', *Feminism and Psychology* 12, 4: 525–30.

Landman, J. 1993. *Regret: The Persistence of the Possible*. New York: Oxford University Press.

Lauzen, M.M., and M. Dozier. 2005. 'Maintaining the double standard: Portrayals of age and gender in popular films', *Sex Roles: A Journal of Research* 52, 7/8: 437–46.

Lee, C., and J. Porteous. 2002. 'Experiences of family caregiving among middle-aged Australian women', *Feminism & Psychology* 12, 1: 79–96.

Levin, J. 2001. *God, Faith and Health*. New York: John Wiley & Sons.

Levinson, D.J. 1978. *Seasons of a Man's Life*. New York: Knopf.

———— and J.D. Levinson. 1996. *The Seasons of a Woman's Life*. New York: Ballantine Books.

Lewchuck, W., and D. Robertson. 2006. 'Listening to workings: The reorganization of work in the Canadian motor vehicle industry', in Shalla (2006: 53–73).

Li, Chris. 2004. *Widowhood: Consequences on Income for Senior Women*. Ottawa: Statistics Canada, Catalogue no. 11-621-MIE2004015.

Lock, M. 1995. *Encounters with Aging: Mythologies of Menopause in Japan and North America*. Los Angeles: University of California Press.

Longino, C.F. 2005. 'The future of ageism: Baby boomers at the doorstep', *Generations* 29: 79–83.

Lorber, J. 1997. *Gender and the Social Construction of Illness*. Thousand Oaks, Calif.: Sage.

————. 2005. *Gender Inequality: Feminist Theories and Politics*. Los Angeles: Roxbury.

Lorde, A. 1980. *The Cancer Journals*. San Francisco: Aunt Lute Books.

Lüscher, K., and K. Pillemer. 1998. 'Intergenerational ambivalence: A new approach to the study of parent–child relations in later life', *Journal of Marriage and the Family* 60, 2: 413–25.

Luxton, M. 1980. *More Than a Labour of Love: Three Generations of Women's Work in the Home*. Toronto: Women's Press.

————. 1983. 'Two hands for the clock: Changing patterns in the gendered division of labour in the home', *Studies in Political Economy* 12: 27–44.

Lynn, M. 2001. 'Pilot Project on Midlife Women: Quality of Life and Social and Economic Wellbeing', unpublished research report. Toronto: Centre for Feminist Research, York University.

McDaniel, S.A. 1988. *Getting Older and Better: Women and Gender Assumptions in Canada's Aging Society*. Ottawa: Canadian Research Institute for the Advancement of Women.

————. 2003. 'Family/work challenges among mid-life and older Canadians', in M. Lynn, ed., *Voices: Essays on Canadian Families*, 2nd edn. Toronto: Thompson Nelson, 152–76.

————. 2004. 'Generationing gender: Justice and the division of welfare', *Journal of Aging Studies* 18, 1: 27–44.

Macdonald, B., and C. Rich. 1991. *Look Me in the Eye: Old Women, Aging, and Ageism*, expanded edn.. Minneapolis: Spinsters Ink.

MacDonald, G. 2006. 'Personal questions: Nora Ephron', *Globe and Mail*, 5 Aug., F7.

McGraw, L.A., and A.J. Walker. 2004. 'Negotiating care: Ties between aging mothers and their caregiving daughters', *Journals of Gerontology* 59B, 6: S234–S332.

Mackin, J. 1995. 'Women, stress, and midlife', *Human Ecology* 23, 4: 20–3.

McLaren, L., and D. Kuh. 2004. 'Body dissatisfaction in midlife women', *Journal of Women & Aging* 16, 1/2: 35–54.

——— and J. Wardle. 2002. 'Body image: A life course perspective', in D. Kuh and R. Hardy, eds, *A Life Course Approach to Women's Health*. Oxford: Oxford University Press, 177–84.

McMullin, J.A., and J. Cairney. 2004. 'Self-esteem and the intersection of age, class and gender', *Journal of Aging Studies* 18, 1: 75–90.

Mann, S.A., and D.J. Huffman. 2005. 'The decentering of second wave feminism and the rise of the third wave', *Science and Society* 69, 1: 56–91.

Marable, M. 2004. 'Globalization and racialization', *Z Magazine*. At: <www.zmag.org/content>.

Marcoen, A. 2005. 'Religion, spirituality and older people', in M.L. Johnson, ed., *The Cambridge Handbook of Age and Aging*. New York: Cambridge University Press, 363–70.

Marshall, B., and S. Katz. 2006. 'From androgyny to androgens: Resexing the aging body', in T. Calasanti and K. Slevin, eds, *Age Matters: Realigning Feminist Thinking*. New York: Routledge.

Marshall, K. 2000. 'Incomes of younger retired women: The past 30 years', *Perspectives on Labour and Income* (Winter): 9–17.

———. 2006. 'Converging gender roles', *Perspectives on Labour and Income* 18, 3: 7–19.

Marshall, L. 2006. 'Aging: A feminist issue', *NWSA Journal* 18, 1: vii–xiii.

Marshall, N.L. 2001. 'Health and illness issues facing an aging workforce in the new millennium', *Sociological Spectrum* 21: 431–9.

Martel, L. 2005. *Healthy Aging: Healthy Today, Healthy Tomorrow? Findings from the National Population Health Survey*. Ottawa: Minister of Industry and Statistics Canada.

Martens, A., J.L. Goldenberg, and J. Greenberg. 2005. 'A terror management perspective on ageism', *Journal of Social Issues* 61: 223–39.

Matarazzo, A. 2006. 'When is junior moving out? Transitions from the parental home to independence', *Canadian Social Trends* 82: 8–14.

Miech, R.A., and M.J. Shanahan. 2000. 'Socioeconomic status and depression over the life course', *Journal of Health and Social Behaviour* 31: 398–417.

Milan, A., and B. Hamm. 2003. 'Across the generations: Grandparents and grandchildren', *Canadian Social Trends*: 2–8.

Miller, Arthur. 1991. *The Ride Down Mount Morgan*. New York: Dramatists Play Service.

Moen, P., and L. Han. 2001. 'Constructing a life course', *Marriage and Family Review* 30, 4: 97–109.

——— and R.M. Orrange. 2002. 'Careers and lives: Socialization, structural lag, and gendered ambivalence', *Advances in Life Course Research* 7: 231–60.

———, ———, and D. Dempster-McClain. 1995. 'Caregiving and women's well-being: A life course approach', *Journal of Health and Social Behavior* 36, 3: 259–73.

———, J. Robinson, and V. Fields. 1994. 'Women's work and caregiving roles: A life course approach', *Journal of Gerontology: Social Sciences* 49: S176–86.

Morissette, R., and K. Johnson. 2005. *Are Good Jobs Disappearing in Canada?* Ottawa: Statistics Canada, Analytical Studies Branch, Business and Labour Market Analysis Division.

——— and Y. Ostrovsky. 2005. *The Instability of Family Earnings and Family Income in Canada, 1986 to 1991 and 1996 to 2001*. Ottawa: Statistics Canada, Analytical Studies Branch, Business and Labour Market Analysis Division.

Murphy, B. 2002. *Why Women Bury Men: The Longevity Gap in Canada*. Winnipeg: J Gordon Shillingford.

Naples, N.A. 2003. *Feminism and Method: Ethnography, Discourse Analysis and Activist Research*. New York and London: Routledge.

National Enquirer. 2007. 'Jane Fonda's greatest regret—putting war before kids', 6 Aug., 24.

Nelson, A. 2006. *Gender in Canada*, 3rd edn. Toronto: Pearson Prentice-Hall.

Norris, E. 2006. 'Age matters in a feminist classroom', *NWSA Journal* 18, 1: 61–84.

Nouri, M., and M. Helterline. 1999. 'Narrative accrual and the life course', *Research on Aging* 20, 1: 33–64.

———— and ————. 2000. 'Narrative accrual and the life course', in E.W. Markson and L.A. Hollis-Sawyer, *Intersections of Aging: Readings in Social Gerontology*. Los Angeles: Roxbury, 113–26.

'The numbers game: Are aging boomers going to bankrupt Canada? or does the census show we're going to be in good shape?' 2002. *Toronto Star*, 20 July, E1–E3.

Oppenheimer, V.K. 1988. 'A Theory of Marriage Timing'. *American Journal of Sociology* 94, 3: 563–1.

Palmore, E.B. 1999. *Ageism: Negative and Positive*, 2nd edn. New York: Springer.

————, L.G. Branch, and D.K. Harris, eds. 2005. *Encyclopedia of Ageism*. Binghamton, NY: Haworth Reference Press.

Payne-Stancil, B. 1997. 'Religion and faith development of older women', in J.M. Coyle, ed., *Handbook on Women and Aging*. Westport, Conn.: Greenwood Press, 223–41.

Pearsall, M. 1997. 'Introduction', in M. Pearsall, ed., *The Other within Us: Feminist Explorations of Women and Aging*. Boulder, Colo.: Westview Press, 1–17.

Perrig-Chiello, P., and F. Höpflinger. 2005. 'Aging parents and their middle-aged children: Demographic and psychosocial challenges', *European Journal of Ageing* 2, 3: 183–91.

Phillips, P., and E. Phillips. 1983. *Women and Work: Inequality in the Labour Market*. Toronto: James Lorimer.

Pinquart, M. 2003. 'Loneliness in married, widowed, divorced, and never-married older adults', *Journal of Social and Personal Relationships* 20, 1: 31–53.

Polivka, Larry, and Charles F. Longino, 2004. 'Postmodern Ageing and the Future of Public Policy', in Emmanuelle Tulle, ed., *Old Age and Agency*. Hauppauge, NY: Nova Science, 3–26.

Popay, J. 1992. '"My health is all right, but I'm just tired all the time": Women's experience of ill health', in Helen Roberts, ed., *Women's Health Matters*. London: Routledge, 99–120.

———— and K. Groves. 2000. '"Narrative" in research on gender inequalities in health', in E. Annadale and K. Hunt, eds, *Gender Inequalities in Health*. Buckingham: Open University Press, 65–89.

Portrait of the Canadian Population in 2006, by Age and Sex, 2006 Census. 2007. Ottawa: Minister of Industry and Statistics Canada.

Prince, M.J., R.N. Harwood, R.A. Blizard, A. Thomas, and A.H. Mann. 1997. 'Social support deficits, loneliness and life events as risk factors for depression in old age: The Gospel Oak Project VI', *Psychological Medicine* 27: 323–32.

Ravanera, Z.R., F. Rajulton, and T.K. Burch. 2004. 'Patterns of age variability in life course transitions', *Canadian Journal of Sociology* 29: 527–42.

REAL Women of Canada. 2006. 'Alerts'. At: <www.realwomenca.com/alerts.htm>.

Rebick, J. 2005. *Ten Thousand Roses: The Making of a Feminist Revolution*. Toronto: Penguin Canada.

Reid, A., and N. Purcell. 2004. 'Pathways to feminist identification', *Sex Roles: A Journal of Research* 50, 11/12: 759–69.

Reid, P.T. 1984. 'Feminism versus minority group identity: Not for black women only', *Sex Roles: A Journal of Research* 10, 3/4: 247–55.

Reinharz, S. 1997. 'Friends or foes: Gerontological and feminist theory', in M. Pearsall, ed., *The Other within Us: Feminist Explorations of Women and Aging.* Boulder, Colo.: Westview Press, 73–93.

Rennie, D. 1984. 'An overview of the Canadian work force, 1901–1971', in A. Wipper, ed., *The Sociology of Work.* Ottawa: Carleton University Press, 4–40.

Rind, P. 2002. *Women's Best Friendships: Beyond Betty, Veronica, Thelma and Louise.* Binghamton, NY: Haworth Press.

Robbins, A., and A. Wilner. 2001. *Quarterlife Crisis: The Unique Challenges of Life in Your Twenties.* New York: Putnam.

Robertson, A. 2000. 'Embodying risk, embodying political rationality: Women's accounts of risks for breast cancer', *Health, Risk & Society* 2, 2: 219–35.

Roof, W.C. 1999. *Spiritual Marketplace: Baby Boomers and the Remaking of American Religion.* Princeton, NJ: Princeton University Press.

Ross, C.E., and J. Mirowsky. 2002. 'Age and gender in the sense of personal control', *Social Psychology Quarterly* 65, 2: 125–45.

Rostosky, S.S., and C.B. Travis. 1996. 'Menopausal research and the dominance of the biomedical model 1984-1994', *Psychology of Women Quarterly* 20: 285–312.

Rowe, J.W., and R.I. Kahn. 1997. 'Successful aging', *Gerontologist* 37, 4: 433–40.

Royal Commission on the Status of Women in Canada. 1970. *Report of the Royal Commission on the Status of Women in Canada,* F. Bird, ed. Ottawa: Information Canada.

Rubin, L.B. 1981. *Women of a Certain Age: The Midlife Search for Self.* New York: Harper & Row.

———. 1991. *Erotic Wars: What Happened to the Sexual Revolution?* New York: Harper.

———. 2001. 'Getting younger while getting older: Family building at midlife', in R. Hertz and N. Marshall, eds, *Working Families: The Transformation of the American Home.* Berkeley: University of California Press, 58–71.

Rundle, L. 2006. 'Still ain't satisfied: Despite a Royal Commission', *Herizons* 19, 3: 16–19.

Rupp, L.J. 2001. 'Is feminism the province of old (or middle-aged) women?', *Journal of Women's History* 12, 4: 164–73.

Ruzek, S.B. 2004. 'How might the women's health movement shape national agenda on women and aging?', *Women's Health Issues* 14: 112–14.

Sarton, M. 1982 [1973]. *As We Are Now: A Novel.* New York: Norton.

Schellenberg, G., M. Turcotte, and B. Ram. 2005a. 'Preparing for retirement', *Canadian Social Trends* 78: 8–11.

———, ———, ———. 2005b. 'What makes retirement enjoyable?', *Canadian Social Trends* 78: 12–14.

Schnittker, J., J. Freese, and B. Powell. 2003. 'Who are feminists and what do they believe? The role of generations', *American Sociological Review* 68, 4: 607–22.

Sermat, V. 1978. 'Sources of loneliness', *Essence* 2: 271–6.

Settersten, R.A., ed. 2003. *Invitation to the Life Course: Toward New Understandings of Later Life.* Amityville, NY: Baywood.

Shalla, V., ed. 2006. *Working in a Global Era: Canadian Perspectives.* Toronto: Canadian Scholars' Press.

———. 2006. 'Jettisoned by design? The truncated employment relationship of customer sales and service agents under airline restructuring', in Shalla (2006: 120–47).

Sheehy, G. 2006. *Sex and the Seasoned Woman.* New York: Random House.

Shellenbarger, S. 2005. *The Breaking Point: How Female Midlife Crisis Is Transforming Today's Women.* New York: Henry Holt.

Shelton, S. n.d. 'Beauty standards'. At: <nappystories.com/main/nonfiction/beautystandards. htm>.

Shields, M. 2004. 'Stress, health and the benefit of social support', *Health Reports* 15, 1: 9–38.

Shumway, D.R. 2003. *Modern Love: Romance, Intimacy and the Marriage Crisis*. New York: New York University Press.

Skolnick, A.S., and J.H. Skolnick, eds. 2003. *Family in Transition: Rethinking Marriage, Sexuality, Child Rearing, and Family Organization*, 12th edn. Boston: Allyn and Bacon.

Sontag, S. 1972. 'The double standard of aging', *Saturday Review* 55: 29–38.

Spencer, M. 1993. 'The idea of fate: Literature, history, character, and the modernization of consciousness', paper presented at the Eastern Sociological Society meetings, Boston.

Spitze, G., and M.P. Gallant. 2004. '"The bitter with the sweet": Older adults' strategies for handling ambivalence in relations with their adult children', *Research on Aging* 26, 4: 387–412.

Springer, K. 2002. 'Third wave black feminism', *Signs: Journal of Women in Culture and Society* 27, 4: 1059–82.

Stacey, J. 1996. *In the Name of the Family*. Boston: Beacon.

Statistics Canada. 2000. 'Incomes of younger retired women: The past 30 years', *The Daily*, 11 Dec. At: <www.statcan.ca/Daily/>.

———. 2003. 'Study: Finances in the golden years', *The Daily*, 17 Nov. At: <www.statcan. ca/Daily/>.

———. 2003. 'Canada's demographic situation: Fertility of immigrant women', *The Daily*, 22 Dec.

———. 2005. *Women in Canada, a Statistical Report*. Ottawa: Statistics Canada.

———. 2007. *Portrait of the Canadian Population in 2006, by Age and Sex, 2006 Census*. Ottawa: Minister of Industry.

Stewart, A.J., and E. Vandwater. 1999. '"If I had to do it all over again . . ." Midlife review, midcourse corrections, and women's well-being in midlife', *Journal of Personality and Social Psychology* 76, 2: 270–83.

Stobart, S., D. Dosman, and N. Keating. 2006. *General Social Survey on Time Use: Cycle 19— Aging Well: Time Use Patterns of Older Canadians, 2005*. Ottawa: Minister of Industry and Statistics Canada.

——— and K. Cranswick. 2004. 'Looking after seniors: Who does what for whom?', *Canadian Social Trends* 74: 2–6.

Sussman, D., and S. Bonnell. 2006. 'Wives as primary breadwinners', Perspectives on *Labour and Income* (Aug.): 10–17.

Sweet, R., and N. Mandell. 2004. 'Homework-as-homework: Mothers' unpaid educational labour', *Atlantis: A Women's Studies Journal* 28, 2: 7–18.

Tally, M. 2006. '"She doesn't let age define her": Sexuality and motherhood in recent "middle-aged chick flicks"', *Sexuality & Culture* 10, 2: 33–55.

Teuscher, U., and C. Teuscher. 2006. 'Reconsidering the double standard of aging: Effects of gender and sexual orientation of facial attractiveness ratings', *Personal and Individual Differences* 42: 631–9.

Townsend, M. 2006. 'The new face of retirement: Growing older, working longer'. At: <www.policyalternatives.ca>.

Trethewey, A. 2001. 'Reproducing and resisting the master narrative of decline: Midlife professional women's experiences of aging', *Management Communication Quarterly* 15, 2: 183–226.

Turcotte, M. 2006. 'Parents with adult children living at home', *Canadian Social Trends*: 2–10.

Twigg, J. 2004. 'The body, gender, and age: Feminist insights in social gerontology', *Journal of Aging Studies* 18, 1: 59–73.

Vasil, L., and H. Wass. 1993. 'Portrayal of the elderly in the media: A literature review and implications for educational gerontologists', *Educational Gerontology* 19, 1: 71–85.

Walsh, F., and J. Pryce. 2003. 'The spiritual dimension of family life', in F. Walsh, ed., *Normal Family Processes: Growing Diversity and Complexity*. New York: Guilford Press, 337–72.

Walters, V., and M. Denton. 1997. 'Stress, depression and tiredness among women: The social production and social construction of health', *Canadian Review of Sociology and Anthropology* 34, 1: 53–69.

Walz, Toman. 2002. 'Crones, dirty old men, sexy seniors: Representations of the sexuality of older persons', *Journal of Aging and Identity* 7, 2: 99–112.

Washington Post. 2007. 'Miss ability: Judging disabled women's beauty', 2 Jan. At: <thegimp-parade.blogspot.com/2007/01/miss-ability-judging-disabled-womens.html>.

Wekker, G. 2004. 'Still crazy after all those years . . .: Feminism for the new millennium', *European Journal of Women's Studies* 11, 4: 487–500.

Wethington, E. 2000. 'Expecting stress: Americans and the "midlife crisis"', *Motivation and Emotion* 24, 2: 85–103.

———, H. Cooper, and C.S. Holmes. 1997. 'Turning points in midlife', in I.H. Gotlib and B. Wheaton, eds, *Stress and Adversity over the Life Course: Trajectories and Turning Points*. New York: Cambridge University Press, 215–30.

Wheaton, B., and I.H. Gotlib. 1997. 'Trajectories and turning points across the life course: Concepts and themes', in Gotlib and Wheaton, eds, *Stress and Adversity across the Life Course: Trajectories and Turning Points*. New York: Cambridge University Press, 1–25.

White, T., and M.F. Sherman. 2002. 'Silencing the self and feminist identity development', *Psychological Reports* 90: 1075–83.

Williams, C. 2004. 'The sandwich generation', *Perspectives on Labour and Income* 16, 4: 7–14.

———. 2005. 'The sandwich generation', *Canadian Social Trends* (Summer): 16–21.

——— and J. Normand. 2003. 'Stress at work', *Canadian Social Trends* 70 (Fall): 7–13.

Williams, R., and M.A. Wittig. 1997. '"I'm not a feminist, but . . .": Factors contributing to the discrepancy between pro-feminist orientation and feminist social identity', *Sex Roles: A Journal of Research* 37, 11/12: 885–904.

Wilson, L., S.J. Wilson, A. Duffy, and N. Mandell. 2006. '"She could be anything she wants to be": Mothers and daughters and feminist identity', *Journal of the Association for Research on Mothering* 8, 1/2: 171–9.

Wilson, S.J. 1996. *Women, Families and Work*, 4th edn. Toronto: McGraw-Hill Ryerson.

Wolf, N. 1997. *The Beauty Myth*. Toronto: Vintage Canada.

Woodward, K.M. 1998. *Figuring Age: Women, Bodies, Generations*. Bloomington: Indiana University Press.

Worcester, Nancy. 2004. 'Hormone replacement therapy (HRT): Getting to the Heart of the Politics of Women's Health?', *Journal of Women and Aging* 11, 4: 57–73.

Wray, S. 2003. 'Women growing older: Agency, ethnicity and culture', *Sociology* 37, 3: 511–27.

———. 2004. 'What constitutes agency and empowerment for women in later life?', *Sociological Review* 52, 1: 22–38.

———. 2007. 'Women making sense of midlife: Ethnic and cultural diversity', *Journal of Aging Studies* 21: 31–42.

Wright, C.L. 2006. 'Retirement? what retirement?', *Globe and Mail*, 17 Nov., C9.

Wright, J. 2005. 'Coaching mid-life, baby boomer women in the workplace', *Work: Journal of Prevention* 25, 2: 179–83.

Wrosch, C., and J. Hechausen. 2002. 'Perceived control of life regrets: Good for young and bad for old adults', *Psychology and Aging* 17, 2: 340–50.

Young, J.E. 1982. 'Loneliness, depression and cognitive therapy: Theory and applications', in L.A. Peplau and D. Perlman, eds, *Loneliness: A Sourcebook of Current Theory, Research and Therapy.* New York: Wiley, 379–405.

Zahn, H.J. 2005. 'Aging, health care, and elder care: Perspectives of gender inequalities in China', *Health Care for Women International* 26: 693–712.

Zucker, A.N. 2004. 'Disavowing social identities: What it means when women say "I'm not a feminist, but . . .", *Psychology of Women Quarterly* 28: 423–35.

Zukewich, N. 2003. 'Unpaid informal caregiving', *Canadian Social Trends* (Autumn): 14–18.

Index